CHRONICLES OF NOTRE DAME DU LAC

CHRONICLES
OF NOTRE DAME DU LAC

EDWARD SORIN, C.S.C.

TRANSLATED BY
JOHN M. TOOHEY, C.S.C.

EDITED AND ANNOTATED BY
JAMES T. CONNELLY, C.S.C.

A NOTRE DAME SESQUICENTENNIAL BOOK

UNIVERSITY OF NOTRE DAME PRESS
NOTRE DAME   LONDON

Copyright © 1992 by
University of Notre Dame Press
Notre Dame Indiana 45665
All Rights Reserved

Manufactured in the United States of America

Library of Congress Cataloging-in-Publication Data

Sorin, Edward.
    Chronicles of Notre Dame du Lac / Edward Sorin : edited
and annotated by James T. Connelly.
        p.   cm.
    "A Notre Dame sesquicentennial book."
    Includes index.
    ISBN 0-268-00789-6
    1. University of Notre Dame—History—19th century.
2. Sorin, Edward.   I. Connelly, James T., 1937–   . II. Title.
LD4113.S67   1992
378.772'89—dc20   91-51114
                                                      CIP

TABLE OF CONTENTS

ABBREVIATIONS

Several of the sources and repositories cited in the notes are abbreviated as follows.

AMS = Archives of the Marianite Sisters of Holy Cross, Le Mans, France.

ASHC = Archives of the Sisters of the Holy Cross, Saint Mary's, Notre Dame, Indiana.

CHCHC = Annual Conference on the History of the Congregations of Holy Cross.

GA = General Archives of the Congregation of Holy Cross, Rome.

IPA = Archives of the Indiana Province, Congregation of Holy Cross, Notre Dame, Indiana.

M.g. = Matricule générale de la Congregation de Sainte-Croix.

EDITOR'S PREFACE

The history of what would come to be known as the University of Notre Dame may be said to have begun on August 5, 1841, in Le Mans, France, when a group of seven men began a ten-week journey that would take them to Vincennes, Indiana, in the interior of North America. The leader of this band was a young French priest, Edward Frederick Sorin, and his *Chronicles of Notre Dame du Lac* describes the audacious enterprise undertaken by these seven Frenchmen and their associates from the time that they set out for North America until 1866, when the end of the American Civil War ushered in a new era for both their frontier college and the country as a whole.

All of these men belonged to the Congregation of Holy Cross, one of the many Catholic religious orders founded in France in the aftermath of the French Revolution. In 1820 Jacques Dujarié, parish priest of Ruillé-sur-Loir in the diocese of Le Mans in the west of France, had been charged by his bishop with the task of founding a religious institute of laymen who would undertake to serve as teachers in the rural parishes of the diocese and thus help to reestablish the system of primary schools in the country villages which had been devastated by the Revolution. Dujarié formed the young men who came to him into a religious community, the Brothers of St. Joseph, and governed them for fifteen years, until infirmity, old age and a rash of internal

problems led him to offer his resignation to the bishop of
Le Mans, Jean-Baptiste Bouvier.[1]

In 1835, Bishop Bouvier gave the direction of the
Brothers of St. Joseph, by then about fifty strong, to another of his priests, Basile-Antoine Moreau, thirty-six, a
professor of Sacred Scripture in the diocesan seminary.
Moreau had just founded a group of clerics, two priests and
two seminarians besides himself, which was known as the
Auxiliary Priests of Le Mans. Within weeks Moreau moved
the novitiate of the Brothers from the village of Ruillé-
sur-Loir to a house which he owned in Sainte-Croix, a
suburb of the city of Le Mans. When he joined the Brothers
of St. Joseph and the Auxiliary Priests together into one
institute in 1837, the new community took its name from
the neighborhood of Sainte-Croix, where its motherhouse
or headquarters was located, and became the Congregation
from (of) Sainte-Croix (Holy Cross).[2]

Originally intended to serve the needs of the church
in France, Moreau was persuaded by the bishop of Algiers
to send a contingent of seven Brothers and three priests
of Holy Cross to Algeria, a French colony, in 1840. When
two of the Brothers died within a year and the bishop was
unable to make good on his promise of financial support,
the others returned to France in June 1842.[3] By then another French missionary had come knocking on Moreau's
door to ask for help, Celestin de la Hailandiere, the new
bishop of Vincennes, Indiana, in the United States.

Born in Brittany, Hailandiere had been a lawyer in
Rennes when he chanced to hear a French missionary
from the United States speak about the need for priests in
that new nation. The young man thereupon discerned his
calling, left the practice of the law, and entered a seminary.
When he was ordained in 1836, he offered himself to
the missionary who had been instrumental in his vocation, Simon Bruté de Rémur, sometime spiritual director

1. Etienne Catta and Tony Catta, *Basil Anthony Mary Moreau*,
2 vols. (Milwaukee: Bruce Publishing Company, 1955), 1:277–318.
   2. Ibid., 319–37
   3. Ibid., 457-489.

of St. Elizabeth Seton and the first bishop of Vincennes, Indiana. Hailandiere's talents and legal training made him a logical choice for vicar general in the new diocese. While on a visit to France in 1839 to collect money and to recruit workers for the diocese, he received word from Rome that Bishop Bruté had requested his appointment as coadjutor bishop with the right of succession.[4]

Overwhelmed by the prospect of shouldering this heavy burden, Hailandiere was at first inclined to refuse. However, after consulting Gabriel Mollevaut, the Sulpician priest who served him as spiritual director, Hailandiere decided to see the will of God in this appointment and accepted it. One month later, while still in France, he received word that Bishop Bruté had died and that he was the new bishop of Vincennes. He returned to Mollevaut for consolation and advice and, among other things, the aged spiritual director suggested to the new bishop that he go to Le Mans, where another of Mollevaut's spiritual sons, Basile Moreau, was in the process of founding a religious community. Perhaps Moreau could alleviate the personnel needs of the new bishop's diocese on the American frontier.

It was thus that Hailandiere made his way to Sainte-Croix in August 1839, the first of several prelates from North America to do so. Moreau, however, had already agreed to help the bishop of Algiers. Though sympathetic, Moreau replied that he had no one to send and promised only to keep Indiana in mind. It was not until two years later that the founder of Holy Cross could seriously consider the United States as a field of endeavor.[5]

Bishop Hailandiere had come to Sainte-Croix seeking Brothers to organize schools for the children of his diocese. By the summer of 1841 Moreau had a group of six Brothers ready to go to Indiana. The eldest among them was Brother Vincent (Jean Pieau), forty-four, who had joined the Brothers of St. Joseph in 1821 and had endured all the years

---

4. Charles Lemarié, *Monseigneur Bruté de Rémur, premier évêque de Vincennes aux Etats-Unis (1834–1839)* (Paris: Librairie C. Klincksieck, n.d.), 227-229.

5. Catta, 1:490–499.

of trial when Dujarié's community first flourished, then
almost disbanded and then revived under Moreau's leadership. Three of the Brothers, Joachim (Guillaume-Michel
Andre), thirty-two, Lawrence (Jean Menage), twenty-six,
and Marie (Rene Patoy), twenty-one, whose name was later
changed to Francis Xavier, had finished their novitiate and
professed vows only a few days before leaving for North
America. The other two, Brothers Anselm (Pierre Cail-
lot), sixteen, and Gatien (Urbain Monsimer), fifteen, were
still novices when the group set out from Sainte-Croix on
August 5, 1841, the feast of Our Lady of the Snows.[6]

The members of this group seem to have been carefully
chosen with regard to their skills so that the new foundation might be as self-sufficient as possible. Brother Vincent
was a licensed teacher and had been the first director of the
boarding school which Moreau had opened at Sainte-Croix
in 1836. He had also served as one of Moreau's councillors,
as he had done for Dujarié before 1835. Brother Lawrence
was a farmer, while Joachim was a tailor and Francis Xavier
was a carpenter. The two younger men were expected to
serve as teachers and appear to have been selected because
Bishop Hailandiere believed that young people would learn
English more quickly. As superior of this group, Moreau
appointed Sorin, who was twenty-seven years old, three
years ordained and had entered Holy Cross only two years
before, in 1839.

The seventh of nine children born to a prosperous
family in Ahuillé, a village near Laval in the Department
of Mayenne, about sixty miles west of Le Mans, Edouard-
Fréderic Sorin de la Gaulterie belonged to the rural gentry,
who were accustomed to playing a commanding role in
the affairs of the French countryside.[7] While he was by
all accounts a charming and vigorous man who had real

6. Garnier Morin, *From France to Notre Dame* (Notre Dame,
Ind.: Dujarié Press, 1952), 32-35.

7. On Sorin's family, see Charles Lemarié, *De la Mayenne à
l'Indiana, le Pere Édouard Sorin (1814–1893)* (Angers, France: Uni-
versité Catholique de l'Ouest, 1978), 5–10, and Catta, 1:501–503.

talent for leadership, Sorin also appears to have been one of those people who assume that they should be in charge and proceed accordingly. From the time that Moreau appointed him to lead the expedition to Indiana, Sorin was always in a position of authority in the Congregation of Holy Cross. For the last twenty-five years of his life, 1868 to 1893, he served as superior general.

The prospect of being a missionary seems to have attracted Sorin early in life. He once claimed that, after God, he owed his vocation to Bishop Bruté, whom he had heard speak while a student in the seminary at Le Mans. Six months before leaving for Indiana he wrote to Bishop Hailandiere:

> My body is in France; but my mind and heart are with you. . . . I live only for my dear brethren of America. That is my country, the center of all my affections and the object of all my pious thoughts.[8]

These sentiments would prove to be more true than Sorin could have known at the time.

After several days' rest in New York City, the seven missionaries set out for the interior of the United States.[9] They could have started west by rail from Philadelphia, but to save money they chose the longer water route: up the Hudson River by steamboat to Albany, across New York state on the Erie Canal to Buffalo, by steamer across Lake Erie to Miami, Ohio, on the Maumee River near Toledo. From the steamboat they transferred to wagons for a rough, two-day journey to Providence, Ohio, where a canal had been completed. There they boarded a boat for the trip to Fort Wayne, their first stop in the state of Indiana.

In 1841 Indiana had already been a state for twenty-five years. More important, though, for the future of the Congregation of Holy Cross, the native American tribes had been removed from their lands in the northern part of the

8. Sorin to Hailandiere, undated, University of Notre Dame Archives.

9. On the journey from New York City to Indiana, see Morin, 63–90.

state by the federal government only four years before, in 1837. The territory in the northern and northwestern parts of Indiana was then opened to settlement and a stream of people from the eastern states and Europe was beginning to find its way onto this fertile land. In 1841 the whole state plus eastern Illinois as well, including the growing trading center of Chicago, was under the ecclesiastical jurisdiction of the bishop of Vincennes, an old French trading post on the lower Wabash River in southwestern Indiana. When the Holy Cross missionaries arrived in Fort Wayne on October 1, 1841, the bishop of Vincennes had approximately twenty-five priests, one quarter of them French missionaries like himself, to serve the scattered Catholic population of this vast territory, one-fifth the size of France.[10]

From Fort Wayne the seven Frenchmen pushed on overland to Logansport on the Wabash River where they were given food and shelter by August Martin, a Breton priest who had come to America only two years before and who knew both Father Moreau and Brother Vincent. Martin accompanied them as far as Lafayette, Indiana, where they boarded a river boat for the trip down the Wabash to Vincennes. Finally, on Sunday, October 10, just after dawn, the travelers reached Vincennes. They had been en route for sixty-seven days. Making their way from the river up to the cathedral, they presented themselves to the bishop, and after mass they sang the Te Deum in thanksgiving for their safe arrival.

The day after the missionaries arrived, Bishop Hailandiere began to show Sorin various sites near Vincennes where the Brothers might locate. Sorin selected Black Oak Ridge near St. Peter's Colony, a predominantly Catholic settlement twenty-seven miles east of Vincennes in Daviess County, Indiana. By the end of the week, the Brothers had moved into two log buildings and had taken charge of a school begun some years before by the Sisters of Charity from Nazareth, Kentucky.[11]

10. Charles Lemarié, *Les missionaires bretons de l'Indiana au XIXe siècle* (Montsurs, France: n.p., 1973), 199–205.

11. Morin, 98–106.

When the Brothers arrived at St. Peter's, they found the school being conducted by a young German immigrant, Charles Rother, who wanted to join their community and whom the bishop had sent there to await their arrival. The recruitment of candidates for the Congregation of Holy Cross in the United States thus began immediately. In early November 1841 Rother received the habit as Brother Joseph and began his novitiate. Before the end of the year, three others—an Irish-American born in New Orleans, an Alsatian, and a German—were accepted as postulants. Less than a year later, in August 1842, these three plus four others received the habit as novices and three more were accepted as postulants.[12]

While the number of new candidates was impressive, there were serious problems with their formation for life in the Holy Cross community. Brother Vincent was the only one of the Brothers who had come from France who had spent more than a year in the community and who had much experience of the religious life. Moreau had sent him to America to direct the Brothers' novitiate, and when the bishop insisted that Vincent return to Vincennes in December 1841 to conduct a school for the French-speaking children of the town, the novitiate was left in the hands of Brothers who themselves had lived the religious life for scarcely more than a year. Sorin, as parish priest, was engaged for most of the week in visiting the scattered Catholic families. Moreover, while the Brothers who had come from Sainte-Croix were struggling to learn English, some of their new recruits spoke neither French nor English but German.[13] Sorin confessed to Moreau, "It is almost necessary for us to make the exercises in three different languages at the same time or that the Holy Spirit repeat the miracle of Pentecost."[14] What effect all this had on the formation of these first American novices can only be surmised.

12. Morin, 106–108, 114, 118–123, 131, 140, 143–144. See also M.g.

13. Morin, 119–133.

14. Sorin to Moreau, St. Peter's, Indiana, Dec. 10, 1841, cited in Morin, 118.

How to train the numerous candidates who were coming to join them was only one of the concerns facing the
Brothers. Father Moreau and Bishop Hailandiere had not
made a written contract about the Brothers, and the bishop
took the position that they had been given to him to
be the nucleus of a diocesan congregation directly under
his authority. Moreau insisted that the seven men who
had come from France in 1841 and any other religious of
Holy Cross, men or women, who might subsequently join
the original contingent should remain dependent upon the
motherhouse at Sainte-Croix.[15]

Financial considerations were crucial in determining
that this first American foundation would continue to be
part of the larger Congregation of Holy Cross and not
become an autonomous community. When he had first
come to Sainte-Croix in 1839, Bishop Hailandiere had
promised to pay for the missionaries' travel expenses to
Indiana. When he was presented with the bill, he said that
although he had had the money in 1839, he no longer had
it in 1841.[16] Moreau held a lottery in Le Mans to raise
the money for the group's passage. When the bishop was
unable to support the growing community at St. Peter's,
Moreau sent additional funds from France. He also sent
Hailandiere a letter saying that the Holy Cross religious
in Indiana would remain dependent on Sainte-Croix so
that the bishop would have the advantage of their labor
without having to support them. Moreau also promised not
to remove the Congregation from Hailandiere's diocese "so
long as they will be able to live there."[17]

During the spring and summer of 1842, the Brothers
had been busy cutting timber, baking bricks, and gathering
stones for the buildings which they intended to erect at
Black Oak Ridge to house the boarding school that they
were planning to open. Their plans ran afoul of the bishop's

15. Morin, 106–111, 125–126, 139–140, 142–143. Catta,
1:507–508.

16. Morin, 111–112.

17. Morin, 111–114, 147–148. Catta, 1:508–515.

promise to the Eudists, another congregation which he had recruited for his diocese and to which he had given his word that if they would establish a college in Vincennes, he would permit no other college under Catholic auspices to be set up nearby which might compete for students. Bishop Hailandiere was unyielding on this point and when Sorin pressed the issue, the bishop offered a compromise.[18]

Hailandiere held title to a piece of property in northern Indiana. If the community would establish there in two years' time a novitiate for the Brothers and a school, Holy Cross could have the land. The offer was accepted and in early November 1842 Sorin and seven Brothers set out for the north with three hundred dollars from the bishop and a letter of credit to a Mr. Coquillard, a merchant in the village of South Bend, a few miles from the property.[19] By thus putting more than three hundred miles between themselves and Bishop Hailandiere, the Brothers were able to establish their independence of the bishop's direct control in fact, if not in the bishop's mind.

The land which the Holy Cross missionaries received from Bishop Hailandiere had been given to him by Stephen Badin, the first priest ordained in the United States. After his ordination in 1793, Badin had spent the next twenty-six years of his life on the western frontier in Kentucky. In 1819 he had retired to France, but he had come out of retirement in 1828 at the age of sixty, had returned to North America, and had offered his services to the bishop of Detroit. In 1831 he had been sent to serve the Potawatomi Indians in southwestern Michigan and northern Indiana, a tribe first evangelized by Jesuit missionaries in the seventeenth century.

In 1833 Badin had purchased the 524 acres which later came into the hands of the Congregation of Holy Cross with the intention of opening an orphanage for the children of the Indians and settlers. In 1835 Badin retired to Cincinnati, but the Potawatomi Indians continued to be

18. Morin, 148–153.
19. Ibid., 152–161.

served by resident priests until 1838, when the newly ordained pastor, Benjamin Petit, twenty-six, died in St. Louis
after accompanying his Indians to Kansas, where the federal
government had forced them on to a reservation. Badin had
deeded the land to the bishop of Vincennes on condition
that he would reimburse Badin for improvements made
on the property and that he would establish an orphan
asylum "or other religious, charitable institution." The college which Sorin proposed to open would fulfill the latter
stipulation.[20]

Sorin, Brothers Gatien and Francis Xavier and five of
the novices recruited during the past year at St. Peter's
arrived at the northern property on November 26, 1842,
and lived through the winter of 1842–43 in a log cabin
which they found standing on the land and which had
been used as a chapel. On the property were two good
sized lakes connected by a marsh. Looking out over the
frozen lakes and the snow-covered landscape, Sorin had
dedicated both the property and their undertaking to Mary,
the Mother of God. The place would henceforth be known
as Notre Dame du Lac.[21]

When the priest who had been serving as their chaplain quarreled with Bishop Hailandiere and left the diocese in February 1843, Brothers Vincent, Lawrence, and
Joachim took six of their novices and two postulants and
left St. Peter's Colony for the north, where they arrived
after a two-week trek in midwinter. Brothers Anselm and
Celestine, a novice, stayed behind in Vincennes to teach in
the bishop's school. Thus, by the spring of 1843 there were
nineteen living in the log cabin at Notre Dame du Lac.[22]

The construction of larger and more permanent buildings was imperative, and in the spring and summer of 1843

20. Ibid., 161–168. See also Lemarié, *De la Mayenne à l'Indiana*,
29–35.
21. Sorin to Moreau, Notre Dame du Lac, Dec. 5, 1842, cited
in Edward L. Heston, translator, *Circular Letters of the Very Reverend
Basil Anthony Mary Moreau*, 2 vols. (Notre Dame, Ind.: Ave Maria
Press, 1943), 1:58–60.
22. Morin, 169–177.

a two-story brick house was erected near the log chapel and a larger building was begun which was occupied in January 1844. During the summer, three priests, a Brother, and four Sisters arrived from Sainte-Croix, sent by Moreau to reinforce the American Holy Cross foundation. A larger wooden church building had been erected in the spring of 1843 and a second story was added to provide living quarters for the Sisters. In the autumn, the boarding school received its first students.[23]

Soon after their arrival at Notre Dame du Lac, the Holy Cross community began to receive orphans sent by friends and families in the frontier settlements. A manual trade school was opened to give instruction to the boys which would fit them to earn a living as adults. The character of the foundation was further altered when the local member of the Indiana State Legislature offered to procure a charter from that body establishing the boarding school as a university with the right to grant degrees. Sorin was agreeable and in 1844 the legislature granted the charter. Thus began the University of Notre Dame du Lac, only the third Catholic school in the United States to be legally incorporated.[24]

The original band of Holy Cross missionaries in the diocese of Vincennes had settled in northern Indiana in 1842 in order to open a school. What they created over the next decade was an apostolic center which served the Catholics within approximately a hundredmile radius of Notre Dame du Lac in a variety of ways. Boys were sent to Notre Dame and girls to the Sisters at Bertrand, Michigan (after 1855 at St. Mary's), for an education, and orphans were received and cared for at both sites. Young men and women who wished to devote themselves to religious life were trained and sent out on mission from these centers.

23. Lemarié, *De la Mayenne à l'Indiana*, 36–44. See also *A Story of Fifty Years from the Annals of the Congregation of the Sisters of the Holy Cross, 1855–1905* (Notre Dame, Ind.: Ave Maria, n.d.), 20.

24. Arthur J. Hope, *Notre Dame: One Hundred Years* (Notre Dame, Ind.: University Press, 1943), 58–60. Catta, 1:528.

When the number of Catholic families in a location war-
ranted it, schools were established by the Brothers and
Sisters in places such as St. John's in Lake County, Laporte,
and Michigan City, Indiana. In addition to teaching at the
"university," the Holy Cross priests rode a circuit through
northern Indiana and southwestern Michigan providing
a sacramental ministry and organizing the Catholics into
parish communities.

Before long the Congregation of Holy Cross began
to extend its activites well beyond the diocese of Vincennes and the state of Indiana. An attempt to staff a
college in central Kentucky in 1846 failed, but in 1849 the
Holy Cross community made a permanent foundation in
New Orleans. In 1851, the congregation was established
in Cincinnati. A house was opened in New York City in
1855, and in 1856 the congregation took over a college in
Susquehanna, Pennsylvania, another in Chicago, several
parish schools in Philadelphia and an orphanage in Washington, D.C. By 1859 there was a foundation in Baltimore.
In less than twenty years the frontier college in the forests
of northern Indiana had become the national center of
a network of institutions in various parts of the country.
As the *Chronicles* recount in some detail, these endeavors
were not accomplished without stress and setbacks, but, all
things considered, the expansion was remarkable.

The Congregation of Holy Cross received papal approval in 1857, thus making it a religious community of
pontifical right, under the direct authority of the pope
rather than that of the various bishops in whose dioceses it
might be working.[25] Rome, however, was not keen on having men and women together in the same community and
insisted that Moreau establish the Sisters as an autonomous
congregation, distinct in its governance and in its finances
from the priests and Brothers. This Moreau did, but the
actual working out of the separation took years to accom-
plish and eventually resulted in the establishment of three
women's communities, the Marianite Sisters of Holy Cross,

25. Catta, 2:166–258.

which took in the Sisters working in France and Louisiana; the Sisters of the Holy Cross, which included the Sisters in the American Midwest, Baltimore, and Washington; and the Sisters of Holy Cross and the Seven Dolors, which gathered together all the Sisters in Canada. Suffice it to say that these separations generated some hard feelings that would persist into the twentieth century.

The founder of Holy Cross, Basile Moreau, made his one and only visit to the houses of his community in the United States and Canada in the summer and autumn of 1857.[26] Although the *Chronicles* describe his visit as ushering in an era of harmony between the American Holy Cross community and the motherhouse in France, the reconciliation was short lived. The chronicler frequently complains of a lack of appreciation on the part of Sainte-Croix for the situation of the houses in the United States, and if anything, the complaints became sharper after 1857. Opposition to Moreau's leadership began to grow in France, and the motherhouse was saddled with a crushing debt because of the mishandling of funds by the steward of the community's college in Paris. The American houses were vexed by internal dissensions, a severe national financial crisis, and the Civil War. The *Chronicles* end in 1866 with the resignation of Moreau as superior general. His successor, Pierre Dufal, held office for only two years before resigning. An extraordinary general chapter in 1868 elected Sorin as the third superior general of the Congregation of Holy Cross. By then, the community's foundational years had come to an end.

* * *

The Rules of the Congregation of Holy Cross prescribed that in each house of the community a chronicle would be kept recounting "all that is pertinent to the enlightenment of the general administration as to persons, things and important events and is of such a nature as to edify the community." In France, the chronicler for each

---

26. On Moreau's visit to North America, see Catta, 2:303–318.

house was to bring a draft of the chronicles for the year with him to the annual retreat. Once approved, the chronicles would then be copied into a book kept at the motherhouse. Back at the house from which a particular chronicle came, the approved draft was to be copied into another book that would be kept at that house.[27]

When Sorin's successor as superior general, Rev. Gilbert Français, made his first visitation at Notre Dame from October or November 1894 to March 1895, he was shown the *Chroniques de Notre Dame du Lac*. It would appear that he had never seen them before and he wanted to take them with him when he returned to France. The provincial superior of the United States, Rev. William Corby, asked that a translation into English might be made which could be kept in America. The man assigned to make the translation was Rev. John Toohey, C.S.C.[28]

Toohey began work on the translation in January 1895, working in the rectory of St. Vincent de Paul parish in Allen County, Indiana, where he was pastor. Reassigned during the summer of 1895 to St. Bernard's parish in Watertown, Wisconsin, he continued work on the translation and completed it in October 1895. By that time, Français had returned to Paris. Whether the original manuscript was ever sent to France is questionable.[29]

Toohey worked from a bound copy of the manuscript and complained that parts or whole words were cut off in the binding process.[30] Presumably, this was the same manuscript which is in the possession of the Indiana Province Archives Center at Notre Dame, Indiana, and from

27. *Congrégation de Sainte-Croix, Régles communes & particulieres* (Le Mans, 1858), Régle LIII, 1, 10.

28. Toohey to Corby, St. Vincent, Indiana, Jan. 17, 1895; Mar. 21, 1895. William Corby Provincial Administration, IPA.

29. Toohey to Corby, Oct. 17, 1895. On Français's itinerary, see Français to Corby, Neuilly, France, July 12, 1894, and Aug. 23, 1894; Watertown, Wisconsin, Mar. 1, 1895; Montreal, May 18, 1895; Neuilly, Sept. 26, 1895, IPA.

30. Toohey to Corby, Watertown, Wisconsin, Oct. 17, 1895. IPA.

which this edition has been prepared. Toohey also noted that he was "aiming to be as literal as possible without making the translation too Frenchy."[31] In preparing this edition, Toohey's translation has been checked against the original French manuscript. While his translation has been retained for the most part, clauses and sentences which he omitted have been restored and passages which he translated so freely as to alter or obscure the meaning have been rendered more literally.

The original manuscript tends to use semicolons instead of periods and to let paragraphs run on for a page and more. Toohey's division of the original into sentences and paragraphs has been retained for the most part. The original manuscript contained marginal notes indicating the subject matter of the adjacent text. Toohey omitted these, but they have been restored in this edition. On the whole, about 85 percent of the text in this edition corresponds to Toohey's translation.

While the rules of the congregation instructed the chronicler to remain anonymous and to speak of himself only in the third person, there seems to have been no doubt in Toohey's mind that Sorin was the author of the Notre Dame chronicles.[32] Indeed, the chronicle for 1853 identifies the chronicler as Father Sorin himself as does that of 1861.[33] While these instances as well as much internal evidence point to Sorin as the author, the manuscript was written by several different hands. The first seven chapters appear to have been written by the same person, someone other than Sorin. Chapter eight (1849) appears to be in Sorin's handwriting, but a third hand appears to have taken over in chapter nine (1850). In subsequent years, still other hands are evident.

In the Indiana Province Archives is a copybook entitled "Journal kept by the Secretary to serve in the Com-

31. Toohey to Corby, St. Vincent, Indiana, Mar. 21, 1895. IPA.

32. Rule LIII, 4. Toohey to Corby, St. Vincent, Indiana, Jan. 21, 1895, IPA.

33. See pp. 120 and 255.

position of the Chronicles of N.D. du Lac." A note at
the bottom of the title page states that this journal was
"ordered by the Council of Administration on the eleventh
of January, in the year of our Lord one thousand eight
hundred & forty seven" and the note is signed "Bro. Gatien,
Secr'y." The entries in this copybook run from February 8,
1847, to January 10, 1849. While additional journals of this
sort are not extant, there may well have been others that
were destroyed when the information that they contained
had been used.

Although the congregational rules stated that the
chronicler in each house should have his chronicles ready
to hand in at the time of the annual retreat at the end
of the school year, the Notre Dame chronicles, with the
exception of the first three years, are written in chapters
which correspond to the calendar year. Internal evidence
suggests that the chronicle for each year was written after
the year had ended and sometimes after a lapse of several years.

In chapter three, which covers 1844, the chronicler
mentions the transfer of the Brothers' novitiate to Indianapolis in November 1846 and Bishop Bazin, who presided over the diocese from October 1847 to April 1848.
Later in the same chapter, the number of orphans received
up through 1848 is given.[34] Thus, it would appear that the
chronicle for 1844 was written in 1849 and the chronicler may have made use of the journal of Brother Gatien
referred to above.

In one instance the chronicler specifically identifies
the date on which he is completing the chronicle for the
preceding year. The last page of chapter thirteen, which
covers 1854, indicates that the last part of that chapter,
and possibly the whole of it, were written on April 24,
1855.

In summary, internal evidence and community tradi-
tion indicate that Sorin was the author of the chronicles. The handwriting in the original manuscript indicates

34. See pp. 42 and 48.

at least three different scribes, Sorin among them. While most of the chapters were probably composed within a few months of the end of the year that they chronicle, some chapters may not have been written until several years later. In either case, a journal of events may have been used to refresh the chronicler's memory.

Finally, the reader ought to be advised that the *Chronicles of Notre Dame du Lac* is the personal account of a twenty-five year period in the history of the Congregation of Holy Cross written by one of the principal figures in the events described. While Father Sorin no doubt believed that he saw things as they were, others saw the same things differently and were just as convinced that their view was correct. When he came to translate the sections pertaining to the history of the congregation in New Orleans, Toohey remarked that that section was of great personal interest to him because he had entered the community as a sixteen-year-old Irish immigrant in Louisiana in 1856 and was acquainted with many of the people mentioned in the chronicle of that difficult period. He urged the provincial superior, Father Corby, to ask the superior general for the chronicles of the motherhouse in Le Mans.

> Every question has two sides; and whilst I do not call in question anything written by Fr. Sorin, I think the historian of Notre Dame ought to have an opportunity, if possible, of hearing the other side.[35]

The reader is well advised to remember that there is another side to the story recounted in the *Chroniques de Notre Dame du Lac.*

*   *   *

While I must bear full responsibility for the final shape of the text and the notes, I owe a word of acknowledgment and thanks to several people. James Langford of the University of Notre Dame Press has shown interest, given encouragement, and patiently awaited the finished product

35. Toohey to Corby, St. Vincent, Indiana, Mar. 21, 1895. IPA.

since first I proposed the publication of the Sorin chronicles. I have been helped immeasurably in the preparation of the manuscript by several members of the Decio Hall typing pool at the University of Notre Dame, most notably Margaret Jasiewicz, Sherry Reichold, Cheryl Reed, and Nancy Kegler, and, at a later stage, by Diane Jaeckel. I am indebted to Charles Lamb of the University of Notre Dame Archives for his assistance in gathering photos to illustrate this volume. Sister M. Campion Kuhn, C.S.C., gathered photos from the archives of the Sisters of the Holy Cross. Jane Pitz prepared the two maps and Barbara Cohen made the index. My provincial superior, Rev. Carl F. Ebey, C.S.C., encouraged me to undertake the preparation of the Sorin chronicles for publication, and my associates at the Indiana Province Archives Center, Jacqueline Dougherty and Thomas Balaz, C.S.C., patiently bore with me during the months that I was working on the manuscript.

Last, but by no means least, my interest in the history of the Congregation of Holy Cross was first whetted and sustained by Thomas T. McAvoy, C.S.C., and my mentors in American religious history were Jerald C. Brauer and Martin E. Marty at the University of Chicago. While these three are in no way liable for the defects in this work, they are largely responsible for whatever merit it may have.

James T. Connelly, C.S.C.

November 26, 1991
Notre Dame, Indiana

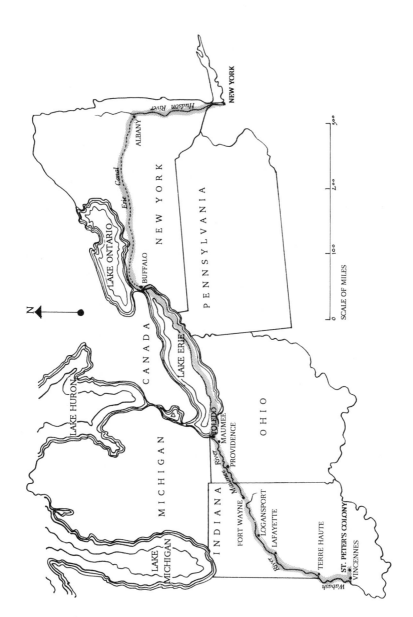

Westward route of the first colony of Holy Cross religious in North America, September 17–October 10, 1841.

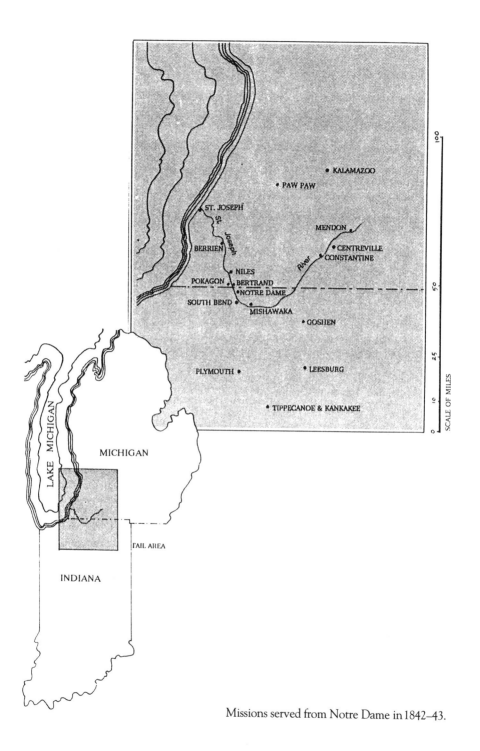

Missions served from Notre Dame in 1842–43.

Chroniques de
N. D. du lac

CHAPTER 1

August 5, 1841 – St. Peter's

For two years the Brothers of St. Joseph had been expected at Vincennes; during all that time, it had been impossible for Reverend Father Moreau, their Superior General, to comply with the urgent requests of Bishop De la Hailandiere. At last, on 5 August, the feast of Our Lady of the Snows, the first colony took its departure after a most impressive and touching ceremony. The novelty of the event had attracted a numerous gathering of patrons and friends of the community. On this occasion, Fr. Moreau seemed to surpass himself, and he communicated to all his listeners his own emotions.

Departure of the first colony, August 5, 1841; Fr. Sorin and six Brothers. Their difficulties at Le Havre

This first colony was composed of Fr. Sorin and Brothers Vincent, Joachim, Lawrence and Mary, professed, with whom were associated two young novices of fifteen, Brothers Gatien and Anselm,[1] who were destined to become teachers.

The instructions issued by the Mother House in the beginning appear not to have extended any farther than to the establishment of a novitiate for Brothers, at the expense and risk of the diocese which asked for them. It would even seem that, according to oral agreements (for there never existed anything in writing on the subject), the Brothers and the priest were simply given to Bishop De la Hailandiere, then bishop of Vincennes, on condition that

1. See Editor's Preface, pp. xiii–xiv.

1

he should pay for their supplies and also the expenses of their journey from New York to Vincennes. Fr. Moreau reserved no other jurisdiction to himself than the right to recall them later, but not without replacing them immediately. In the course of this narrative it will appear to how many difficulties this absence of a regular contract gave rise.

The delay of two years in the departure of the colony was caused not so much by lack of subjects as by want of pecuniary resources to meet the expenses of departure. The delay would probably have been prolonged indefinitely had not Providence inspired a pious lady of Le Mans with an idea, whose execution unexpectedly furnished Fr. Moreau with the means of starting the new missionaries on their journey. Mme. [no name given] put up a golden chair to be disposed of by lottery for the new colony, which produced fifteen hundred francs. A sum almost equal to this was added by private donations and it was with this modest capital that the seven travelers started on their journey of fifteen hundred leagues under the protection of Our Lady of the Snows and of their Guardian Angels.

From the very start they found it necessary to place all their reliance on the protection of heaven. For, besides the narrow limits of their pecuniary resources, their ignorance of the language of the country as well as of the manners and the character of the New World and the consciousness of their own incapacity had made them put their hopes in protection from on high. Moreover, according to their ideas, America was a land of savages, where besides death and *la cangue*,[2] a missionary might expect at every step to have to make extraordinary sacrifices. However, their ignorance did not always result in disastrous consequences. If it prevented them from appreciating beforehand their future position in Indiana, on the other hand the extraordinary

2. *La Cangue* was a punishment which consisted of a four-foot square wooden collar weighing anywhere from twenty to sixty pounds which the offender had to wear around his neck night and day for the duration of his sentence. See "La Cangue," *Encyclopedia Britannica*, 14th ed. (1950).

sufferings and privations for which they had been looking prepared and encouraged them to meet a thousand lesser crosses chosen for them by God and of which they had never thought.

Hardly had they arrived in Le Havre when difficulties of all kinds obliged them to seek help by the recitation of thousands of Ave Marias. This devotion had been taught them by the excellent Mr. Dupont[3] of Tours, who had the kindness to accompany them from Le Mans to the sea and who rendered them invaluable services till the very last moment.

Difficulties on departing

The first difficulty was in regard to their passports, which were not perfectly in order, and they were within a little of being all obliged to return to Le Mans to have them corrected. At last, by dint of earnest prayers and after experiencing many fears and making the rounds of the authorities, the pious travellers succeeded in having the matter of the passports arranged. This was only the beginning of their little trials.

The agent of the community at Le Havre, not knowing how slight were their resources, had secured places for them in the cabin at five hundred francs each, more money than they possessed. The agent, however, without the remotest idea that there would be any difficulty, had had all their baggage put aboard, and nobody made any objection.

Father Sorin was awaited at Le Havre by five Sisters of the Sacred Heart who had engaged their passage several months beforehand in order to have a priest with them on their voyage. Now it so happened that these Ladies, although they had secured their places on a vessel to sail on the day fixed upon, August 8, found that their passage was engaged on one vessel and that of the Brothers on another. Rather than lose the fifteen hundred francs which they had already paid on their places, they preferred to sacrifice

The Ladies of the Sacred Heart loan 1,000 fr.

3. Leon Papin-Dupont, a lawyer of Rennes and known as "The Holy Man of Tours," had a young relative studying at Our Lady of Holy Cross, the mother house in La Mans. Widely traveled himself, Dupont was of great assistance to the Holy Cross colony. See Garnier Morin, *From France to Notre Dame*, 40, 44–45.

a thousand francs; otherwise, they would have lost both what they had advanced and the opportunity of taking passage with a priest. They had been forbidden to start otherwise.[4]

Once freed from their first engagements, the Brothers felt at liberty to act for themselves, and instead of a cabin passage, they were content with a little compartment for themselves of twenty by ten feet between decks amongst the poor emigrants. By means of this new arrangement, instead of a deficit of five hundred francs, they should have in New York a little reserve of fifteen hundred francs. It is true that, humanly speaking, they paid for this economy by some sacrifices and inconveniences; but in the dispositions in which the little band were at the time, they considered themselves fortunate, and each day of their passage they blessed God with all their hearts.

Moreover, amongst the crowd of nearly two hundred persons that were traveling with them in the steerage, they found constant opportunities to do some good. Poor as they were themselves, they were rich in comparison with many of the passengers, and soon, through their little donations to the most indigent, the good Brothers came to be looked upon as the Benefactors of the steerage.

The *Iowa*, the packet boat that carried them from Le Havre to the United Sates, was a large vessel and a good sailor. It was commanded by Captain Pell, an American Episcopalian, liberal and free from bigotry. Not only did he allow Fr. Sorin and his companions to go up on deck, a privilege reserved exclusively for cabin passengers, but all along he showed them the same consideration as he gave to the Ladies of the Sacred Heart.

Their joys and troubles at sea

It was on Sunday, 8 August, at three o'clock in the afternoon, that the ship left port; and hardly had it got five hundred feet from shore, when a little boat put out in pursuit with a letter that had just arrived for

4. The Sisters of the Sacred Heart loaned the Holy Cross colony one thousand francs so that the latter might book passage on the *Iowa*, the same vessel as the Sisters. See Morin, 44–45.

Fr. Sorin. This letter contained the final wishes for a happy voyage from their dearly beloved Fr. Rector.[5] Never perhaps was a letter received at a more opportune time, nor with greater joy and gratitude. Twenty times did they charge their guardian angels to bear back the ardent prayers which they addressed to heaven for his happiness and long life. God thus seemed to wish to make them forget their first apprehensions and by a concurrence of circumstances, as unexpected as they were agreeable, he was pleased, we may say, to cause tears of gratitude and admiration to take the place of those tears of sorrow which the exile's heart feels the need of shedding when he leaves the native soil to which he may never return.

Agreements and consolations

Eight days passed and still they had not left the English Channel, and those eight days were bad days for the whole crew. Although the sea was not in one of its furious moods, the rolling was greater than usual and all the passengers suffered much. Only one escaped sea-sickness for a time, and his services were all the more valuable to his companions because, were it not for him, they would have had to suffer without any assistance. Whoever has had experience of the sea knows how it paralyzes and in a sense annihilates the physical and moral powers of even the most courageous. Hardly had the little colony regained a little health and energy when Br. Vincent, whose attentions were no longer indispensable, needed to be waited on himself, which was cheerfully done.

This truly paternal watchfulness of Providence, which was experienced by them more than once, not only on really critical occasions but sometimes even in the ordinary details of life, this solicitude full of tenderness did not escape their notice; perhaps it might be said that nothing contributed more to excite in the depths of their souls that confidence and that unreserved abandonment of themselves to this same Providence which watched so attentively over them.

5. Basil Moreau was also referred to as "Rector" of the Institute of Holy Cross which he had founded.

The sea had its pleasures for them as well as its little annoyances; even when they were hardly able to stand or to raise their heads, they did not altogether lose that gaiety which always accompanies a conscience at peace with itself. It was amusing to hear them ask one another, between the throes of those revolutions that were going on within them, whether they still thought the world big enough to bear any proportion to their courage.

Once on the open sea, the sickness left them, their strength returned, and then came those days of joy which they will love to recall till their dying day.

On deck there was a little room, eight by six feet, for the cabin passengers. The Ladies of the Sacred Heart and the Brothers had the exclusive use of this room in turns for their religious exercises. There instructions were given and even the chapters were held; there confessions were heard; there, whenever the sea permitted it, the Holy Sacrifice of the Mass was offered and each of our pious pilgrims came to sit at the table of the Angels and to be fortified with the precious viaticum against the daily and nightly dangers of the treacherous elements; and this was done eleven times during the sea voyage.

To relate all the sweet emotions of this happy family on those solemn occasions would not be easy. It will be much pleasanter for them to call to mind, throughout their whole lives, the extraordinary consolations bestowed upon them in this dear and charming little floating sanctuary. It is there that it pleased Our Lord to begin to fulfill the promises that he made to all those that shall have left father, mother, etc., for his sake. There in truth each one must have felt that he already received the hundredfold of what he had left.

Piety everywhere commands respect and esteem. Aboard the *Iowa*, besides a great number of Protestants of all sects, there was a troupe of comedians going from Paris to New York. Generally speaking, even in France, comedians can hardly be said to be partial to religious. But here the latter had no reason to complain. Like all the other passengers they showed themselves most respectful and attentive to those whose profession was in such marked contrast with their own.

An unexpected event brought into strong light the general sentiments of the ship towards the little band. A child of two years of age, daughter of a German Protestant, fell sick and it soon became evident that there was no hope of recovery. After many fruitless pleadings, the Ladies of the Sacred Heart finally succeeded in obtaining the consent of the father to have her baptized. The hour was agreed upon and all was got in readiness. Mme. Batilde Sallion, their superioress, and the patriarch of the Brothers were chosen as sponsors and the ceremony took place in the little room on the deck. The event caused a great sensation amongst all the ship's company but especially amongst the Brothers and the Sisters whose joy was almost unbounded. Two days later, the new Christian went to take possession of the heritage that had just fallen to her.

Baptism of a child

The burial was another event in which all the passengers took part. The captain himself invited Fr. Sorin to perform the funeral ceremony, assuring him beforehand that everything would be carried out in silence and with decorum. At the hour appointed, the body was borne by four sailors on a plank five or six feet long. It was made to rest on the edge of the vessel until the priest had recited the usual prayers and during all that time the crew and passengers stood uncovered and silent as if they had been in a church. The prayers being finished and the signal given to the bearers, the plank, which was a sort of catafalque, was raised at one end, the little corpse slid gently off and the next instant it was heard dropping into the sea. But the soul which had taken its departure was already in heaven.

Her death and burial

This little event called forth sentiments of gratitude amongst our pious travellers and caused them to say many a fervent prayer to the new tutelary angel whom they had sent to God. The little Mary, they said to one another, owes us much; she will not forget those who have made her so happy. Many years afterwards, they still loved to recall their little Mary, who on her side appears not to have forgotten them.

The frequent and regular exercises of these good Religious could not fail to draw upon them the attention of their fellow travellers. Without transgressing the bounds of politeness and respect, they more than once addressed questions to Fr. Sorin, which called for explanations of some length; twice, amongst others, they gave rise to public controversy, which each time happily terminated in favor of the truth. The reasons brought forward seemed to make a deep impression on a worthy American gentleman and his daughter, who both promised to study the Catholic religion seriously. The captain himself appeared to be shaken in his convictions. Some years afterwards it was reported that he was converted. However this may be, he certainly deserved well of the little family, who have always gratefully remembered him.

In Le Havre he had been very insistent with Fr. Sorin that he take a place amongst the cabin passengers and the refusal of the latter seemed even to provoke him. On the eve of landing, taking Fr. Sorin aside on deck, he said to him, "You doubtless remember, sir, how I urged you at Le Havre. Permit me today to congratulate you. You have edified me, sir, amongst your poor. I thought the place was unbecoming to your character. Today I feel with you that you did well to remain there. You were right."

Finally, the voyage was nearing its end; the land of America, so fervently desired, began to appear in the distance. Then it was that our young missionaries could judge of the happy results of their correct deportment and of their little donations, both amongst the passengers in the cabin and those in the steerage, by the affectionate manner in which every one bade them good-by with thanks and wishes of happiness in the New World. Strangers might have mistaken those poor religious for veritable benefactors of all the passengers. Many begged to be remembered in their prayers, and all promised never to forget them. Even the comedians came to assure them of their esteem and their good wishes. Such is the power and efficacy of virtue that wherever it appears genuine and unpretentious, it soon wins all hearts.

Arrival in New York

On 13 September the vessel entered New York bay, probably one of the most beautiful in the world. It would be hardly possible to describe the sentiments of joy of the pious band at sight of this strange land which they had come so far in search of, through so many dangers and fatigues. It was a little after sunset when Fr. Sorin set foot on land with a few of the passengers, the general landing being deferred till next day. One of his first acts on this soil so much desired was to fall prostrate and embrace it as a sign of adoption and at the same time of profound gratitude to God for the blessing of the prosperous voyage.

Sept. 13th, Eve of the Exaltation of the Holy Cross, a happy portent

The arrival of the new missionaries could not have taken place at a more striking and propitious time. It was the eve of the Exaltation of the Holy Cross, so that Fr. Sorin was able to celebrate his first mass in America on the day of the feast. This happy coincidence was of a kind to make a deep impression on the heart of the young religious of Holy Cross, who himself had placed all his confidence in the power of the Holy Cross and who desired more than he feared to suffer for the love of Christ. He therefore gladly accepted the portent of the circumstance by which heaven seemed to tell him, as formerly it told the apostle, that in this land he would have to suffer. Long afterwards, he would remember that it was in the name of the Cross that he took possession for himself and his comrades of this soil of America.

Here we must mention the names of Mr. and Mrs. Byerly,[6] who received the Brothers with a heartiness that surprised as much as it edified them. Mr. Byerly was a merchant of New York, a convert to Catholicism of just one week. The fervor of his first sentiments, added to the

6. Samuel Byerley, born in England, was a customs officer in New York. See Morin, 56–61. In 1843, Byerley and his family moved to South Bend, Indiana. See Franklin Cullen, *Holy Cross on the Gold Dust Trail* (Notre Dame, Ind.: Province Archives Center, 1989), 2; also Herman J. Alerding, *A History of the Catholic Church in the Diocese of Vincennes* (Indianapolis: n.p. 1883), 575.

natural goodness of his heart, caused him, during the three days of their stay in New York, to be most eager to do them any and every service that they might need.

The City of New York at this time contained about three hundred and fifty thousand inhabitants, at least fifty thousand of whom were Catholics. The Brothers had the honor of being presented to the venerable Bishop Dubois and of spending nearly a day with him at the residence of the pastor of St. Paul's in Brooklyn. He died two years afterwards. He was the first Bishop of New York, where he had spent more than twenty years.[7] There was already in this city a rather numerous French congregation, but the members were neither edifying nor were they zealous for the triumph of the truth.

Generally, one is surprised on arriving from Europe to find in a land not long since inhabited by savages, a city whose streets and stores might compare, sometimes even favorably, with those of Paris and London. Although yet inferior in population to those two queen cities of the world, New York cannot fail before long to rival both of them, since it surpasses them in the promises of the future on account of its maritime and commercial location.

Departure from New York

On the third day after their arrival, having purchased their little provisions, the Brothers started for Vincennes, from which they were still three hundred leagues distant. Bp. De la Hailandiere had instructed his agent in New York to give them three hundred dollars for their traveling expenses. This was more than enough, but they were as sparing as possible. In order to save expenses they preferred to take a slower and cheaper mode of traveling, so that they

7. John Dubois was the third bishop (1826–1842) of New York. Born in Paris Aug. 24, 1764, he had been ordained in France and had emigrated to America in 1791. After doing pastoral work in Virginia and Maryland, he directed Mother Seton's Sisters of Charity. He died Dec. 20, 1842. See Joseph B. Code, *Dictionary of the American Hierarchy (1789–1964)* (New York: Joseph F. Wagner, Inc., 1964), 74.

did not reach their destination until twenty-five days after their departure from New York.

Notwithstanding the anxiety of all to see Vincennes, the journey was in general agreeable—everything was new and interesting, especially from Albany to Buffalo, a distance of one hundred and fifty leagues, which they made by canal in seven days and a half. But their journey was especially a pious one. Their religious exercises were carried out just as on the sea, including the chapter. As to confession, it was made once at the foot of a fallen oak, while the boat was preparing, or rather waiting, to pass a lock.

Before reaching Buffalo, Fr. Sorin, who had long wished to visit the Falls of Niagara, thought that he ought not to lose the opportunity to do so. He took with him his dear Mentor, Brother Vincent, and both of them started for Niagara by train, by which they reached the Falls in several hours. After the sight of the ocean, never a spectacle appeared to them more worthy of admiration.[8] When they had studied it to their heart's content, they hastened to rejoin their fellow-travellers, and the two parties arrived at Buffalo at the same time. They remained there for twenty-four hours with the excellent German pastor, the Rev. Mr. Pax.[9] Fr. Sorin had the happiness of celebrating the holy mass in his new church and several of the Brothers that of receiving holy communion there.

Fr. Sorin and Br. Vincent visit Niagara

Thence they proceeded to Toledo by a steamboat on Lake Erie, where they had a great deal to suffer for nearly thirty-six hours. On their arrival at Miami, a short distance from Buffalo,[10] they were greatly embarrassed as none of them spoke any English; it was harder for them to understand than to make themselves understood.

The perils of travel

8. Sorin described the visit to Niagara Falls in a letter to Moreau of Sept. 26, 1841, GA.

9. Alexander Pax, a German-born, French-speaking priest, was assigned to Buffalo by Bp. Dubois in 1838 and had built a new church which he named St. Louis. See John Timon, *Missions in Western New York and Church History of the Diocese of Buffalo* (Buffalo: Catholic Sentinel Printing Company, 1862), 237.

10. Instead of Buffalo, the chronicler probably meant Toledo. See Sorin to Moreau, Oct. 1, 1841, in GA.

From Miami they went on to Providence, where the steamer ended its trip, and they had to hire two carriages for themselves and their baggage in order to reach the Miami canal, which was not finished that far. It was especially during this portion of the journey, which lasted two days, that they had occasion to remember the care that heaven took of them. The roads were terrible amongst those forests, whose centenarian trees were sometimes thrown across the way so that the drivers were often obliged to make a new path. Every turn of the wheel in those sloughs and ditches appeared to them as a new evidence of protection from on high and called forth new expressions of gratitude. Finally, they reached Junction and then Fort Wayne, the first Catholic station in the diocese of Vincennes.

There they visited the good Mr. Hammion,[11] whom they found dying. He was a saintly missionary. God grant that he may have already received his reward.

The town of Fort Wayne had at that time a population of about fifteen to eighteen hundred inhabitants with a parish of eight or nine hundred souls. The Rev. Mr. Benoit,[12] the first pastor, had recently left for France. Two days afterwards, they were at Logansport, the residence of the Vicar General, the good and pious Mr. A. Martin,[13] who received them with all the amiability and cordiality

11. Joseph De Mutzig Hammion had been ordained by Bp. De la Hailandiere on Aug. 16, 1840, and died early in 1842. Herman J. Alerding, *The Diocese of Fort Wayne* (Fort Wayne, Ind.: Archer Printing Company, 1907), 114.

12. Julian Benoit, born in Septmoncel, France, in the Jura Mountains on Oct. 17, 1808, had emigrated to America in 1836. Ordained in 1837 by Bp. Bruté of Vincennes, he arrived in Fort Wayne on Apr. 16, 1840, where he served until his death on Jan. 26, 1885. See Alerding, *Fort Wayne*, 60–62.

13. August Marie Martin, born in Brittany in 1803 and ordained there in 1828, had emigrated to America in 1839 and was pastor of St. Vincent de Paul Church in Logansport, Indiana, from 1841 to 1844. He did not become vicar general until 1842. Martin was consecrated bishop of Natchitoches, Louisiana, in 1853 and served there until his death in 1875. See Alerding, *Fort Wayne*, 146; Morin, 87–89.

of a genuine Frenchman, waiting on them at table with
his own hands after himself doing the cooking. As he
explained, he was too poor to pay a housekeeper, and for
this reason he had to make do with the services of a little
boy of twelve.

Not only did he afford them hospitality for two days,
but the good missionary accompanied them as far as
Lafayette, where he saw them safely embarked for their
last station, Vincennes itself.

The final portion of their journey took them another
week, during which nothing happened worthy of mention.
They passed by Terre Haute, from which the Sisters of
Providence[14] were only two leagues away, but they could
not afford themselves the pleasure of visiting them. They
were anxious to see Vincennes.

At length, about sunrise on the second Sunday of
October,[15] they beheld the tower of the new cathedral of
Vincennes. They were so filled with joy that they seemed to
forget all their previous fatigue and pains, and they blessed
God who had at length granted them to see with their own
eyes that city of which they had so often spoken during the
last few months.

Arrival at Vincennes

It was October eighth—a bright autumn sunrise. Bp.
De la Hailandiere appeared to be well pleased at the arrival
of the good Brothers for whom he had asked so often
during the last two years. Although somewhat fatigued,
Fr. Sorin was able to say mass and the Brothers to receive
communion. It was a veritable feast day for all. They could
hardly believe their eyes and convince themselves that they
were at Vincennes.

14. The Sisters of Providence, founded in Ruillé-sur-Loir in
the diocese of Le Mans, France, by Rev. Jacques Dujarié in 1812.
They had been recruited for the diocese of Vincennes by Bp. De
la Hailandiere and had made their first American foundation near
Terre Haute, Indiana, in 1840.

15. The actual date was Oct. 10, 1841. See Sorin to Moreau,
Oct. 14, 1841, in GA.

The Brothers had expected to find in Vincennes or elsewhere in the diocese a house ready for their occupation, but the good bishop, who had several places in view, did not wish to decide by himself without first giving them a choice. The next day, he proposed to visit one of the places with Fr. Sorin at Francisville[16] on the Wabash river, four miles from Vincennes. The location did not please Fr. Sorin, who at the request of His Lordship started that evening with a priest of the diocese, the Rev. Mr. Delaune,[17] to examine another farm of one hundred and sixty acres called St. Peter's, situated twenty-seven miles from Vincennes between Washington and Mount Pleasant.[18] It was a place difficult of access but in the midst of several Catholic congregations. It was even one of the oldest missions of the diocese.

At St. Peter's, Oct. 14th: The Bishop gives 160 acres of land

Fr. Sorin arrived there Tuesday morning about nine o'clock. St. Peter's had a little frame church in good repair; two little rooms had been added to it, one for the sacristy and one for the priest. A little further on were two old log shanties such as are quite common in this country, one answering for a kitchen and the other used as a school. The school was taught by a certain Charles Rother, a young German who wished to become a Brother and whom the Bishop had sent there whilst waiting for the Brothers. Thus he had been living with Mr. Delaune at St. Peter's for some time. Although there was no engagement entered into for the Brothers, it became evident that they were expected there rather than anywhere else; and perhaps St. Peter's was the best choice they could make at the time.

Besides, although removed from communication with the outside world and from the river, and though buried in the woods, St. Peter's had a cheerful look. The buildings and the garden were situated on an eminence, and to all appearances the air was salubrious. There was at least room

16. Francisville is in Illinois, below Vincennes.

17. Julian Delaune was born in Paris and had emigrated to the United States in either 1840 or 1841. See Morin, 98n.

18. Montgomery in Daviess County, Indiana.

enough to pass the winter there and, without taking time to look elsewhere or to wait, the order was sent to the Brothers to come at once. On the evening of the fourteenth the little band was gathered together in the chapel of St. Peter's to offer thanks to God in common.

St. Peter's

As has been seen, St. Peter's was already known as a Catholic center. Some years before there had even been a school taught there by the Sisters of Charity,[19] who had not been able to make their living and had withdrawn. The Catholic congregation was of about thirty-five families, all of whom were poor except about five or six. But all, Catholics and Protestants, appeared to be well pleased at the arrival of the Brothers. All the neighbors on whom Fr. Sorin could call during the first weeks with the pastor of the place received him most cordially.

Without delay they all set to work, one on the little farm, another at the garden, a third in the kitchen, and the others to study the language. They felt the need of this more fully than ever.

The conduct of this little community was truly edifying. Those good Brothers were often in want of everything except food and clothing; but, according to the precept of the Divine Master, everyone appeared to be content. At no period of their Society, perhaps, will there be more privations, more wants, and less dissatisfaction; and likely also fewer complaints and murmurs. Long afterwards, when an abuse is to be corrected or a disagreeable duty to be enforced, the fervor of these happy beginnings might be called to mind. During the first two months all had to sleep on the floor and to practice many another act of mortification of a like nature. Yet all were habitually gay and happy in their lot. Where fervor and devotion reign, a sacrifice is a joy rather than an affliction.

19. The Sisters of Charity of Nazareth, Kentucky. See Thomas T. McAvoy, *The Catholic Church in Indiana, 1789–1834* (New York: Columbia University Press, 1940), 191.

Postulants

Before long, Providence sent them some helpers. Besides Mr. Rother, who, as has been said, was expecting them, two young men of the neighborhood presented themselves and were received into the Novitiate. Some months later two others of a more advanced age came to increase the number of the children of St. Joseph; in the following spring, several others arrived from Jasper [Indiana] and from New York, and these were also received. A year had hardly passed before nine vocations were already admitted to the Novitiate.

Eight of these were received into the Society by the conferring on them of the religious habit at the close of the first general retreat, August 21, 1842. Mr. Rother had received the habit in the month of December of the previous year; three other postulants also took the habit the following November. Thus, twelve took the habit at St. Peter's in the space of fifteen months. Seven years later, only half of them remained.

In general, vocations in this country can inspire but very limited confidence until after profession. They are mostly Irish and Germans that present themselves. The former are by nature full of faith, respect, religious inclinations, and sensible and devoted; but a great defect often paralyzes in them all their other good qualities: the lack of stability. They change more readily than any other nation. The latter are ordinarily less obedient, prouder, more singular in their tastes and less endowed with the qualities of the heart; but they are more persevering.

As to genuine Americans, there is no hope of finding subjects amongst them for a religious house of this kind. We might look upon it as a miracle of grace for a young American to persevere in the humble and difficult employment of a Brother of St. Joseph. The spirit of liberty as it is understood in the United States is too directly opposed to the spirit of obedience and submission of a community to leave any hopes for a long time to come of any addition of subjects in a country in which the nature of the men appears to offer so few dispositions towards the religious life. Hence it comes to pass that the young men who spend some time amongst the Americans soon imbibe their spirit and manners and become in reality all the more unfitted for the religious life the more years they have passed in the New World.

Foundation of Vincennes

The entrance of the first postulants should have retained the good Br. Vincent in the community, since he had come from France only for this important purpose, to train the Novices. Yet it became necessary for us to make other arrangements. The Bishop of Vincennes insisted on having this good Patriarch to teach his own school in Vincennes. It was necessary to obey. The Brothers had found it advisable from the very first to try to retain the good graces of their bishop.

Nov. 15th, Br. Vincent in Vincennes

The joy caused by their arrival was greatly diminished when the bishop was presented with a bill of three thousand and several hundred francs, the sum due for their expenses. This sum was to be paid by Bp. De la Hailandiere as soon as possible after the arrival of the colony. His Lordship looked surprised and even offended at the amount, and after telling Fr. Sorin that he would not pay it, he added that he would write to Father Rector to decide the important question: shall the Brothers be subject to the direction and the jurisdiction of the Ordinary? Do they belong to your house of Le Mans or to the diocese?

Doubts on the question of on whom the Brothers depend

The answer of the Rev. Fr. Moreau was somewhat vague and settled nothing for the present. This uncertainty on the one side and on the other could not but be injurious to the establishment of the Brothers, who, having no resources of their own and depending, even for the necessaries of life, on their Mother House and on the diocese, hardly dared to ask help from anyone before ascertaining definitely to whom they should look. On their side, neither the diocese nor the (Mother) House was in a hurry to act until this question was settled. The diocese, however, made this determination much more clearly manifest. Whilst Fr. Moreau continued to do all that he could for them, Bp. De la Hailandiere maintained a kind of reserve, as much as to say that he would have been willing and able to do more if the Brothers' establishment had been placed entirely in his care.

Collection by Mr. Delaune

Mr. Delaune collects $3000 in ten months

The state of destitution of the little colony thus deserted on both sides and left to its own fate would soon have been a very sad one had not Providence shown the same readiness as in a thousand other circumstances to step in and rescue our good Brothers from their embarrassing situation. The Rev. J. Delaune had not yet started for the new post assigned him by the bishop at Shanetown, but he was preparing to do so in a few days. Conversing one evening with Fr. Sorin about his pious projects for his future parish, the latter said to him laughingly that he would perhaps be doing better if he took the staff and sack of a beggar and went to friendly houses to collect for the Brothers whom he had received into his house without being able to assure them against soon dying of hunger. God permitted that the words were taken more seriously than they were intended.

Having afterwards discussed the matter at their leisure, permission was asked of the bishop, who, contrary to the expectations of Mr. Delaune himself, granted him permission to try to make a collection in the East and in Canada for the Brothers of St. Joseph, on condition, however, that one fourth of the proceeds should be applied to the debt on a church built by the zealous missionary at Mount Pleasant.

He started at once. God blessed his devotedness during nearly a year of his charitable expedition, and he sent the Bishop nearly fifteen thousand francs, not to speak of some bales of goods and some postulants whom he secured. These resources were more than enough to keep life in the young community.

By the advice of His Lordship, a portion of this sum was employed in clearing eighty acres of land; soon afterwards they had a magnificent field of eighty acres planted with corn. Unfortunately, the Brothers, who had very little knowledge of agriculture in this country, simply wore themselves out without much benefit. They were possessed by the idea that they knew much better than the Americans what practical farming was, and in all things they preferred their French ways to what they saw and heard around them. However, experience soon taught them that a plan, excellent for a country like France, might be very imperfectly adapted to the requirements of a strange soil, and that precautions called for in France were a mere waste of time in the United States. Here time is everything, land nothing; in Europe it is just the contrary. Hence, the immense difference between the method of cultivation in France and that in America. Thus, it appears that devotedness is not always the sole requisite, but that an experienced guide is needed, otherwise devotedness will wear itself out to little purpose.

The Brothers clear 80 acres of land. Different ways of cultivating

During this first year, our good Brothers did not spare themselves and yet they reaped but little. They often employed means of saving things that are saved in France but they did not understand that to save ten cents they wasted half a day which was equal to fifty cents.

Be this as it may, the more they labored on this new soil of St. Peter's, the more they grew attached to it. The Catholic congregation and their Protestant and infidel neighbors seemed all to be attached to them. The question arose of building a college and all appeared delighted with the idea, ready to help in carrying it out, each according to his means. The materials to construct it were gathered almost immediately and the following spring one hundred thousand bricks, ten thousand feet of lumber and some thousands of feet of cut stone were got ready for this purpose.

Let us say a word here about the great attachment of this little family to the Mother House of Sainte-Croix. It was one of their usual thoughts, and in nearly all their

*Attachment
of this first
colony to the
Mother House*

recreations Sainte-Croix or the Rev. Fr. Rector formed the staple of their conversations. For about six weeks after their arrival they received no news from France and Fr. Sorin made a trip to Vincennes in the hope of finding a letter there from the Rev. Fr. Moreau. At length, towards the end of November, he received one which transported them all with joy. It was opened and read before the Blessed Sacrament and it filled them with consolation. It is probably to this filial affection that they owe the fact of their remaining under the jurisdiction of the Mother House instead of passing altogether under that of the ordinary.

Conversions

*Protestants
convert*

It is something quite remarkable that during those first months after their arrival, those poor religious, destitute of all human means of pleasing and drawing to themselves prejudiced people, succeeded, even though hardly able to make themselves understood, in bringing to the knowledge of the truth about twenty of those Protestants, some of whom had held out against the most eloquent sermons. Several entire families at St. Peter's applied to Fr. Sorin for instruction and baptism. Assuredly God wished in this manner to sustain their courage amid their little trials.

Some weeks after their arrival, the Father set to work as well as he knew how to prepare and preach sermons in English every Sunday. Sometimes he was told on the following day that half of what he said was not understood; but nothing discouraged him, and towards the end of the year nearly all understood him.

Entrance of Mr. Chartier[20]

For six months, this priest had been superior of the Seminary of Vincennes. Having been invited by the Brothers to preach their retreat in August, his acquaintance with

20. Etienne Chartier was born in Montreal in 1809. He entered the Congregation of Holy Cross on Oct. 12, 1842, and withdrew Feb. 9, 1843. M.g.

the house resulted in his application to be received as a member and in the following month he was admitted as a candidate. Retreats had been promised by him to St. Mary's, Mount Pleasant and Washington on the occasion of the jubilee in favor of Spain. Mr. Chartier preached them all successfully as he had at St. Peter's. In a word, he could have made himself very useful to the Society, had he not, in an argument with the Bishop, defended the interests of the house too warmly, going so far that he was afterwards ashamed to retract. He was a man of talent but too hot-headed.

Departure from St. Peters

Without being actually in conflict with the Bishop, we *Nov. 16th* could not expect much encouragement or help from him. No sooner did he hear the first word about our desire to begin a college than he opposed it and declared positively that he would not consent, alleging that we were too near the college of the Eudists at Vincennes, whose superior in France, Mr. Louis, had his promise that he would not grant permission to erect any college except at such a distance as would not interfere with his.

Fr. Sorin made a journey to Vincennes about the end of October to treat of the matter. The Bishop repeated to him what he had already expressed in writing and ended by saying that if he wished to build a college, he would give him the lake property near South Bend, in the northern part of the diocese. Having obtained the necessary information in Vincennes, Fr. Sorin considered the matter as being very serious and asked the Bishop to give him some time to reflect on it.

On his return to St. Peter's the Father assembled the council of administration and laid the Bishop's offer before it. Several days were spent in ineffectual deliberations; finally the offer was accepted, and the day, hour and mode of departure were agreed upon.

On 16 November, seven of the most industrious of the Brothers set out with their superior for South Bend.

The eight days of their journey were days of hardship; the air piercingly cold, as the little band moved north on a direct line.

Mr. Chartier falls out with the Bishop and departs

The rest of the community were to remain at St. Peter's till the following spring, under the direction of Mr. Chartier. But contrary to the expectation of Fr. Sorin and of the Brothers, Mr. Chartier again fell out with the Bishop, and the consequence of this disagreement was that he refused to remain any longer in the diocese of Vincennes, which he left about the middle of February.

Brother Vincent, being thus at the head of the rest of the community, made arrangements and took advantage of the season to remove from St. Peter's to Notre Dame du Lac, whither it would have been much more difficult to come some months later. They therefore set out and reached the end of their journey the Monday before Ash Wednesday much fatigued and after great hardship but overflowing with health and good spirits. They arrived a few hours ahead of Fr. Sorin, who was returning from a visit to a tribe of savages. This separation had lasted only four months, but it seemed to them like four years.

CHAPTER 2

N. D. du Lac 1842-1843

1. Topographical Description

It was on November 26, 1842, that Fr. Sorin arrived *Nov. 26, 1842*
at Notre Dame du Lac with seven Brothers, Mary, Gatien,
Patrick, William, Basil, Peter and Francis,[1] after a journey
of more than one hundred leagues through the snow. This
property was then known as St. Mary of the Lakes. It is
situated on the left bank of the St. Joseph River,[2] half a
league from South Bend, the county seat of St. Joseph
County, one league from the northern boundary of Indiana; about twelve leagues from Lake Michigan, thirty-
five leagues from Chicago, seventy from Detroit and four
hundred from New York.

It contains about five hundred and twenty-four acres of
land or nearly one-third of a league square, only ten acres
of which were then under cultivation, the rest being virgin
forest with the exception of about eighty or ninety acres,

---

1. Br. Mary, whose name was later changed to Francis Xavier,
and Br. Gatien were among the original colony that had come from
France the previous year. The other five Brothers had joined the
community at St. Peter's and were still novices. Four were Irish
immigrants: Brs. Patrick (Michael Connelly), 44; William (John
O'Sullivan), 27; Basil (Timothy O'Neil), 32; and Peter (James Tully),
34. Br. Francis (Michael Disser), 17, was born in the Alsace region
of France. See M.g.

2. The property is actually on the right bank.

the center of which was occupied by two charming lakes fed
by springs and about twenty-five feet deep. The banks contain an inexhaustible supply of white marl, which, when
worked like loam, is employed in making lime.

Without being very rich, the ground here is suitable
for raising wheat, corn, potatoes, clover, buckwheat and
all kinds of edible roots. The only residence was an old log
cabin, forty by twenty-four feet, the ground floor of which
served as a room for the priest, and the story above for
a chapel for the Catholics of South Bend and environs,
although it was open to all the winds. To this little cabin
had been added some years before a little frame building of
two stories, a little more becoming and somewhat more
habitable than the first, in which resided a half breed
with his family, who, when necessary, acted as interpreter
between the priest and the savages. Add to this a neat little
house eight feet by six, and you have all the buildings then
in existence near the Lake.

2. Its Religious Condition. Its Past

There were at that time around this poor little sanctuary, the only one in northern Indiana, about twenty
Catholic families scattered in a radius of two leagues. Two
leagues above South Bend and also on the river is situated a
little town noted for its wrought and cast iron works and of
about the same size as the former, a thousand inhabitants.[3]
At the same distance below South Bend is the village of
Bertrand, formerly a very flourishing place but then without
any commerce whatever, Niles, a league and a half down
river, having absorbed it all.

Although there was a little brick church at Bertrand
which could easily have been finished, still, as there was
never more than one priest at a time in the neighborhood,
the Catholics of those four little towns and of the neighbor-

3. The present city of Mishawaka, Indiana, part of which was
originally known as St. Joseph Iron Works. See Timothy Edward
Howard, *A History of St. Joseph County Indiana* (Chicago: Lewis
Publishing Company, 1907), 1:319–323.

ing country were accustomed to look for spiritual aid to the church at the Lake. Consequently, it was there that the retreat of the Jubilee was made by all the Catholics from miles around to the satisfaction and edification even of Fr. Sorin. The cold was intense, and yet the exercises were regularly attended. For two years there had been only very rare visits by a priest from Chicago. The Catholic religion was thus little known as yet in all this part of the diocese. The few ceremonies that could be carried out, being necessarily devoid of all solemnity and even of decency, could have hardly any other effect in the eyes of the public than to give rise to a thousand offensive and sarcastic remarks against Catholicism. There was scarcely a single Catholic in all the country able to defend his faith against these insults and the conduct of many often served as foundation and proof of the blasphemies of the malicious and the ignorant. All the surroundings were strongly Protestant, that is to say enemies more or less embittered against the Catholics.

At Mishawaka, as well as at South Bend and Niles, there were already three or four sectarian churches. As soon as the arrival of our new missionaries and their object became known, one might have said that a cry of alarm could be heard and all those pulpits of falsehood resounded every Sunday with the most heated invectives against the twelve Popish priests and the twenty monks of the Lake, passion thus multiplying their numbers in order more effectively to put everybody on his guard. Moreover, it was added that the Pope of Rome had already sent Fr. Sorin ninety thousand dollars and that he would send another ten thousand to make the even number. A little later, when the walls of the college began to appear, people seemed to take a delight in saying that we might go ahead with our college, but as soon as it was completed they would burn it down.

There was nothing very encouraging in this reception. To look at it from a human standpoint, it would have been wiser to retreat without delay; but even though they anticipated still greater opposition in the future, our pious champions, who knew how to hope against hope, cheered themselves with the expectation of a future more meritorious and more glorious for their holy cause. They placed all their confidence in heaven and let their neighbors talk and rave.

Let us say some words about the past history of Notre Dame du Lac. The ground was purchased in 1830, 1831, and 1832 by Mr. S. T. Badin,[4] the first priest ordained in the United States. Sold afterwards by him in 1836 to the venerable Bishop Bruté,[5] founder of the diocese of Vincennes, it was afterwards transferred by the latter to the Rev. Mr. Bach[6] on condition that a college should be built thereon within the space of two years. Which condition not having been complied with, Bp. De la Hailandiere was in a position to offer it in 1842 to the Society of Notre Dame de Sainte-Croix with the proviso that in the same space of time a college and a novitiate for Brothers should be there erected. The land may have been worth fifteen to twenty thousand francs at the time.

It was, therefore, Mr. Badin who in 1830 had made it the center of some Catholic settlements scattered over northern Indiana and western Michigan. He had also found and gathered together a considerable number of savages, mostly of the Potawatomi tribe, whose first apostle he was in this country and with not a little success.

4. Stephen Theodore Badin, born in Orléans, France, in 1768, emigrated to America in 1792 and was ordained in Baltimore by Bishop John Carroll the following year. See J. Herman Schauinger, *Stephen T. Badin: Priest in the Wilderness* (Milwaukee: Bruce Publishing Company, 1956). On the purchase of the land see Morin, 161. McAvoy, 187, dates the construction of a chapel and cabin by Badin at St. Mary of the Lakes in 1834.

5. When the diocese of Vincennes, Indiana, was created in 1834, Simon Guillaume Gabriel Bruté de Remur, a French Sulpician priest who was on the faculty of Mount St. Mary's College, Emmitsburg, Maryland, was appointed the first bishop. He died in 1839. See Charles Lemarié, *Monseigneur Bruté de Remur*.

6. Ferdinand Bach was a member of the Fathers of Mercy, a French religious institute introduced into the United States in 1839. See Arthur J. Hope, *Notre Dame: One Hundred Years*, 51; *The Catholic Encyclopedia* (1907–1914) 5:795.

Especially after he received Fr. Deseille[7] as his assistant, the savages were converted by the hundreds. The former lived in these parts for only a few years. Fr. Deseille seemed destined to have a much longer stay, but death carried him off from his dear Indians in 1837. It was in the poor hovel described above that he terminated his pious career after administering holy communion to himself.

The excellent Mr. B. Petit,[8] a young lawyer of Rennes, who had become a missionary of the diocese of Vincennes, was sent the day after his ordination to replace the zealous departed priest. He also took up his abode at St. Mary of the Lakes where he lived but a few months, death cutting down this excellent priest at the very beginning of his career when he had become exceedingly endeared to all that had anything to do with him. He died at St. Louis on his return from an expedition to the West which he had undertaken with his dear Indians to whose welfare he had evidently sacrificed his life.

During his short residence amongst them, he himself baptized more than three hundred Indians and had had as many as two hundred confirmed at one time in the little building mentioned above as the chapel. When Fr. Sorin arrived, there remained only about two hundred, all the others having been removed at different periods to Mississippi. The saintly Mr. Petit was succeeded by a Canadian missionary from Detroit, who spent nearly three years in the country, which he did not edify as his predecessors had done.[9]

7. Louis Deseille, a young Flemish priest, came to assist Badin in 1832 and carried on Badin's work among the Potawatomi. See McAvoy, 184.

8. Benjamin Mary Petit, born in Rennes, France, in 1811, emigrated to America in 1836 and was ordained a priest by Bp. Bruté on Oct. 14, 1837. He died in St. Louis, Feb. 10, 1839, on his return from the lands in Kansas whither the federal government had moved the Potawatomi. See Alerding, *Fort Wayne*, 160–161.

9. The Potawatomi were removed beyond the Mississippi to Kansas. See Morin, 163–165. Parish sacramental records contain

3. The Missions

For five or six years, the priest of St. Mary of the Lake was accustomed to visit several places in the neighborhood at stated times and to say mass for the people. Those places were already known as missions, although in some of them there were only one or two Catholic families. In Indiana, towards the south, going up river from South Bend and Mishawaka for a distance of about ten leagues, you find the little town of Goshen, which had then about two hundred inhabitants, twenty or twenty-five of whom were Catholic; six leagues further, that of Leesburg, still smaller in total and in Catholic population. A little more to the southwest, at ten leagues from the Lake, there was also a little Catholic congregation whose center was at Plymouth. To the east in Michigan was Bertrand, two leagues from St. Mary's; a little lower, the little town of Niles, which also formed a congregation; four leagues further, the town of Berrien, where the priest said mass for three families; and six leagues farther on, still on the same river, the town of St. Joseph, which formed one of the finest missions of the country.

At twenty-eight leagues, on the way towards Detroit, Kalamazoo is situated, with a population of twelve or fifteen hundred inhabitants, at least a hundred of whom are Catholics. In Michigan, St. Mary's also attended another little congregation of ten or twelve families at Nantowossibi at twenty leagues; another of two or three families at Centerville at seventeen leagues; another at Constantine at fifteen leagues; and finally that of Pokagon's Indians at twelve leagues, that of Paw Paw at eighteen leagues, that of Kankakee and that of Tippecanoe[10] containing altogether a little more than two hundred souls.

---

the names of four priests who served the congregation between Petit and Sorin, namely, Ch. Bauwens, 1839, S. A. Bernier, 1839–1841, M. Shawe, 1841, and Anthony Kapp, 1841.

10. Kankakee and Tippecanoe are in southeast Marshall County, Indiana. See "Missions served from Notre Dame, 1842–1854," Sacred Heart Parish Collections, IPA.

Most of these different little parishes desired very much to have a priest amongst them, but this was an impossibility. A great deal of activity was necessary to visit them all three or four times a year, and unless they are visited at least once a month, nothing can be done in this country.

4. Advantages

St. Mary's of the Lake was at that time of easy access. In a day it could communicate with Chicago, which was distant by forty leagues; in two days with Detroit, eighty leagues away, and in four days with New York, four hundred leagues distant. Vincennes, one hundred leagues away, required a week. The St. Joseph River facilitated importation and exportation of goods and produce. Moreover, the two lakes were a source of enjoyment and of profit to the community and to a college by their fish and their beds of marl, from which lime could be made and bartered. Besides, there were the advantages of the baths for the students in summer and the amusements on the ice in winter. Finally, although in itself quite ordinary, the soil of the Lake can be kept fertile by means of marl and lime.

If the missions should develop, they will be an additional benefit to the locality, and as there was then no Catholic college in all the surrounding country, not even in Detroit or Chicago, the hopes of their finding the means of making a livelihood encouraged the missionaries from the beginning to build that which one sees there today.

5. Preparations for the College

Fr. Sorin arrived at the Lake with about two thousand francs; the bishop, who had himself received the collection of Mr. Delaune, could put at their disposal four or five thousand francs, including two thousand six hundred francs granted that year by the Propagation of the Faith. This was indeed but little towards establishing a community consisting already of more than twenty persons and which expected a new colony of priests, Brothers, and Sisters towards the beginning of the following season.

However, neither the small amount of their present possessions nor the barrenness of the place nor the thousand difficulties inseparable from such an enterprise in a center almost wholly Protestant could discourage our hardy pioneers. They hardly stopped to consider the idea of modifying the magnificent plan of building which they had brought with them from St. Peter's. The college was to be in the shape of a double hammer, 160 feet long, 36 feet wide and four and a half stories high.

The erection of a college being the first condition of their holding the Lake property, one of their first concerns was to get ready to carry it out at once. Sixty thousand feet of lumber, two hundred and fifty thousand bricks and the necessary lime were engaged for the following spring. Moreover, the Bishop's architect,[11] who had made the plan, also made and sent in his bid for the work. All having been done under the supervision of the bishop, his bid was accepted without long deliberation.

The end of winter was ardently desired that work might begin. Unfortunately, that year it was of a length and severity almost unheard of in the United States. For five whole months the snow covered the ground, and during all that time there was not an intermission of even one week of the intense cold. The consequence of this for the enterprise was unfortunate, because the whole country was impoverished to a considerable extent.

6. The First Church, December 10, 1842

Although the college has first been spoken of, it was found necessary before attending to it to prepare a suitable place in which the Christians of the area might assemble. In the beginning of December, an appeal was made to all the Catholics of the congregation, but what could be

11. Hope, 55, identifies the architect as Mr. Marsile.

expected of people so poor, and, let it be said, with such little zeal as most of them were animated with? The result of the appeal was a subscription payable in so many days of work! In three weeks, trees enough were cut down and hauled to the place to put up a building forty-six feet by twenty. On the day appointed, the men assembled and raised the walls of the new temple. The efforts of their liberality did not go beyond that. Fr. Sorin had to have the building finished at his own cost, otherwise no church would have been there for years. This was an expense of one thousand francs for the community. The church was opened on 19 March, the feast of St. Joseph.

The other members of the community were soon to arrive from St. Peter's, contrary to the will of the bishop, who wanted them to maintain both St. Peter's and the Lake. But Fr. Sorin could hardly see in the resources of himself and his associates the means of adding a house and positively refused to open two foundations one hundred leagues apart. By order of their superior, the Brothers, eleven in number, left for St. Mary of the Lakes in the first days of February and arrived on Mardi Gras. Their reunion was a joyful day for all.

It was particularly to their assistance that was due the completion of the chapel at the date already mentioned. Insignificant as was this building, it was necessary at the same time to devote it to still another use. A second story was carried through its entire length in order to lodge in it the Sisters that were to arrive the following spring or summer. The old dormitory that had been used as a chapel was assigned to the Brothers and one of the priest's rooms was joined on to the new church with the intention of also adding the other room the following year, which would then furnish a space ninety by twenty feet. We shall say nothing of the height of the first story. It was not necessary to be very tall in order to touch the rafters with your head.

7. Arrival of the Second Colony

Frs. Cointet,
Marivault, and
Gouesse, one
Brother and
four Sisters

The second colony started from Notre-Dame de Ste-Croix May 27, 1843, and was composed of Father F. Cointet,[12] the Rev. Mr. Marivault,[13] priest, Mr. l'Abbe F. Gouesse[14] for the Society of priests, Br. Eloi[15] for the Brothers' Society, and Sisters Mary of the Heart of Jesus, Mary of Bethlehem, Mary of Calvary and Mary of Nazareth.[16]

Their voyage was pleasant enough, although at times a little disagreeable. They reached Detroit towards the end of the first week of July. There they were near losing their leader, Fr. Cointet. He fell from the balcony of the bishop's residence and by all rights could not have been expected to get up alive, considering the height of the balcony and the hardness of the ground where the accident took place. But Providence seems even then to have had a special design of protection and love towards this zealous missionary. The only penalty he paid was to remain some weeks in Detroit

12. François Louis Cointet was born Feb. 26, 1816, at La Roë (Mayenne), France, and had been ordained a priest for the diocese of Le Mans in 1839. A seminary classmate of Sorin, he joined the Congregation of Holy Cross and began his novitiate upon his arrival at Notre Dame in August 1843. See M.g. and Hope, 69.

13. Théophile de Lascoux-Marivault was born Feb. 9, 1809, at Le Blanc (Indre), France, and was already a priest when he entered the Congregation of Holy Cross in August 1842. M.g.

14. François Gouesse was born May 17, 1817, at Courbeville (Mayenne), France, and was already in minor orders when he entered the Congregation of Holy Cross in January 1842. M.g.

15. Br. Eloi (Jean-Marie Leray) was born Apr. 23, 1818, at Autrain (Ille-et-Vilaine), France. M.g.

16. All four Sisters were French: Mary of the Heart of Jesus (Marie Savary), 19, was born in Quelaine (Mayenne); Mary of Bethlehem (Marie Desneux), 45, was born in Ruillé-sur-Loir (Sarthe), was probably illiterate and had been one of the very first Sisters at Ste-Croix; Mary of Calvary (Marie Robineau), 25, was born in Parce (Sarthe?) and was one of the first four women to receive the habit as Holy Cross Sisters in August 1841; and Mary of Nazareth (Marie Chauvin), 21, was born in Paris. ASHC. See also M. Georgia Costin, "Beginnings in America: The Bertrand Years, 1843–1853," in Costin, ed., *Fruits of the Tree* (Notre Dame, Ind.: Sisters of the Holy Cross, 1989), 2:29–30.

to recover, whilst at the same time he became known there and edified all that had the opportunity to wait on him.

His traveling companions meanwhile continued their journey, leaving Br. Eloi and Sr. Mary of Calvary to take care of the patient. Their arrival at St. Mary of the Lake made a sensation impossible to describe, both on those that were there already and on the new arrivals. This moment may serve as a point of comparison to represent to themselves what they will one day experience when they meet in heaven.

A single room was placed at the service of the priests and the Sisters had to themselves the ground floor below the chapel where they spent nearly two years. Except for the fact that there was only one window and that in consequence of the close atmosphere there was a large stock of fleas and bed bugs, they were, as they say in America, pretty comfortable.

This timely reinforcement would, if need had been, infuse new courage into the old missionaries; but there was one circumstance that was embarrassing. None of the three ecclesiastics had made a novitiate. That was the first thing to be attended to, but it afforded no relief to Fr. Sorin. On the contrary, it meant more work. Moreover, the needs of the times were such that it was out of the question for them to shut themselves up and devote themselves exclusively to the exercises of the Novitiate. The attempt was made to have the two work together but without being able to throw the blame on any one, it was soon found that, with the best will in the whole world, the old proverb held good of *one thing at a time*.

Br. Eloi, as his name suggests, was a farmer and locksmith, and could render great services to the house. A shop was immediately provided for him and tools put at his service. Once he had started to work, he rendered some services but not as much as he could. An ungovernable temper often paralyzed the skill of his hands. Perhaps he got even more pay for his services than he earned till he left the house in 1845.

Br. Eloi is of little use. The Sisters soon make themselves useful

As to the Sisters, there is no doubt that their services were a benefit felt by all. The wardrobe had necessarily been neglected as, up to this time, there was no one to look after it except the Brothers. In some months everything about it was orderly and clean, and all were content.

8. First Brick Building

The expenses for bricks, lumber and lime had hardly been met, together with the necessary outlay for the running of the house, when it was found that the treasury of the house was exhausted. On the other hand, the architect, unfaithful to his promises, allowed the season for building the college to pass by. The fear of not being able to do anything towards the college this year and the consciousness of many other urgent needs caused it to be determined to put up some brick building that would serve as a bakery and a dormitory for a few boarders and for the Brothers for whom there were no accommodations.

This was the origin of the first brick building, which was originally erected for two stories, and to which new needs caused two other buildings to be added in succession, and two additional stories as it exists at the present day for the use of the Sisters. Meanwhile it served for nearly a year for its first purpose and even for the classes.

9. The College Begun

The general retreat of the Brothers was just over. About a month previously, the idea of beginning the college this year had been abandoned. Neither the time nor the resources appeared to be sufficient when, on 24 August, the architect arrived from Vincennes with two workmen. Mr. Byerley offered a credit of ten thousand francs at his store and a loan of 2500 francs. The Rev. Mr. Marivault offered to draw on his family for six thousand francs due him. Everyone was urgent, and on the twenty-eighth, the feast of St. Augustine, the corner stone of the college was blessed in the presence of a considerable number gathered together to witness the translation of Mr. Deseille's remains.

A subscription was taken up on the occasion which amounted to about a thousand francs. This was on Thursday and work was deferred until the following Monday. But from that day until 20 December, work was rushed forward as fast as possible. Fortunately, the autumn of this year was extremely favorable, and when snow and cold came, the college was under roof. The plastering could not be done till the following year, but it required only a few months, and some of the rooms were occupied from the beginning of June, and all was in readiness at the return of winter.

No need to tell the joy felt by those poor religious at sight of the building so much desired, surmounted by the cross which topped the highest trees of the forest. They had for this year only a few boarders along with seven or eight little orphans.

10. Charter as a University

The walls of the college had not reached the third story when the member of the Legislature for St. Joseph County came to personally offer his services to Fr. Sorin, assuring him that he could obtain from the State Legislature a full charter for a University and another incorporating the Manual Labor School of the Brothers. Mr. Defrees[17]—this is the name of the legislator—was not a Catholic but, quite the contrary, a Methodist. But in this case God was pleased to cause him to lay aside for once the prejudices of his sect and even his personal animosities, to make him useful to his country even in favoring his enemies. To the surprise of many and to the general rejoicing of the Catholics as well as to the vexation of their enemies, the two documents were secured. The two charters, each in its kind, conferred

Obtained by Mr. Defrees, an infidel then a Methodist

17. Senator John Dougherty Defrees represented St. Joseph County in the Indiana State Legislature. Born in Tennessee of French-Irish ancestry, from 1831 to 1834 he had published, together with his brother, Joseph, a local newspaper. He later practiced law in South Bend, served as editor of the *Indianapolis Journal* and was appointed public printer by President Lincoln. See Howard, 1:194, 464–466; 2:624, 715.

all the privileges that could be granted by the government and they will remain in the archives as the most precious monuments that could be in its possession.

11. Financial Condition

Poverty. Loan of 10,000 fr.; Grant of 17,000 fr.

The resources furnished by the diocese were soon exhausted. The buildings erected during the year cost nearly thirty thousand francs without mentioning the necessary and ordinary expense of the house. The Rev. Mr. Marivault's draft was protested in France, with six hundred francs costs added. Fr. Sorin had already drawn on the Rev. Father (Moreau) in November for five thousand francs, but it was necessary to add thereto a loan of ten thousand francs, which was secured by the pastor of Ft. Wayne, Mr. J. Benoit. Moreover, in Mr. Byerley's store there was an account current of about eight thousand francs.

Fortunately, the Propagation of the Faith granted this year, at different intervals, the sum of seventeen thousand francs. Besides, Mr. and Mrs. Beaubien of Detroit donated to Fr. Sorin a piece of ground that was sold some time afterwards for about fifteen thousand francs. The gift was made in favor of the Sisters but left to the donee entire liberty to use it otherwise should it be judged proper. When the act was signed, Fr. Sorin was asked by Mrs. Beaubien if he would consent to give an education to two little orphans to which he readily agreed.

Another expense of the same year was the clearing of forty acres, about two thousand francs. At the end of this period the debts of the house amounted to between twenty and twenty-two thousand francs.

12. General Remarks

The first year at Notre Dame du Lac was remarkable: 1. for the devotedness and piety of the house in general; 2. for the animosity of the Protestants against the institution; 3. by the nature of the various undertakings; 4. by the donations that were received; 5. by the two charters; 6. by the assistance received from the Mother House. Many had to suffer, but all were ready for sufferings. The prospect of the college sustained the weak while changing them. Although less unfamiliar with the manners and customs of the country than at St. Peter's, the good Brothers were still far from acting with the liberty and the opportunism of the Americans. No one knows how to live and to manage things like the Americans.

The house was sometimes in a state of confusion, but at the same time a truly religious spirit reigned everywhere. The community was more than once visibly protected. It is rare that works of the kind undertaken are continued to the end without accident, but there was no such thing as a fall or a wound during all this time.

Towards the middle of December, when the college was yet filled with pieces of wood and rubbish, fire broke out in a partition on the first story and had even time to make some progress before it was discovered. Of course in the condition in which things then were, all seemed destined to become the prey of the flames. Providence was doubtless watching over the house whilst all were sleeping. The alarm was very great; but after half an hour the danger was arrested by the efforts of the Brothers and the workmen, and all joined in returning thanks to God.

Fire stopped. A coal furnace to heat the whole college

The college was built with the view of being heated in all parts by means of a large furnace enclosed in the sand under the first floor. It was through one of the pipes that a partition took fire. For two years this furnace was the only fire in the building. At last, no one having the satisfaction of getting even a smell of the heat that it diffused all around, it became necessary to put up stoves.

Furnace abandoned after two years' trial

The following year all came near burning down through the imprudence of a boy in meddling with one of those stoves. There was great alarm and the danger was really imminent.

A third fire threatened to reduce everything to ashes in 1846, and this time it was due to the imprudence of Fr. Sorin himself. He wanted to have the stoves in the rooms along the corridor replaced by little chimneys and had too readily trusted the word of a mason. After eight

New fire prevented

or ten days one of these chimneys started a fire, and once more the college was within an inch of becoming a total ruin. God be praised for not having more severely punished the house by the thoughtlessness of its head.

The question was often raised, even from the very beginning, of furnishing the college with a lightning rod. Fr. Sorin and his council preferred to trust to the guardianship of the Blessed Virgin. They had been likewise advised *Fire insurance* to have the college insured. It was only in 1848 that they *of 15,000 fr.* consented to take out an insurance policy and then for only fifteen thousand francs.

This same year was rendered memorable by conversions that were much talked of and by the baptism of ten adult savages.

Brother John, an Englishman by birth, had been deputed to go in search of the new colony, but on his arrival at Le Mans he found that they had just left. He himself returned with a Sister infirmarian, Mary of Prov- *Fr. Moreau's bell* idence, towards the end of November.[18] With him also came the bell donated by the Rev. Fr. Moreau. It was solemnly blessed a few days afterwards and mounted on the college, whence it is to be removed to the church tower as soon as the latter is built. It has, perhaps twice, saved the college from complete destruction when it was threatened by fire.

18. Br. John (Jeremiah Cronin) was born in Dover, England, in 1820, was a convert to Catholicism and entered the Congregation of Holy Cross in June 1842 at St. Peter's. See his file in Midwest Province Archives, Notre Dame, Indiana. Sr. Mary of Providence (Marie Daget) was born in Symphronde (Sarthe?), France, on Mar. 22, 1806. She received the habit Aug. 28, 1843, at Ste-Croix and professed vows Jan. 22, 1847, at Bertrand: ASHC. They arrived at Notre Dame in November 1843.

CHAPTER 3

1844

---

1. Chapel of the Novitiate

In the month of November 1843, as Fr. Sorin was making his retreat on a little island beyond the Lake, he found the place admirably suited for a Novitiate for the Brothers, and as there remained only one year more, according to the contract of donation, to build the house, he did not think he was wasting his time by spending his leisure hours in drawing up the plan of the Novitiate as it was afterwards carried out.

Dedicated to the Most Sacred Heart of Mary

The cornerstone of the chapel contained in this plan was blessed in May of the following year. The building of this chapel was in fulfillment of a vow made by Fr. Sorin on the occasion of the sickness of one of the Sisters.[1] The work on the university did not permit the continuance of that on the chapel before the month of November. But then, such was the activity of the workmen in this matter that in seven and a half days the walls were up and eight days more sufficed to build those of the Novitiate, the third part not having been added until the following autumn.

Begun in May 1844 in fulfill-ment of a vow

The chapel and the Novitiate were blessed on 8 December of this same year under the title of the Most Holy and Immaculate Heart of Mary, and on the same day the

Blessed on Dec. 8th; Arch-confraternity established. Profession of two Sisters

---

1. This was Mary of Calvary, who had been in danger of death. See Sorin to Moreau, Nov. 8, 1843, GA.

Archconfraternity was there solemnly established. On the same day also, two Sisters, Mary of the Five Wounds and Mary of Bethlehem, made their profession and one postulant, Mary Coffee, received the habit with Fr. Moreau's name, Sr. Mary of St. Basil.[2]

From this time, until the end of 1848, when the new church was dedicated, this little sanctuary became the favorite spot of the whole house. There the community assembled in times of distress or of rejoicing; there were published the general prescriptions or regulations in regard to the common welfare; there each year the retreat of the Brothers was made and even that of the priests. There also, later on (after March 19, 1847), they came to venerate the precious relics, the holy body of St. Severa, presented to this chapel by Bp. De la Hailandiere on his return from Rome in 1845; thither also, they came to honor the Passion by making the Way of the Cross, which was there canonically erected on March 14, 1845.

The usual place for meetings of the community

The following year, the same mystery was there recalled in a manner equally touching and eloquent by the erection of the celebrated group of Our Lady of the Seven Dolors given to Fr. Sorin by Mr. Dubuguay in Paris. A little later, the same chapel was enriched by the Forty Hours, which made of this little enclosure the treasury and center of all the spiritual privileges and goods of the community.

Group of the Seven Dolors

It was thither that the pious visitors of the house were in preference taken and there that the Bishops of Detroit, Milwaukee and Cincinnati successively celebrated holy mass, to the great satisfaction of the community and also to their own. During all this time, it was the best thing there was in every respect in the institution. Mrs. Byerley

Visit of the bishops of Detroit and Milwaukee

2. On Mary of Bethlehem, see chapter 2, note 16. Mary of the Five Wounds (Elizabeth Paillet) had arrived from France in late October 1844. Born at Breuvannes (Haute Marne), France, on Sept. 15, 1812, she had entered the Congregation of Holy Cross at Ste-Croix, Sept. 5, 1843, and received the habit, June 6, 1844. AMS. Costin, 37, 39–40, identifies the new novice as Bridget Coffey. She was born Feb. 19, 1824, in Ireland. ASHC.

had furnished it with a magnificent carpet and Br. Mary
had skillfully decorated it on every occasion.

It has been thought proper to dwell at some length on
this chapel of the Novitiate because during these four years
it was the constant object of the religious attentions, not
to mention of all the affections, of the community. Where
should we stop were we to recount all the favors that each
one believed himself to have there received?

2. The Novitiate

The first, we might almost say the only, aim of the
Brothers of St. Joseph in coming to the United States was
to establish a novitiate and thereby to assure to religion
in this country some good religious teachers. The sphere
of their movements became enlarged, at least in prospect,
almost as soon as they arrived. The important object of
their mission was not on that account lost sight of. It must
be here confessed, however, that the needs of a college just
coming into existence, as well as poverty and the necessity
to procure a living, long prevented all that was required for
success from being done for the novitiate. Want of time,
of a place, of a Master of Novices, of rules in English, and
likewise of fit subjects, turn by turn or simultaneously rendered impossible the development of this precious branch
and even the keeping of the postulants that entered and
who would probably have remained had they been solidly
formed to the religious life.

This was the first object of the Brothers. Diffi-culties. Poverty. The language. Fewness and inconstancy of candidates

I will not here repeat what I have already stated in
Chapter One in regard to vocations in this country, but I
will add that by means of the inexhaustible resources of a
good novitiate in conformity with the new Constitutions,
most of those national and individual defects that candidates may bring with them on their entrance would soon
disappear and make place for solid virtues. It is unquestion-
able that the greater number came with good will. Now
everybody knows how much work a skillful master can do
with a man well disposed—*bonae voluntatis.* The fact is that
for a long time, in consequence of their poverty and their

Means of success

fewness to carry out the enterprises begun, the Brothers could hardly make a trial of this conviction.

Novitiate finally begun on St. Mary's Island

Until the building of the novitiate on St. Mary's island, nothing could be done for four years except to give an imperfect outline of the institution so called. It was not completed for want of candidates and because the Master was still too much occupied with other things. The following list gives a precise idea of the resources of the country in the matter of vocations. The vestures are thus given in the Registers of the house: one in 1841; eleven in 1842; four in 1843; nine in 1844; eight in 1845; four in 1846; three in 1847; and three in 1848. In all, there were forty-three postulants in the space of seven years. Of this number, seventeen afterwards left the Society and three died. Thus, only one-half are today members of the community.

Transfer to Indianapolis

In the month of November 1846, the Brothers' Novitiate was transferred from Notre Dame du Lac to Indianapolis, where it remained only until the following spring. It was at the request, or rather at the imperious urging, of Bp. De la Hailandiere that this change had been made. Bp. J. S. Basin[3] was of an entirely different opinion and the novitiate was brought back to St. Mary's Island after having occasioned an expense of four thousand francs without any result, not to speak of a house purchased for 22,300 fr. which has not yet been disposed of.

What kind of people present themselves

Not only are vocations rare, but one-third of the time they do not present the qualities necessary to put the men to study. One-half are too old and the others too ignorant to begin the necessary studies. And then they have less desire than they seem to have in France to become teaching Brothers. During the first years at Notre Dame du Lac it was almost impossible to form and maintain a regular novitiate. But as soon as the house was finished in 1844, Fr. Sorin

3. John Stephen Bazin, third bishop of Vincennes, succeeded De la Hailandiere on the latter's resignation in 1847. Born at Duerne in the vicinity of Lyons, France, in 1796, he emigrated to America in 1830 and worked for seventeen years in Mobile, Alabama. He died in Vincennes on Apr. 23, 1848, after only six months as bishop. See: Alerding, *Vincennes*, 186–189; Code, 11.

fixed his own residence there among the novices and the candidates for six months, whereupon his place was taken by Fr. Granger as soon as the latter could make himself understood in English.

Fr. Sorin passes six months there and is replaced by Fr. Granger

Before the arrival of the Brothers in the United States there was no novitiate of religious men of the same kind in the country. In 1845, the Brothers of the Christian Schools unsuccessfully attempted such an establishment in Baltimore. In the following year, the Brothers of St. Patrick repeated the experiment in the same city and appeared to succeed pretty well. Perhaps to this diversion of attention may be attributed the diminution of the number of candidates.

The greater number of those candidates are poor, sometimes even carrying all their property on their persons. Hardly five thousand francs were brought into the Society by all of them together. Here, even more than in Europe, those that succeed in making money in the world do not think of giving it up. It would be better for some years to come to bring young postulants from beyond the sea, who are unacquainted with the spirit and the morals of the Americans. These would be easily formed and would offer a better assurance of perseverance.

3. Orphans or Apprentices

Although orphans had been received into the house the previous year, still it was only from 1844 that they can be considered as forming a distinct class in the institution, having their own teachers and their special rules. However important this establishment of apprentices may seem at the present day, it must be confessed that it was not the result of long reflections. When Providence sent the first of those little abandoned ones, pity caused them to be received. Once they had become inmates of the house, it was necessary to think of giving them something to do. They were therefore successively placed in the shops that were already opened and maintained by the Brothers. Soon the idea occurred to teach them a trade which would enable

Apprentices established without thought or plan

Pity causes the first to be received and the Good Lord blesses the work

them one day to secure for themselves an honorable place in society.

*The Admin-
istration sees
the means of
doing good*

A certain number having thus been at first imposed, as it were, on the house, their future, as well as the responsibility assumed, called for the serious attention of the Council of Administration. It was believed that in this act of charity so imperatively commanded there was a means of securing some vocations for the Brothers, perhaps even for the priests. The carrying out of any plan for this purpose required an immediate outlay, but left a hope that this outlay would be afterwards repaid by the very products of the trade they had been taught.

A charter was therefore asked for from the Legislature and obtained by the same member who had taken charge of that of the college, under the title of Manual Labor School of the Brothers of St. Joseph. This charter constituted the Brothers as a legal body in the eyes of the public and as such

*The nature of
the charter and
its conditions*

they could legally enter into contracts with regards to their Apprentices, make regulations and conditions for them and enforce them by law. This was a valuable privilege.

Shortly afterwards, a legal form and engagement was drawn up and printed to be signed by the guardians, the children and the superior. One of the principal clauses was that the Apprentices were to remain in the house until the age of twenty-one years and that the house should furnish them at their departure with two complete suits of clothes. It is understood as a matter of course that at the end of their time they should have received a good common education and that, when it was possible, the relatives or guardians should, at the entrance of the child, pay the sum of two hundred francs.

*The appren-
tices separated
from the college*

The Apprentices were at first left with the boarders of the college, whose number they helped to swell. The necessity of separating them was soon felt, but the resources of the house did not permit a complete separation to be made at once, given the expense that would be entailed. It was therefore necessary to keep them together in the college but without allowing any communication between them.

Except for two hours and a half per day and on Sundays and festivals, the Apprentices spend all their time at work in their respective shops, in which some have already made remarkable progress in their trades. No child is admitted under the age of twelve. It is astonishing to see what sympathy this establishment has called forth among thoughtful Catholics.

Lately, the Brothers of St. Patrick, not long since established in Baltimore, also opened a school of arts and trades after the same plan. The Bishops of Cincinnati and New York wish to have some of our Brothers as soon as possible to open similar institutions in their cities. God only knows how much good can be done in this manner in those great centers of population.

Desire of the bishops of Cincinnati and New York for similar establishments

In nearly every large city in the United States there is an orphan asylum, nearly all of which are in charge of the Sisters of Charity. This is an immense benefit to Catholic children up to the age of twelve or thirteen. But what will then become of them? Are they ready to enter fearlessly into the world wherein are so many dangers for their faith and morals? It is then as a complement of all those pious asylums that this of Notre Dame du Lac was established so that those children might simply pass from the hands of the daughters of Charity to those of the Brothers of St. Joseph.

This establishment complements the orphanages of the U.S.

There are eighteen of them at present and, if means permitted others to be received, it would be easy to multiply their number. Except as to classes and studies, the regulations for them are the same as for the students of the college for rising and retiring, for rest and recreation.

Those dear children seem to be growing daily more and more contented in a condition which they appreciate more and more in proportion to their growth and to the development of their reason. In general, they afford as much consolation as they give trouble and, according to the last statement of their expenses and their work, it can hardly be said that they are a burden to the house. God be blessed who thus, even in the performance of a charity that was almost forced upon the institution, provided a genuine resource for the future.

4. The Sisters of Holy Cross at Bertrand (Mich.)

As soon as he arrived at St. Peter's in 1841, Fr. Sorin had manifested his desire to the Rev. Fr. Rector to have Sisters of Holy Cross for the service of the mission. It was only two years later, however, that it was possible for the Mother House to send him any. They came, four in number, under the guidance of Fr. Cointet, who led the second colony. We have already mentioned where they were placed and in what they were employed in the beginning at Notre Dame du Lac. The good effects of their coming only created in some sort new needs. Four Sisters were not enough to perform all the work that it was desirable to entrust to them.

They dream of forming a novitiate

Moreover, requests were received from persons whom it was advantageous to accept. In brief, a Novitiate of their order was considered as a desirable establishment. But whether the Bishop would consent to this was very doubtful, or rather more than doubtful. He feared it himself, as he answered when the subject was first broached to him.

The bishop is opposed

Despairing of obtaining anything from Vincennes, Fr. Sorin, who had just received a confidential letter from the Rev. Father in regard to the difficulties opposed to him by Bp. Bouvier[4] relative to the Sisters at Sainte-Croix, whom the bishop would not so much as hear mentioned, addressed himself to the bishop of Detroit, who seemed to be delighted to have the Sisters established in his diocese and who gave encouragement to this effect.

They establish themselves in Bertrand, Michigan

Not content with this first approbation of the bishop of Detroit, Fr. Sorin, who had some presentiment of what later happened, asked, before making the change, to have a confirmation of this favor. Hereupon, he considered himself justified and sent two Sisters and three postulants to Bertrand, two leagues from the Lake, in the diocese of

---

4. Jean-Baptiste Bouvier was the bishop of Le Mans, France. The motherhouse of the Congregation of Holy Cross was in his diocese and the superior of the congregation, Basil Moreau, was subject to his authority. On Moreau's dispute with Bouvier over the Holy Cross Sisters, see Catta, *Moreau*, 1:770–776.

Detroit. His object was to establish them as near as prudence would allow so as to be able to supervise them
himself without difficulty and to obtain from them some
services for the community and the college.

Bp. De la Hailandiere no sooner learned of this than,
thinking a sharp trick had been played on him, he immediately wrote to the bishop of Detroit in such a severe and
imperious manner that the latter was frightened and lost
no time in withdrawing the permission and authorization
he had given to establish the Sisters at Bertrand.

*The bishop
of Vincennes
intimidates the
bishop of Detroit,
who at first
yields; Fr. Sorin
goes to Detroit
and obtains a
continuation
of what has been
done at Bertrand*

On receipt of this disagreeable news, Fr. Sorin went
to Detroit to lay the matter more fully before the bishop.
During this time, the bishop of Cincinnati came there on a
visit, and the matter was submitted to him.[5] The great argument of the bishop of Vincennes was that the proximity of
the two establishments was dangerous. Bishop Purcell was
of a different opinion, and Fr. Sorin returned, confirmed in
what he had done, which, after all, was according to the
prescribed conditions. The Sisters remained at Bertrand,
but the bishop of Vincennes did not forget.

*The Sisters rent
a house for 18
months*

It was in the middle of the summer of 1844, thirteen
months after their arrival from France, that the Sisters went
to their new post. They were first lodged in a house rented
from a Catholic, where they remained until the spring of
1846. There they received a certain number of postulants
and also a few pupils. But being at the same time cramped
for room, having no persons of talent and experience and
no pecuniary resources, their house could hardly develop.
The following year a grant of five thousand francs was made
in their favor by the Propagation of the Faith. They made
the attempt to build a house for themselves. A piece of land
of seventy-seven acres had been given them at Bertrand on
which they set up their new residence on the banks of the

*77 acres is given
to the Sisters but
later Fr. Sorin
has to pay for it
himself. A new
house for the
Sisters*

---

5. The bishop of Detroit to whom the chronicler refers is Peter
Paul Lefevere, the coadjutor bishop and administrator of the diocese from 1841 to 1869. John Baptist Purcell, born in Ireland and
educated in the United States and in France, was the bishop, later
archbishop, of Cincinnati from 1833 to 1883. See Code, 164, 243.

St. Joseph river, three minutes walk from the church. This was a frame building, which could not be finished till the spring of the following year.

They had just moved in when Fr. Sorin returned from France in 1846. He brought back with him the former superioress and eight other novices and postulants. Among the novices of this colony was Mary of the Cenacle, soon afterward superioress.[6] Under her energetic government, good order and religious discipline were re-established in the whole house. It had suffered much in the absence of its first superioress during fifteen months and still more during Fr. Sorin's trip to Europe.

General retreat

The general retreat of the Sisters in the month of September 1846 was remarkable for all the instructions that were published and which more clearly defined the spirit of the Society than could have been done before. Three Sisters, one of whom was Mary of the Cenacle, were admitted to profession.

Orphans received for the sake of charity

From the beginning of 1844, the Sisters of Holy Cross, after the example of the Brothers and for the same motives, saw themselves, as it were, compelled to receive some little orphan girls. The first year they had three or four, in the following year six, in 1846 eight and in 1848 the same number. Either because they were younger or for the lack of discipline amongst them, these little orphan girls did not in general give as much satisfaction as the boys at the Lake. However, there appears to me to be no doubt but that this branch of charity might be developed advantageously even as much as the former.

Foundation at Pokagon

In 1844, the Sisters made a foundation at Pokagon amongst the savages of the Potawatomi tribe, who numbered one hundred and ninety. Two Sisters were sent there with a priest and they opened a school of English, which

6. The absent superioress was Mary of the Five Wounds, whom Sorin had sent back to France to raise money. See Etienne Catta and Tony Catta, *Mother Mary of the Seven Dolors* (Milwaukee: Bruce, 1959), 75–76. Mary of the Cenacle (Louise Naveau) was born Aug. 10, 1810, at Chateau-Gontier (Mayenne), France, received the habit June 23, 1846, at Ste-Croix and professed vows Sept. 10, 1846, at Bertrand. ASHC.

has been kept up since and which seems to be doing well. The Indians are attached to them and would be very much grieved if they were to leave.

From this very first year in Bertrand there were always some Sisters especially charged to visit the sick in the village and the neighborhood, whenever they were wanted. By this means the Sisters on many occasions became instruments of the conversion of many infidels who otherwise would probably have died in their unbelief. However, it must be confessed that if the necessity of looking after the Novitiate and of obtaining from it some labor for the college had not been so urgent in the beginning, it would be hard to understand this foundation at Bertrand which was, and will be for a long time to come, nothing more than a dead town.

The Sisters do good by visiting the sick

The future of Bertrand: unsuitable for a boarding school, good for a Novitiate

A novitiate may succeed there, however; a boarding school hardly. Still, the latter has not been seriously attempted. It is only a few months since a mistress really qualified has been given charge of the studies. In a few years hence, one can form a better opinion.

5. The Farm

The farm of Notre Dame du Lac having been always considered as one of the first resources of the community, it will not be uninteresting to devote a separate article to it and to enter into a few details.

A capital resource

On the arrival of the first Brothers at the Lake, there were about ten acres under cultivation, and the soil was completely worn out. About fifty acres were broken in 1843. The following year it was resolved to open twice as much. The ordinary cost of this work is from forty to fifty francs an acre when it is ploughed and well fenced. Hence, it is easy to judge that the expense for the land was considerable that year. The largest part was sown in wheat in the autumn of that same year and the rest in potatoes, maize and some acres of Indian corn.

Cleared at great cost, it raises pigs, calves, sheep, horses, etc.

The farm raises pigs to the number of about 140, eighty-five sheep, seventeen cows, and seventeen calves, not to mention twelve to sixteen oxen that have been here for two years and ten horses almost constantly at work, either on the farm or for the house.

The following year the Brothers wished to avoid the expenses for similar work. They bought a plough for forty dollars, fourteen or sixteen oxen and grain to feed them. This year they did almost all the work themselves and thus they saved a considerable amount. The products, in consequence of the bad years that have just occurred, were slight. It was fortunate indeed that real losses were not suffered. Up to the present time expenses have been recovered but little beyond that.

During the first five years, the expenses equal the products

Wheat in ordinary years yields from fifteen to eighteen bushels an acre; Indian corn from twenty-five to thirty; potatoes from sixty to seventy-five. It was really only from the spring of this year that the farm may be considered as established on a regular basis. From this date we were also obliged most of the time to keep two workmen besides the Brothers that were sent there, and although everything was calculated to make our Americans smile, still the profits of the farm always more than covered the expenses.

If the worms and the flies had not destroyed a part of the crops of 1845, 1846 and 1847, and the blight that of 1848, the profits on the farm would have been considerable each year. On the other hand, though it may not appear to be the immediate product of the soil, we should place to the credit of the farm all the expenses that the college and the community would regularly have to make without the help of the farm.

In the autumn of the year 1843, about two hundred trees had been planted near the Lake. Later on, in 1845, nearly four hundred saplings were added and about three hundred peach-trees.

CHAPTER 4

1845

---

1. The Barn

Poverty alone had caused the question of a barn to be left so long as a mere project. On a farm of such an extent, everybody agreed that it was an immediate necessity; but it would be an expense of about four thousand francs. Finally, the matter having been agreed upon in council, the foundations were dug at the beginning of this summer, and everything was in readiness for the harvest.

Old barn was pulled down in 1896;[1] 80 x 40 ft. with a basement; it can store 2000 bushels of wheat, 1000 of oats, 500 of barley, etc.

The dimensions were eighty by forty feet. Under the entire length and breadth of the building is a basement of eight feet in height, which can winter two hundred sheep and in which all the potatoes and other roots that the farm produces and that need to be protected from freezing may be stored away.

This barn is the finest in the whole surrounding country. The ground floor can hold in sheaves, two thousand bushels of wheat, one thousand bushels of oats, five hundred bushels of barley, etc., leaving in the middle plenty of room for threshing, winnowing, etc. In a word, it is the bank and the treasury of the farm, solid enough to last twenty-five or thirty years.

1. Marginal note made by someone other than the chronicler.

2. Lime

The Brothers, on their arrival at the Lake, thought that they saw a great advantage to be derived from utilizing the rich banks of their lakes to make lime out of the marl. The first years did not pay expenses, either on account of their ignorance of how to proceed or through mistakes. In 1845, the idea was adopted that by forming a vast reservoir into which the lime could be drawn directly from the kilns so as not to delay the workmen in the fair season, there would be better prospects of success. About three hundred francs were expended on this project and a shed was even put up for the workmen. But things did not turn out as had been expected.

To make the lime, measure it, sell it, and have it paid for was a constant source of annoyance. However, it was not until 1847 and 1848 that it was recognized that the making of lime here was the most sterile of enterprises. Then at last, that is to say, six years too late, it was resolved to let out the job even at very low rates.

No one, however, can fail to see that it is in reality one of the resources of the property and will always be found to be a very valuable asset. Besides, should the neighboring towns increase in population and if Notre Dame du Lac can succeed in purchasing the farm that separates it in one direction from the river, this resource will be quite considerable and will become a monopoly which will be controlled with a sense of justice.

3. First House of the Sisters (Bertrand)

The Sisters of Holy Cross, as has been said in the preceding chapter, had entered the diocese of Detroit in the year 1844; and they remained there for some time in a rented house. In order to secure them to their village, the inhabitants of Bertrand offered Fr. Sorin seventy-seven acres of land for the Sisters. The offer was accepted, and the old frame building that had stood there for ten or twelve years was found to occupy the most charming site on the banks of the St. Joseph river. The sisters added to it a new building also of wood but more elegant and large enough to accommodate a little community. It was a house of two stories, forty by twenty feet, with an addition of one story, twenty-five by twenty feet, for a kitchen. Add a fine brick cellar and you have the first house of the Sisters, which was named Our Lady of the Seven Dolors. It cost about five thousand francs and was finished only in the spring of 1846.

4. The Print Shop

The necessity of having the Constitutions for the Brothers and Sisters printed in English made Fr. Sorin desirous for some time to be able to do it at Notre Dame and not to have to put such papers in the hands of Protestants. The other printed matter that had often to be given out in the Society, not to speak of classical works and religious books that it was desirable to print and sell cheaply in the country, made the administration of the Lake resolve on buying a press at Niles that happened to be for sale at 3500 fr. with three years' schooling.

The first publication that was issued from this press was the Rules and Constitutions of the Brothers, which was printed by Brother Joseph[2] under the direction of a regular printer; then an abridgement of Murray's little grammar, then the Epistles and Gospels, then the first volume of Mrs. Herbert and then the rules of the Archconfraternity, besides some single sheets.

Unfortunately, it was impossible to continue the work as it ought to be done. The expenses were not sufficiently justified and the attempt was given up. The following year, in January 1847, the press was sold again for about the same amount as it had cost, and the idea of printing at the Lake was abandoned, at least for the time being.

2. Br. Joseph (Charles Rother), born July 11, 1808, at Riedesheim in Germany, was the schoolteacher mentioned in chapter 1, who was awaiting the Brothers at St. Peter's and who became the first novice in the United States. See M.g.

No doubt but that with a man who knew how to judge and manage things, the press would have made a considerable gain. The absence of such a man caused the undertaking to be abandoned together with all the hopes to which it had given rise. It is to be regretted that the institution could not by itself carry all those expenses. There would have been plenty of work for two or three little apprentices. The boys would have been of the greatest service there and would have been learning a useful trade.

5. Life Pension of Mr. Badin

The Very Rev. Mr. Badin gives the community two lots worth $6000. Numerous difficulties with the good old man. He wrongs the college and complains everywhere. He chooses Mr. Benoit to terminate his business with N.D. du Lac. Mr. Benoit settles things but not to his satisfaction and he continues to complain

About the middle of July of this year, the Rev. Mr. Badin of Kentucky, the first priest ordained in the United States, arrived at Notre Dame du Lac, admired all that has been done there since his last visit in 1836, and offered to give Fr. Sorin two lots in the city of Louisville in order to help to support and develop the work for the orphans, as well as to purchase a plot of two hundred acres between Notre Dame and the river. This was on condition, however, that a yearly allowance should be made him of four hundred dollars or two thousand francs and that one year after his death the same would be paid to his universal heir.

In the month of August, Fr. Sorin went to Louisville to try to dispose of the lots but instead of the twelve or fifteen thousand dollars that Mr. Badin had given him to expect, he, together with the local magistrates, could not value them at more than six thousand dollars. Three months later the lots were actually sold for this amount by Mr. Badin's own agent, whom Fr. Sorin had retained as his agent at the recommendation of the former.

Mr. Badin complained that the lots were given away at half their value. Meanwhile, Mr. Badin had three thousand dollars offered for the property, but Fr. Sorin, who knew that a title-deed could not be obtained from the seller, fortunately put a stop to the whole affair in time. He then left for France.

Mr. Badin, who never agrees with anybody, began now to criticize and condemn everything that he himself had approved and admired at Notre Dame du Lac. He complained, he grew excited, he charged ingratitude, he accused Fr. Sorin to the Rector, and he started off with two Sisters whom he took travelling with him on the plea of health to Milwaukee and Southport, after having given Fr. Granger, who was replacing the absent superior, an endless amount of trouble.[3]

On his return, Fr. Sorin was greatly pained to learn of the malicious pranks of Fr. Badin. He met him at St. Joseph in October and agreed to renew the contract of the previous year. He gave a mortgage on the Lake property to guarantee the annuity of two thousand francs and procured legal authorization to take all the time that he might judge reasonable to purchase the property already mentioned; but when he wished to regulate his accounts with Mr. Badin, he found the claims of the latter so unreasonable and insisted on so obstinately, that after having wasted some weeks in trying to bring Mr. B. to a friendly settlement without any success, on the suggestion of Mr. B. himself, the matter was placed in the hands of two lawyers, designated by name and accepted on both sides in writing. Some days afterwards Mr. Badin refused the man chosen by Fr. Sorin, and went (to await Mr. Benoit for fifteen days in Ft. Wayne first of all) to carry his complaint to the bishop of Chicago, then to New Orleans, etc.

The following year, he returned with the same claims and the same obstinacy. Fr. Sorin insisted on his rights and let him talk, although he knew on good authority that he was taking measures to ruin his reputation. He left, threatening to go and accuse Fr. Sorin to the archbishop of Baltimore. On his way he stopped at Fort Wayne, where he waited fifteen days for the Rev. Mr. J. Benoit.

3. Alexis Granger, born June 19, 1817, at Daon (Mayenne), France. Ordained a priest for the diocese of Le Mans on Dec. 19, 1840, he had entered the Congregation of Holy Cross in October 1843. He arrived at Notre Dame in the autumn of 1844. M.g.

Toward the beginning of October, Mr. Benoit arrived at the Lake, legally provided with all the powers of Mr. Badin, and secretly assured by Mr. Badin of a fee of two thousand francs if he succeeded in gaining the cause for him and winning the four thousand francs that he claimed.

Mr. Benoit met Fr. Sorin and for two days scrupulously examined the whole series of accounts. So far from finding a debt of four thousand francs in favor of the plaintiff, he was obliged to acknowledge him a debtor to Fr. Sorin to the amount of three hundred francs. It is said that Fr. Badin was very much displeased with his agent and that he afterwards arrogantly accused him of being in complicity with Fr. Sorin of whom he continues to say all the evil he can. Nonetheless, the money question remains and will remain as it was settled and signed at this time by Mr. Benoit.

From the end of 1845, Fr. Badin was evidently angry with Fr. Sorin. The latter was well aware of the cause, which was not a matter of Dollars, but one that must be kept to himself, leaving it to God to settle accounts whenever it is his good pleasure to do so.

6. Completion of the Novitiate

The plan for the Novitiate is completed by an addition that makes this dwelling a building very pleasing to the eye

Until the autumn of this year, the Brothers' novitiate had remained incomplete; that is to say, it consisted of the chapel and the central house, in which the novices, to the number of sixteen, had been lodged. Mr. Badin, seeing the inconvenience occasioned by the want of room, and the beauty that would belong to the establishment on its completion, offered three hundred francs toward finishing it; in consequence of this offer it was resolved to complete the part corresponding to the chapel. However, the inside could not be finished until the following spring and this was taken by Mr. Badin as sufficient reason to withdraw his subscription.

The original intention was to dedicate this third part to St. Joseph and to have a chapel in his honor there, which is deferred for the present but not entirely given up. If the administration of Notre Dame du Lac succeeds some day in lowering the waters of the Lake and in drying the marshes that separate the novitiate from the college, this dwelling place will unquestionably be one of the most agreeable that could be desired.

7. The Infirmary

It had been begun in the autumn of 1844, but it was only in the course of 1845 that it was finished such as it is today, namely, a brick building, sixty by twenty feet, of two stories. Part of it was at first occupied by the print shop. It was only on the return of Fr. Superior in 1846 that it was systematically divided into separate apartments in such a way as to meet the needs of an infirmary. There are four rooms on the ground floor and four upstairs, that is to say, amply sufficient for the usual needs of the college and the community. Up to the present time it has been necessary to use one half of those rooms to lodge persons for whom there is no accommodation elsewhere.

Although built in several stages and partly occupied by several tenants, the infirmary is suitable for its purpose

Under the present heading it is proper to say something about the maladies and the deaths that have successively afflicted the mission.

On their arrival at the Lake, the Brothers were informed that the place was considered unhealthy. The following spring two of them were the proof and the victims, Brothers Joachim and Paul,[4] whose death contributed much to confirm the bad reputation of the place as regards health. The year 1845 was marked by a great deal of sickness, nobody dying but many being down with daily fevers. It is true that the Society this year had to mourn the premature death of Br. Anselm,[5] who drowned in the Ohio while bathing with Mr. Delaune; but no one thought of charging this death to the unhealthiness of Notre Dame du Lac, as was done the two following years.

At first, there were many illnesses at N.D. du Lac, several deaths and numerous sick, proving that the spot is unhealthy; nevertheless, one hopes that the future will be better

4. Br. Joachim, who passed away Apr. 13, 1844, was the first of the original contingent from France to die. See Editor's Preface. Br. Paul (John Bray De la Hoyde) was born in 1816 in Ireland and joined the community at St. Peter's. He died May 27, 1844. M.g.

5. Br. Anselm was one of the original contingent from France. See Editor's Preface. He had been assigned to teach at Fr. Delaune's parish school in Madison, Indiana. M.g.

The autumn of 1846 was marked three times by death: that of Br. John the Baptist, then that of Br. Anthony and of Mr. Garnier, a postulant lately arrived from France.[6] Some time in the following winter occurred the death of a pupil, Mr. Richardville. The autumn of 1847 was visited by more sickness, but fewer fatalities. Sr. Mary of Carmel was the only one to pay the debt of nature.[7]

If truth be told, about this same time almost the same maladies afflicted the whole country, and it would perhaps be difficult to prove that they were really produced by the climate. Still, it cannot be called into question that the number of deaths in so few years did considerable harm to the house in the public estimation. These two years, especially 1846 and 1847, quite a number of boarders went home with fever and not only did they not themselves return but kept others away through fear.

In 1848, the vacation of the college was put a month earlier on this account, and thus the danger of which the sad experience had been made the two preceding years was avoided. Nevertheless, it is not yet proved that there is not really something unhealthy that makes a residence at Notre Dame du Lac dangerous to some constitutions. During six years it would be difficult perhaps to find a single day on which there was no one sick.

6. Br. John the Baptist (William Rodgers): born in Ireland in 1815, he had entered the community at Notre Dame on Oct. 15, 1844, and died there Oct. 13, 1846. Br. Anthony (Thomas Dowling): born in Ireland in 1780, he had entered the community at Notre Dame in 1843 and died there Jan. 10, 1847. Joseph Garnier, who is described in chapter 5:2 as a postulant for the Brothers, died at Notre Dame Oct. 1, 1846. M.g.

7. Mr. Richardville, 15, was an Indian orphan whose father had been chief of the Miami tribe and had resided at Huntington, Indiana. See Br. Gatien, "Journal Kept by the Secretary to Serve in the Composition of the Chronicles of N.D. du Lac," Mar. 28, 1847. IPA. Sr. Mary of Mount Carmel (Marie Dougherty), born Aug. 21, 1805, in Ireland, had been among the first group of women to receive the habit in America at Bertrand, Michigan, on Sept. 8, 1844. She died Aug. 1, 1847, the first Sister of Holy Cross to die anywhere in the world. See ASHC and Costin, 37, 48.

CHAPTER 5

1846

---

1. Voyage of Fr. Sorin to France

Of all the endeavors of Fr. Sorin since his arrival in the United States, none perhaps was more injurious to him than his voyage to Europe at a time when his presence was far more necessary to his house than he could have imagined. During his absence which lasted for about six months, from February until the end of August, the evil spirit made ravages in his flock which even two years later he had not been able to repair. Not that Fr. Granger, who took his place, was negligent or spared himself in any way, but being overburdened with duties and having daily to fight against bad will, which took advantage of the superior's absence to heap difficulties in the way, he could not oppose a sufficiently strong resistance to the passions of others which had become more exacting, nor maintain everywhere the spirit of submission and of peace.

Bad effects of his absence

Of the five seminarians whom he left in the Novitiate at his departure, he found only two on his return. The Sisters, being without a mother for fifteen months, felt deeply the effects of this absence during which they seriously compromised their reputation in the eyes of the public as far as regards good order, charity and the religious spirit. The Brothers perhaps suffered least.

The college shared in the effects of a general impression to the disadvantage of the institution. The print shop was closed and the affairs of Kentucky gave the administration no little trouble, whilst Mr. Badin alone caused us as much annoyance as all the rest put together. Some merchants would give no peace until they had received the full amount of their bills. In a word, during almost all this time there reigned in the house a feeling of uncertainty, embarrassment and torment.

Little success in France

On the other hand, the resources that Fr. Sorin had hoped to find in Europe could not be realized according to his designs. A delay of several weeks at sea prevented him from visiting Ireland, to which country he had several recommendations that carried weight with them and where he would have found vocations for the mission.

When he reached the Mother House, whither more than one calumny had preceded him, he, perhaps too readily, looked upon it as beneath him to justify himself against charges whereof he had never been guilty; his silence was looked upon as a tacit confession of the things laid to his charge. The settlement of accounts between the Mother House and himself did not in the least remove these dispositions on the one side or the other, but on the contrary seemed to confirm each one in his own ideas.

Acquisition of Sr. Mary of the Cenacle; her virtues

Financially, this journey was hardly more successful; he made his expenses and very little over. The only thing that consoled Fr. Sorin in those painful circumstances was the acquisition of Sister Mary of the Cenacle, known in the world as Louise Naveau. She often made him forget all his vexations. She was a woman of tried virtue, of more than ordinary merit for her knowledge of the world, of tact, zeal, devotedness, obedience, the spirit of faith and of confidence in God, whom she loved with all her heart.

Her presence of mind and her prodigal activity made her present wherever her presence was desirable and useful. In a word, she alone was a real resource for the establishment. Would to God, that she had not been called away so soon![1]

1. Sr. Mary of the Cenacle died on Apr. 28, 1848, in Fort Wayne, Indiana, whither she had gone to consult a doctor. See Costin, 51–52.

With her, eight other Sisters or postulants left France for the mission of Notre Dame du Lac;[2] in addition, there was a priest and a seminarian plus three professed Brothers and one postulant.[3] The new colony did not bring much money with them, but they did bring sixty chests which contained a number of articles of actual need in the house.

The passage was fortunate, although rather long—forty days. Fr. Sorin had the good fortune on landing in New York of availing himself of the last day of grace to prevent the protest of a draft for five hundred dollars drawn by Fr. Granger three months before, during his absence.

After celebrating the feast of the Assumption in New York, he and his company traveled rapidly and cheaply, having all the facilities and advantages of the season in their favor.

Eight other Sisters or postulants; three Brothers, a priest and a seminarian. Arrival at New York on Aug. 15 and at N.D. du Lac on Aug. 24

2. General Retreats

The first necessity as well as the first duty to fulfill on the arrival of Fr. Superior was to put everybody in turn on retreat as soon as possible and in succession. The Brothers

2. Five of these Sisters can be identified, of which one, M. of the Infant Jesus (Elizabeth Godfrey), was born in Monroe, Michigan, and had accompanied Sr. M. of the Five Wounds to France in 1845, where she had received the habit at Ste-Croix on Dec. 8, 1845. The other four were French: Cenacle (Louise Naveau), see chapter 3, note 6; Ascension (Mathurin Salou), born Feb. 5, 1826, and received the habit at Ste-Croix Dec. 8, 1845; Joseph (Ernestine Potard), born Feb. 25, 1822, and received the habit June 21, 1846, at Ste-Croix; Dositheus (Thérèse Octavia Dussaulx), born Dec. 8, 1819, at Lisieux and received the habit Sept. 20, 1845, at Ste-Croix. ASHC.

3. The priest was Louis Baroux, born Mar. 25, 1817, at St. Michel de Chavagnes (Sarthe) and ordained a priest for the diocese of Le Mans. He entered the community in July 1845. The seminarian was Emile Dusaulx, born Dec. 11, 1820, at Lisieux (Calvados). Two of the Brothers can be clearly identified as Placid (Urbain Alard), born Feb. 2, 1812, at Voivres (Sarthe), and Theodolus (François Barbé), born Feb. 20, 1818, at Jublains (Mayenne). Both entered the community in 1838. The third was probably Br. Charles Borromeo (Auguste-Marie Thebaut), born Mar. 4, 1818, at Izé (Ille-et-Vilaine), who received the habit at Notre Dame in March 1847. The postulant was Joseph Garnier. M.g.

After his arrival, Fr. Sorin put everyone on retreat, the Brothers first, then the Sisters, and finally the Priests; several profess vows

began first, three days after the arrival of the colony; then the Sisters, whose retreat ended on 8 September. Three of the Sisters made their profession as did one of the recent arrivals, Sr. Mary of the Cenacle, who was then only second assistant but who was to become superior a few months later. Finally came the retreat of the priests.

The more trouble there had been this year, the more each one seemed to take to heart the making of this retreat well, and at the same time it seemed to be a pleasure to them. Thus far, greater recollection or more good will had not been seen. All the regulations and usages of the Mother House, as far as practicable, were proclaimed and received with the most perfect submission. The obediences were assigned in the Minor Chapter[4] and were accepted by all, without exception, with humility and submission. The accusations were made this year, as always, with a frankness and candor truly edifying and full of hope for the coming year.

Fr. Sorin had obtained permission to admit to perpetual vows at this retreat Messrs. Cointet, Marivault and Gouesse. These professions were deferred to the solemnity of Christmas.

Happiness of all at the end of the retreats

The first months appeared all the happier because one felt that he was actually living the life of Sainte-Croix. Never had the consolations of faith been more necessary for the house. Without going over what has been said above as to the troubles caused the administration in the autumn by Mr. Badin, sicknesses and death came by turns and together to try to the utmost the patience of this poor family.

The community is tried and loses three members

Bros. John the Baptist and Anthony, and Mr. Garnier, an excellent postulant for the Brothers, who had come from France with the last colony, were successively carried away in the space of two months.[5]

Grant of 15,000 fr.

The grant of fifteen thousand francs made this year by the Propagation of the Faith, of which they learned towards

4. The minor chapter, composed of selected Brothers and priests resident in the local community, served as a council of advisors to the local superior.

5. See chapter 4, note 6.

the end of autumn, was a great consolation for all amidst their vexations and sufferings.

3. Acquisition at Indianapolis

Ever since 1842, Bp. De la Hailandiere had the idea that the novitiate of the Brothers should be established at Indianapolis. At that time it was evidently impossible to carry out this project. During the bishop's trip to Europe in 1844, he entered into an agreement with the Rev. Fr. Moreau by which the house and the bishop of Vincennes bound themselves reciprocally. One of the clauses of this contract was that if the Society, adopting the plans of His Lordship, would transfer the Novitiate from Notre Dame du Lac to Indianapolis, the bishop would give five hundred dollars and three hundred and seventy-five acres of ground near Bertrand, ~~Indiana~~.[6] *Michigan*

A contract between the Mother House and the Bp. of Vincennes regarding the Novitiate projected for Indianapolis

During the absence of Fr. Sorin, it seems that Bp. De la Hailandiere had learned of the project of making a foundation at St. Mary's.[7] As a matter of course, he loudly condemned it from the first, and soon afterwards he made no mystery (of his determination) that if any members were sent from the Lake to Kentucky, he would pack them all off there. As soon as Fr. Sorin had returned from Europe, the bishop urged that the establishment promised for Indianapolis be founded; then he complained that there were such long delays, and finally he threatened to rid himself of the whole community if he could not have this project carried out.

The Bishop of Vincennes opposes the foundation projected for St. Mary's, Ky., and threatens to send everyone away from the Lake

At this time, Br. Joseph was sent to Indianapolis on a new mission which His Lordship was desirous of establishing, namely, to sell Catholic books cheap and thus to fill every house of the country with them. He made hardly any sales; he was more concerned, it seems to me, in buying than in selling.

6. Although the chronicler wrote "Indiana," "Michigan" is surely correct.

7. See chapter 6:2.

Br. Joseph sent as an agent and on his own authority buys land for 22,500 fr.

The community's unhappiness

The fact is that, having been told to look around and see whether there was any property for sale in Indianapolis which might be suitable for a Novitiate, he took this as an authorization to purchase a property of twenty-seven acres for 22,500 fr. The administration of the Lake was equally surprised and pained, but to refuse to sanction what was done would compromise the house in the eyes of the public and especially in those of the bishop. Moreover, by his last letters, Fr. Rector himself seemed to be of the opinion that some sacrifices might be made in order to preserve the last remnants of the favorable dispositions of the bishop. All things having been maturely considered, the purchase was ratified by the Minor Chapter, and notice was immediately sent to Sainte-Croix.

It is hardly necessary to add that the administration of the Lake chose this means only as a lesser evil, leaving to the Mother House, of course, the right to order the property to be resold if that appeared more expedient.

Here the members of the chapter committed an inexcusable blunder in trying to justify this purchase too strongly by the words of the Rev. Father and in not putting in the clearest light the unpleasant predicament in which the stupidity of Br. Joseph had placed them. This was the reason of the famous memorial which will be mentioned in the next number.

The bishop was delighted. He even wrote to the Propagation of the Faith to obtain a special grant for this project and he nurtured hopes of double assistance from that quarter. How great was the disappointment of the Chapter on learning six months afterwards that there would be no grant at all to the Lake this year!

There was nothing for it but to be resigned to this financial crisis. The financial need was greater than it had ever been before. However, God did not permit the house to be at any time in want of the necessaries.

CHAPTER 6

1847

---

1. Arrival of Fr. Saunier

The unexpected arrival of Fr. Saunier[1] from the Mother House in the month of June was an event in the whole community. He was the bearer of a document which he had orders to read in chapter on the very day of his arrival, and he scrupulously carried out this order. With a little tact he might have foreseen the effects of the reading of the document and have softened them; but either he foresaw nothing or he did not choose to do anything in consequence of his foresight and the memorial was read and defended by its bearer wherever it needed it in such a manner as to leave the most painful and regrettable impressions on nearly all the members of the Chapter. For his part, Fr. Sorin can never entirely forget the annoyance that it gave him.

Some days afterwards, Fr. Saunier, who had an obedience for Louisville, or St. Mary's, left the Lake and started for Kentucky.[2] Hardly had he reached there when he wrote

Fr. Saunier arrives and reads the famous document; the comment and the defense, both appropriate and inappropriate. The regrettable impression that it produces. He leaves for Ky. and asks for four Sisters whom he does not get until after the authorization from Rev. Fr. Rector. Br. Theodulus also goes

J MP

---

1. Augustin Saunier, born Dec. 29, 1814, at Pontlieu (Sarthe), had already been ordained a priest for the diocese of Le Mans when he entered the Congregation of Holy Cross in 1838. Along with Sorin and two others, he was among the first four priests, after the founder, Basil Moreau, to profess vows in the community on Aug. 15, 1840. M.g.

2. The foundation was St. Mary's College, between Lebanon

65

for four Sisters, whom he did not get, however, until he had received an authorization from the Rev. Father. Then the sisters went, towards the end of October. Six weeks afterwards, he got Br. Theodulus in the same manner.

Without pretending here to give the history of the Kentucky affair, it is necessary to say something about it in order to make the chronicle of the Lake complete. From first to last one cannot fail to be surprised that a foundation of such importance could be conducted by such a long series of misunderstandings or, let us say the word, of blunders of administration.

Terrible blunders of administration

2. St. Mary's, Kentucky

Bp. Chabrat offers St. Mary's; Fr. Sorin accepts it for Holy Cross if the Propagation grants 20,000 fr. The Bishop gets 2,000 instead of 20,000 fr.

To take up the history of this affair from the beginning, we must go back to the month of January 1846. At the departure of the Jesuits from Kentucky, Bp. Chabrat[3] wrote to Fr. Sorin offering him the institution which was to be left vacant in some months. After communicating the affair to his council, Fr. Sorin answered the Bishop that he thought he could accept St. Mary's to establish there a school of English, perhaps a Brothers' novitiate and a school of arts and trades; on condition, however, that the property just as it was (that is to say, four hundred acres of excellent land on which the Jesuits, according to the Bishop, had just spent fifty thousand dollars and whose buildings could lodge three hundred persons), should be given to the Society of Holy Cross and that His Lordship would do his best to organize at St. Mary's a central novitiate for the United States, sanctioned by all the Bishops of the Union. Fr. Sorin added that he was on the point of embarking for France where he did not doubt that he could have the matter approved, if His Lordship was agreeable to the terms.

---

and Loretto in Marion County, Kentucky, fifty miles southeast of Louisville. Founded in 1821 by William Byrne, a priest of the diocese of Bardstown (Louisville after Feb. 13, 1841), it was under the direction of the Jesuits from 1833 to 1846. See *Catholic Encyclopedia* (1907–1914), 3:93–94; 14:562.

3. Guy Ignatius Chabrat, born Dec. 28, 1787, at Chambres (Cantal), France, was coadjutor bishop of Bardstown-Louisville from 1834 to 1847. Code, 40.

Some days later, Fr. Sorin set out and on his arrival
in New York he found a letter from Bp. Chabrat, who
accepted with acknowledgement the conditions submitted
to him by the administration of the Lake. The bishop
concluded by saying that he regarded the matter as settled and by encouraging Fr. Sorin not to fear the least
disappointment with respect to St. Mary's.

Fr. Sorin, who could not put off his departure, wrote
to Mr. Delaune,[4] one of his old friends, who was residing
at Madison, ten hours from Louisville and a day and a half
from St. Mary's, informing him of what was happening
and requesting him to go in person to St. Mary's and to
send him without delay at Sainte-Croix an account of
the state of the property and buildings with as close an
estimate as possible of the expenses required in order to
establish a community there. At the same time he informed
Bp. Chabrat of the request made to Mr. Delaune and the
next day he embarked for London, being more desirous
than ever of visiting Ireland and seeking subjects there.

Mr. Delaune lost no time in complying with Fr. Sorin's
request but instead of confining himself scrupulously to the
directions that he had received, he considered it so advantageous to act as he thought Fr. Sorin himself would have
done, that he believed he was rendering a great service to
the Society by immediately buying from the Jesuits all that
should necessarily remain for the house of the Brothers,
and in the name of the House he signed an obligation for
9,500 fr. for furniture.

The notice of the transaction, which he at once sent to
Fr. Sorin at Sainte-Croix, surprised and displeased the latter. However, as he stated in this same letter that with the
approval of Bp. Flaget[5] he had written to the Propagation
of the Faith asking for a grant of twenty thousand francs,

4. See chapter 1, note 17.
5. Benedict Joseph Flaget, born Nov. 7, 1763, at Contournat
near Billom in the Auvergne region of France, had emigrated to
America in 1791 and had been appointed the first bishop of Bardstown (Louisville after Feb. 13, 1841), Kentucky, in 1808. Code,
94–95.

Sainte-Croix did not venture to annul his acts in Kentucky before learning the result of his petition. For four months, an answer was awaited from Paris and Lyons, during which time no word was sent to Mr. Delaune, who continued to act as he had been doing, thinking that his course was approved since nothing was said to the contrary.

The time fixed for Fr. Sorin's departure arrived and, no answer having been received from the Propagation of the Faith, Sainte-Croix began to be alarmed in regard to St. Mary's. Fr. Sorin was seriously uneasy about Mr. Delaune, thinking that he might possibly be abandoned in the predicament in which his devotedness has placed him. This idea alone troubled him and made him feel unhappy.

Sainte-Croix, which could not close its eyes to this critical affair and which feared to make any engagement before knowing the answer of the Propagation of the Faith, charged Fr. Sorin with causing the embarrassing position in which they were placed. On his departure from Sainte-Croix he was forbidden to meddle further with this foundation in regard to which Sainte-Croix would in future treat directly with Bp. Flaget.

At the same time, they finally wrote to Mr. Delaune and told him to be patient and that as soon as an answer should have come from the Propagation of the Faith, the necessary personnel would be sent to St. Mary's, some from France and some from the Lake. Mr. Delaune, who had no information until now of the condition on which, it appeared, the ratification of his acts in Kentucky was to be dependent, answered with astonishment, complaining and demanding justice.

Finally, the Propagation of the Faith answered that the two thousand francs requested for the foundation of St. Mary's were granted. Six months were spent in seeking the author and the correction of this numerical error, but no additional grant was made.

On his side, Fr. Sorin, whose hands were tied as regards St. Mary's, was incomprehensible by his silence to Mr. Delaune and to Bp. Chabrat, so that the former ceased to write to him and the latter made known to him through

his secretary that he would not communicate with him in
the future with regard to St. Mary's; as he was soon to start
for France, he would go to Le Mans and speak personally
with Mr. Moreau. It was in the month of October 1846
that he gave this information; in May of 1847 he had not
yet visited Sainte-Croix nor written a word to the Rev.
Fr. Rector.

Finally, at this time, Sainte-Croix, seeing no escape
from its embarrassment and understanding with what delicacy Mr. Delaune deserved to be treated, resolved to send
him a priest to encourage and help him in his distressing
and interesting position. For it must be said that this zealous
missionary, left entirely to himself for the time being, had
not remained idle. In the month of January 1847, in daily
expectation of a colony from Sainte-Croix, he opened the
college with the help of English speaking professors to
whom he gave lessons in Latin or theology. He even succeeded this first year in gathering together about fifty pupils
at the rate of seventy-five dollars each. It was thus, in the
midst of the occupations of managing this college and of
attending to four adjacent congregations, that Fr. Saunier
found him, having been sent to him by the Mother House.

A man of talent, prudence and tact could even then
have succeeded in arranging things satisfactorily. The prospects of the college were encouraging, Mr. Delaune was
willing to remain there for at least another year for the
sake of the Society, on condition that he received a modest
compensation, and before the end of that time all the debts
of the college could have been easily cleared off. We may
as well say it: the prospect of such a fair future turned the
head of the poor newcomer. It appears indubitable that at
his arrival at St. Mary's, he conceived the project of having
himself made president, independent of the Lake, whence,
however, he expected to draw all the necessary help, but
treating directly with Sainte-Croix in everything.

From that time forward, therefore, he represented himself to the bishop and to Mr. Delaune as the agent of
Sainte-Croix. Soon he imagined that he could conduct
the college better than Mr. Delaune himself, and, as if

he had been really invested with all the powers of the Mother House, without saying a word to the Lake, he made a contract with Mr. Delaune and took upon himself, as representative of Sainte-Croix, the whole government and responsibility of the college of which he made himself president, Mr. Delaune figuring simply as a paid agent. And even with all this, he could hardly keep him as such and take upon himself all that he would like to without turning him out.

In the month of October, he wrote to the Lake saying that Fr. Moreau had just accepted St. Mary's and ratified all his doings. As has been said already, on the authorization of the Rev. Father, four Sisters were sent to him towards the end of the same month and, six weeks afterwards, Brother Theodulus. Believing himself stronger, Fr. Saunier conducted himself in a still more hateful manner toward Mr. Delaune. The latter complained to the Rev. Father, who with a stroke of his pen annulled all that Fr. Saunier has done at St. Mary's as representative of the Mother House. Vexation at such a humiliating defeat, which was probably not mitigated by Mr. Delaune, made Fr. Saunier declare that he was going to leave the Society.

Dr. Spalding, aware of the state of things, takes steps to take the College under the control of the bishop

Dr. Spalding, bishop-elect of Louisville,[6] who looked upon Fr. Saunier as a child whose mission seemed to him to be mysterious, said to whomever wished to hear that Sainte-Croix had sufficiently mocked the Bishop of Kentucky, but that the comedy would soon be at an end; that insignificant representatives were sent claiming to be invested with all powers, who soon afterwards were declared to have none.

Meanwhile, fearing to lose the advances already made together with the reputation of the Society in the diocese of Louisville, Fr. Sorin, with the advice of the Chapter of

6. Martin John Spalding, born May 23, 1810, at Rolling Fork, Washington County, Kentucky, had been vicar general of the diocese of Louisville since 1844 and was appointed auxiliary bishop of Louisville in April 1848 to succeed Guy Ignatius Chabrat, who had resigned. Spalding had himself been educated at St. Mary's College. Code, 275–276.

the Lake, proceeded to Louisville at the beginning of April 1848, and came to an agreement with Dr. Spalding that, unless the Rector opposed it, he would furnish the personnel necessary for conducting the college at its reopening the following September. The Doctor (who was even yet desirous of giving St. Mary's to the Society) asked only for an additional priest and a few Brothers.

Fr. Saunier learned that Notre Dame du Lac intended to give him a superior (although up to this time there was only question of sending Fr. Gouesse to help him; perhaps Dr. Spalding, who did not understand how the matter could be arranged otherwise, had hinted this to him) and positively refused to act with anyone whatsoever from Notre Dame du Lac, although he had been asking for Fr. Gouesse for a year.

Dr. Spalding wrote about the matter to the Lake, fearing, he said, that the refusal of Fr. Saunier might break the provisional understanding of April (which had been made for only a year). Fr. Sorin replied that the refusal or the consent of Fr. Saunier personally was immaterial as regarded the carrying out of the agreement made in the spring.

Meanwhile, the Jesuits renewed their negotiations with the diocese of Louisville and returned to their college at Bardstown. The question of St. Mary's was indirectly affected and entirely changed thereby. The Bishop now had to place all the priests whom he had employed at Bardstown. Without waiting to see whether or not the Lake would fulfill its promise, Dr. Spalding announced to Fr. Sorin that, not being able to leave St. Mary's any longer in the uncertainty in which our Society had left it for two years, he considered it his duty to provide for it independently of all previous arrangements with him, since, as had been already done in the case of Fr. Saunier, Fr. Moreau might once more annul this last agreement and thus place the bishop in new difficulties; moreover, he did not see that the diocese had been treated fairly by our Society; finally, that the Lake might call on Mr. Delaune for whatever was due for the Brother and the Sisters. His letter was that of one who had no longer any use for men whom he was lately begging to remain.

Fr. Sorin once more proceeded to Kentucky and met Dr. Spalding at Bardstown. He insisted on the execution of the last agreement and showed that he was duly authorized, as in fact he had been a few days previously by Fr. Moreau. The Doctor replied that he feared a repetition of what had been done in the case of Mr. Saunier and declared that he could now no longer change any of the appointments that he had made and published for St. Mary's.

Some days after his return, Fr. Sorin received a letter from Dr. Spalding, wherein the latter said: "Mr. Paulinus, prior of the Trappists of Mallery, who came with your visitor, has just arrived here. He informs me that your visitor comes with orders to close the doors of St. Mary's, etc." "Therefore," added the Doctor, "I was not altogether in the wrong in fearing this ultimatum of all these misunderstandings." Thus, in this manner terminated this unfortunate affair, which might have become an immense resource for the Society.

Fr. Sorin visited St. Mary's in the month of July, took Br. Theodulus away and allowed the four Sisters to remain for a year, whilst awaiting certain arrangements of the agents of an orphan asylum in Cincinnati where the bishop expected them.

As for Fr. Saunier, he left the Society without saying a word to Fr. Sorin, who met him by chance on the streets of Cincinnati as he was going to St. Mary's, whilst Fr. Saunier was about to go to the Jesuits at New York. With him were two Brothers recently admitted by the Jesuits, of which fact Fr. Sorin had not received even a hint.

When Fr. Blox, the superior of St. Xavier's College in Cincinnati, was questioned by Fr. Sorin in the presence of Fr. Saunier and these Brothers as to how he could thus receive three subjects without informing their superior, even though they had made perpetual vows and had left their posts vacant, he answered that he knew nothing of these circumstances, and that things being so, none of them could be admitted amongst the Jesuits. Fr. Sorin then declared in their presence that he would take none of them back and he left them as he had found them, thinking with Bishop Purcell that the Jesuits were not always particularly delicate towards other religious houses and promising himself that he would not soon forget the lesson he had just received.[7]

3. Transfer of the Novitiate to Indianapolis

In conformity with a decision of the Minor Chapter, Fr. Granger with six novices left Notre Dame du Lac for Indianapolis in the first days of September 1847. Although far from being looked upon favorably by the majority, this step could not be put off without exposing the house to the just indignation of the bishop, who had advanced three thousand dollars to pay for the property and who was not bound to give the five hundred dollars and the 375 acres of land promised until the Brothers had done their part, which he did without delay.

Once in this capital of the state, Fr. Granger seems not to have found much difficulty in establishing himself with his novices according to the Constitutions and the Rules that relate to the novitiate. The property, although half within the city limits, was, nevertheless, removed from the tumult of the streets and offered nearly all the advantages desirable for the end for which it was purchased, except

7. The two Brothers appear to have been Bernard (Patrick Leo Foley) and Mary Joseph (Samuel O'Connell). Bernard, born in Ireland in 1820, entered the Congregation of Holy Cross at Notre Dame in August 1845. He was teaching at the parish school in Madison, Indiana, in June 1848, when he wrote to Sorin requesting a dispensation from his vows. See Br. Bernard to Sorin, June 23, 1848, Edward Sorin Papers, IPA. He was readmitted to the congregation in 1855. See Br. Bernard to Sorin, Aug. 15, 1855, IPA. Mary Joseph, born in Ireland in 1819, had entered the Congregation at St. Peter's, Dec. 4, 1842, and had been teaching at Delaune's parish school in Madison when Delaune moved to Kentucky to begin his affiliation with St. Mary's College. Br. Mary Joseph went to St. Mary's, probably in the autumn of 1846, and left the Congregation from St. Mary's on Nov. 12, 1846. See Delaune to Br. Mary Joseph, Sept. 22, 1846, IPA. See also M.g.

that the brick building which served as the novitiate was too near the public road. With this one exception, all around was silent and the location was agreeable.

Fr. Granger here occupied himself exclusively with his Novitiate, being forbidden to do anything whatsoever for the congregation of the city.

Time soon proved the inopportuneness of this undertaking. With hardly anything to show in return, the expenses for the support of this house were three times as great as at the Lake, and the administration could not support them more than six months without taking measures to arrest them and to recall the Novitiate to Notre Dame du Lac, as will be recorded in the following chapter.

4. Blessing of the Cornerstone of the New Church at Notre Dame du Lac

The need of building a church was every year felt more strongly at Notre Dame du Lac. For two years the pupils could no longer be taken to the old log building and the congregation was afraid, with good reason, to meet there in winter. Without being able as yet to determine on the plan or dimensions of this new temple, seeing that there was hardly money enough with which to begin the foundations, Fr. Sorin, ever full of confidence in the merciful riches of Providence, wished to bless the cornerstone of this new church on the octave of the Assumption.

It was in reality somewhat bold for a man who had nothing collected, nothing even promised for the new enterprise, but it seemed to him a matter of necessity. He left to God the care of finding the resources. Who has ever hoped in the Lord and has been confounded? One year later, the church was up to the great joy of the house and of the whole Catholic congregation, as will be shown presently. And in the month of November of the year 1849, this same church had the honor of being solemnly consecrated under the title of the Sacred Heart of Jesus, as will be mentioned in due time.

CHAPTER 7

1848

---

1. New Agreement with Bishop Bazin *of Vincennes*

The character of the events of this year would appear to be of a more marked importance than whatever had occurred up to the present date. One of the first in chronological order and importance was the new agreement with the new bishop of Vincennes.

It had been morally impossible for Fr. Sorin to assist at his consecration at Vincennes in the month of November previous. Until the month of April 1848, it was equally difficult for him to make the journey to Vincennes. However, at that time he felt more desirous than ever of visiting this worthy prelate and the Minor Chapter happily endorsed the journey.

Once at Vincennes, his first concern was to have cancelled the former agreement which bound the Brothers in such a manner to the diocese that they had no liberty to make any foundations elsewhere, no matter what advantages might be presented. The first point being secured, Fr. Sorin himself drew up a new agreement which the good bishop consented to sign. It contained only five articles but all were highly important for the good of the work.

The first secured an absolute title to (the property of) Notre Dame du Lac with the simple obligation of refunding

The old agreement cancelled; by the new, N.D. du Lac is free to send its subjects wherever it seems well; more foundations with a single Brother. Novitiate recalled and the land sold on condition of a reimbursement of $3000 to the Bishop

75

*The $600 which
the bishop had
promised for
the churches of
South Bend and
Mishawaka given
to that of N.D.
du Lac. A deed
is finally given
for N.D. du
Lac with a mort-
gage of $3000*

three thousand dollars to the Ordinary[1] in case the property
were to be sold and the community to withdraw. The
second permitted the recall of the novitiate to the Lake,
the sale of the property of Indianapolis on condition that
three thousand dollars should be paid back to the bishop
whilst the five hundred dollars and the 375 acres should be
retained, and that the six hundred dollars advanced by the
bishop for the churches of South Bend and Mishawaka go
to the building of that of the Lake.

The third regulated the ordination of candidates of the
Society and their immediate dependence on the jurisdiction of their legitimate superiors. The fourth permitted that
only two Brothers at the least should be sent out together.
The fifth gave assurance of the protection of His Lordship,
especially within the limits of his diocese.

The first article was executed on the spot and the
others will doubtless go into full effect in due time. The
whole house blesses heaven for the happy arrangement,
the only one that could put an end to the ever-recurring
difficulties.

However great was the pain of everyone on learning of
the sudden death of this pious prelate a few weeks later, all
admired so much the more the Providential action on the
house, whose most important interests had been secured by
this worthy bishop almost immediately before he took his
departure from this world of misery and of strife.[2]

2. Death of Mother Mary of the Cenacle

*Mother Mary
of the Cenacle
goes to Fort
Wayne by order
of the Superior
to regain her
health; she dies
there April 29th*

Such is the nature of the joys of this world that they
must be mixed with sorrows and grief. The actual circumstances furnished a striking proof of this to all the
community. Fr. Sorin was rejoicing in anticipation of the
joy that the reading of the new contract would give the
administration of the Lake. But when he came to Fort

1. In canon law, the ordinary is the bishop who is in charge of
the diocese.
2. Bazin died in Vincennes on Apr. 23, 1848. Code, 11.

Wayne, whither he had sent the Mother Superior of the Sisters to be treated by an old physician from Germany who had a great reputation, he was painfully surprised to find her almost dying, at the very time when he so confidently expected to learn that she was cured.

He remained with her four days, not so much to console her as to be himself edified, and at the same time to give her this last proof of esteem and affection which she so well deserved by her devotedness and her rare virtues.

She died three days after the departure of the Father Superior from Fort Wayne, on 27 April, which was the Saturday within the octave of Easter, carrying with her the regrets of all that had known her but especially of Fr. Sorin who owed so many debts of gratitude to her.

Her short life in religion was a long series of virtuous acts of all sorts; her long illness placed in a strong light her great courage and her lively faith, and of her death it was said that if the angels were to die, they would surely die such a death as hers. May she obtain for me that my last moments be like those that closed her angelic life: *Requiescat in pace.*

3. Recall of the Novitiate to Notre Dame du Lac

The return of Fr. Granger and his novices was too earnestly desired to be long delayed once it was possible. In the month of May the necessary measures were taken and the little family returned to their own with sentiments of reciprocal affection which the temporary separation had only made stronger and more perceptible. The whole interior of the novitiate on St. Mary's island was plastered anew for their return. The chapter room, which had never been entirely furnished, also received its final touches.

Fr. Granger returns from Indianapolis with the Novices, June 25th, and the Novitiate on St. Mary's Island is replastered

And this new habitation, which nature has surrounded with all its charms, seemed to put on a fresher and more smiling air than ever for its inhabitants. By all appearances, no attempt will henceforth be made to find elsewhere any better place. If there are some inconveniences in the too great proximity of the novitiate and the college, there are unquestionably more serious ones in a separation of any considerable distance.

4. Regular Visit

*Fr. V. Drouelle,
the visitor, arrives
at N.D. du Lac
Sept. 3rd and
stays there until
Nov. 22nd;
he leaves for
Guadaloupe*

For several years, Fr. Rector gave it to be hoped that he would be seen in person at Notre Dame du Lac. Perhaps he would have actually carried out his intention this year had not the troubles in France made it a duty for him to remain at Sainte-Croix.[3] Fr. Drouelle was named to take his place; after having first brought a colony to Canada and visited Fr. Vérité's establishments,[4] he arrived at the Lake in the first days of September and remained there until 22 November, after which he set out for Guadaloupe where he was to remain with Fr. Dugoujon, who had been named prefect apostolic of this island.[5]

It would be hard to tell all the good done by this visit so long desired, especially by Fr. Sorin, who knew that there was no other way to re-establish the truth often

3. During the Revolution of 1848, anticlerical elements in Le Mans and environs threatened to burn the motherhouse at Ste-Croix and there were repeated threats against Fr. Moreau and the congregation's school. See Catta, *Moreau*, 1:681–725.

4. In 1847, the first Holy Cross foundation in Canada was made at St-Laurent, a village near Montreal. Ibid., 1:570–598. The superior of this Canadian foundation was Fr. Louis-Augustin Vérité. Born Oct. 11, 1815, at Montfort (Sarthe), he was already a priest when he entered the congregation at Ste-Croix in 1839. Victor Drouelle, born at Conlie (Sarthe) on Aug. 9, 1812, was already a priest when he entered the Congregation in 1837. He had served in the community's first overseas mission in Algeria from 1840 to 1842. M.g.

5. Casimir Dugoujon, born Mar. 1, 1810, at Condom (Gers), France, was already a priest when he entered the congregation in 1843. He withdrew from the community in 1846 but returned the following year. Active in France in the campaign to abolish slavery in the French colonies, he was appointed prefect apostolic in the French possession of Guadaloupe, a Caribbean island, in March 1848. He landed on Guadaloupe Aug. 12, 1848, and almost immediately became embroiled with the military governor, who ordered him back to France on Jan. 26, 1849, the day after Drouelle arrived to assist him. M.g. and Catta, *Moreau*, 1:701–706.

calumniated at Sainte-Croix by a bad will and to restore the reputation of the administration of the Lake than by giving a man of intelligence and of uprightness a chance to judge for himself of the real state of affairs.

Fr. Drouelle acquitted himself of his mission with tact and fairness and restored peace and union wherever they were found wanting. The material state of the house appeared to him very encouraging and in spiritual matters, if he did not find all the religious spirit desirable, he had at least the satisfaction, before quitting the Lake, of finding the dispositions in general very consoling. His stay at Notre Dame du Lac, more than anything else, succeeded in restoring a perfect understanding between the Mother House and this foundation.

At various intervals, Fr. Visitor received the vows of nine Brothers and gave the habit to one postulant at Notre Dame du Lac; he likewise admitted to profession three novices of the Sisters at Bertrand and gave the veil to three postulants.

5. Opening of the Priests' Novitiate

It was also during the stay of Fr. Visitor at Notre Dame du Lac that the Novitiate of the Priests, or the Seminary, was opened for the second time, this time under the guidance of Fr. Cointet, whose place on the missions was taken by Fr. Gouesse. It was then begun with nine candidates, two of whom were priests, and seven others more or less advanced in their ecclesiastical and literary studies.

Opening of a Novitiate for Priests; nine Novices under the control of Fr. Cointet, Nov. 10th

In the eyes of all the Brothers of the Lake, as well as in his own, this was an affair of the highest importance. All were separated from the pupils and on 10 November began to follow all the common exercises of the priests of the Society. A set of rules was drawn up for them and their studies and classes were regulated.

In the following spring, it is proposed to have them with their director in a house of their own, but for the present, the best that could be done was to give them rooms on the second story amongst the Fathers and professors. Up to the present time, these young men seem to be animated by the best of good will and promise great consolations.

Experience having shown that there was no well-founded hope of development for the Society of Priests in the United States other than by forming our own subjects from the beginning, the maintenance of a Novitiate for this branch, even more than for the two others, ought to be considered in the rank of the vital resources which should communicate life to the whole work. It is true that unless there is a great change in the subjects that generally present themselves, this establishment will be a burden from the material point of view; but the expenses that it will occasion will not be any less justifiable when compared to the results for the whole Society.

6. School in Brooklyn, New York

Fr. Drouelle and Fr. Sorin go to N.Y. Sept. 15th and promise Brothers to two churches

In September 1847, Bp. Hughes had Fr. Thébaud write a letter to request Fr. Sorin to begin a school of arts and trades in New York, but the lack of the necessary funds had caused the undertaking to be postponed indefinitely.[6] When Fr. Drouelle passed through New York in the month of July, the Bishop requested him to confer with Fr. Sorin. Having done this in chapter, it was resolved that the two Fathers should go to New York and confer with His Lordship in regard to this foundation.

But on their arrival in New York, Bp. Hughes was no longer at liberty to act as at the time of his first proposition to Fr. Sorin. He promised, nevertheless, to do all that he could with a committee of which he was president for the administration of a considerable legacy made in favor of the orphans of Brooklyn. He wished to place those orphans

6. John J. Hughes, born in Ireland June 24, 1797, had been educated at Mount St. Mary's, Emmitsburg, Maryland, and ordained in 1826 for the diocese of Philadelphia. Appointed coadjutor bishop of New York in 1837, he had succeeded Bp. Dubois when the latter died in 1842. Code, 138. Rev. Augustin J. Thébaud, S.J., was the Jesuit superior at St. John's (later Fordham) College in New York. See Thébaud to Sorin, Nov. 17, 1848, Sorin Papers, IPA.

under charge of the Brothers, who would teach them letters and trades.

But the members of this committee not being able to come to an understanding, and proposals having been made by Mr. Parmentier[7] in regard to the schools of different parishes of Brooklyn where there were actually about eight hundred children to educate, the two Fathers, having procured a recommendation from the bishop, visited three pastors of those congregations, who seemed to be delighted with this opening and very desirous to see the Brothers arrive as soon as possible.

A month later, on All Saints Day, five Brothers arrived in Brooklyn. Unfortunately, the Jesuits had learned of these arrangements. One of their Fathers had been employed for some time in the principal parish; they had probably formed their plans for these same schools. In a word, it was impossible then to find employment for more than two (Brothers) and the other three returned at once.[8]

Five Brothers sent to Brooklyn, Oct. 25th; only two find work; the other three return, Nov. 16th

The history of Kentucky and of Cincinnati serve as keys to explain this little phenomenon. However, the Minor Chapter was satisfied even at this price to have a foothold in Brooklyn, one of the first posts in the United States. And what is still more consoling, the first school is in the hands of a very able pastor who is devoted to the house.

7. Blessing of the Church

It took place on 12 November in presence of a numerous concourse of people and of the Fr. Visitor, who

7. André Parmentier was a prominent Brooklyn Catholic. See M. James Lowery, "Model Lay Activity—the Brooklyn Parmentier Family" (M.A. thesis, St. John's University, Jamaica, N. Y., 1940).

8. Brothers Basil (Timothy O'Neil), 38, and Aloysius Gonzaga (Robert Sidley), 18, both Irish-born, kept a school at Assumption parish in Brooklyn from September 1848 until May 1849. They were withdrawn when the pastor, Rev. Mr. Bacon, refused to sign a contract for their services. See Notices of Some Ex-Members (Fathers and Sisters) and Chronicles of (Fallen) Establishments of Brothers in U.S., 43–44, IPA; M.g.

had the consolation of celebrating the first solemn mass there. Fr. Cointet having been authorized about a year before to bless it, the ceremony could not be performed by anyone else. The mass, which the music-master of the college had been preparing for two months, was executed to perfection. The sermon on the occasion was preached by one of the two clergymen candidates, the Rev. Mr. Ivers,[9] who acquitted himself of this duty in a manner to please his entire audience. It was an excellent sermon, but a little long.

The length of the church including the sacristy is ninety feet by thirty-eight feet wide and twenty-four feet high. The style is Greek (*et à plein centre*). There are three arches and six fluted columns, which make a very pretty effect. The tribune, which was built for the use of the Sisters, is in the form of an ellipse, like a sanctuary. It is already enriched by an organ of Mr. H. Erben,[10] which, though somewhat weak for the church, is all the same a principal and very precious ornament thereof.

Fr. Sorin intends, as soon as the means will permit, to have a tower built over the door or the facade in which will be placed a bell whose size is to be determined only by the sum then at his disposition. The joy that this new church has caused in the whole community and in the entire congregation seems to have doubled the religious spirit of everybody.

9. William Ivers, born in Ireland in March 1800, entered the congregation at Notre Dame in 1848 and withdrew June 5, 1849. M.g.

10. This organ was made by Henry Erben of New York City. See Erben to Sorin, Nov. 22, 1848, and Jan. 23, 1849, Sorin Papers, IPA.

CHAPTER 8
1849

1. Development of the Sisters' Academy at Bertrand

Up to this time the school of the Sisters at Bertrand had made hardly any progress because of the lack of really competent Sisters. Hence the arrival of Miss Shea[1] in the month of October 1848 was a real acquisition. In a few months, a prospectus was published and some twenty boarders filled all the places in the young academy. The institution at Bertrand already has a reputation, and if it is only conducted wisely in the future, it will easily succeed. The monthly exhibitions here, just as at the university, will do much good.

Miss Shea arrives at Bertrand, Sept. 25th

2. The New Plan of Studies

The plan of studies followed by the Jesuits[2] was adopted at the return of the pupils in the month of September, but the results could not be clearly perceived until during the course of the following year. They were decidedly

The Jesuits' plan of studies adopted Sept. 1st; monthly exhibitions

1. Catherine Shea, a governess from Ireland, taught at the academy from 1848 to 1850. See Mary Immaculate (Helen) Creek, *A Panorama: 1844–1977: Saint Mary's College, Notre Dame, Indiana* (Notre Dame, Ind.: Saint Mary's College, 1977), 11.
2. The Jesuits' plan has been identified as that in use at St. Louis University. See John T. Wack, "The University of Notre Dame du Lac: Foundation, 1842–1857" (Ph.D. diss., University of Notre Dame, 1967), 184, n.14.

favorable. Whilst giving the pupils more liberty, these became more contented, and their gratitude was shown by a
greater assiduity than they had hitherto displayed.

The spirit of piety grew amongst them in equal proportion; just on the eve of the Distribution, thirty-eight of
them were clothed with the scapular. The month of May
was celebrated in a manner to edify, and the archconfraternity received some new members.

As to the intrinsic merit of the new plan, it consists
chiefly in this, that in all the branches of English the same
studies may be followed by the students of the different
classes without prejudice to their respective classes. Each
branch has its cup rather than wine poured out after the
ancient manner. This new plan presents a great advantage
in the United States, where everyone wants to be free to
study what he likes. It pleases everybody.

The long walks in summer, dinners in the woods, stay-
ing up till nine o'clock in winter for the older students,
contributed to make life in the college agreeable. Moreover,
the monthly exhibitions in public made the institution
known and popular, and this by degrees gained the good
will of the neighborhood.

The acquisition of an apparatus[3] was not without its
favorable results for the college. This year, the number of
pupils was one-third greater than the previous year.

3. Foundation of New Orleans

Br. Vincent leaves with four Brothers and three Sisters on Apr. 15th and arrives at N. Orleans toward the 25th; $125 for each

The fall of the establishment in Brooklyn was preceded
by some weeks by the more advantageous establishment of
New Orleans. Five Brothers, (Vincent, Theodulus, Basil,
Francis de Sales and Louis) and three Sisters (Five Wounds,
Calvary and Nativity) proceeded thither towards the end
of April and on 1 May took charge of the Orphan Boys'
Asylum[4] at a salary of $125 for each and $25 additional

3. Ibid., 196. The apparatus in question was some kind of
scientific instrument.

4. St. Mary's Orphan Asylum had been founded in 1835 by
Rev. Adam Kindelon, a diocesan priest, was incorporated, endowed

for a director and a directress, payable semi-annually in advance.

4. Missions and Church at Niles

The missions had never been better, nor even so well attended as this year. Frs. Cointet, Gouesse and Baroux devoted all their time to them and did much good. These missions were more fruitful in good before God than in money in the eyes of the administration. Most of these recently established little congregations being poor, they can give but litt'. towards the support of the priest. However, Fr. Cointet thought that by the opening of spring he could begin a church at Niles with subscriptions from the Catholics of Niles and from some laborers on the railroad, who had not yet departed.

A church is undertaken at Niles thanks to the community and especially to Fr. Cointet; first stone blessed in May by the Fr. Superior

The church was to be finished about the fifteenth of August. A new railroad will probably be started from South Bend and will supply the means of building some new churches in the north of Indiana.

5. Changing the Brothers from the Novitiate to the College

On July 9, 1849, the annual retreat of the priests was begun (six priests, eight scholastics, and four seminarians from Milwaukee). It ended on the fifteenth and the Novitiate of the Scholastics of the Society was organized on the same day under the direction of Fr. Granger. All the Brothers moved together to the college to be there under the direction of the Father Superior. In order to promote the advancement of the Milwaukee Seminarians in piety as well as in science, they were permitted to live with our members for this year.

---

and received a subsidy from the State of Louisiana. It suffered from poor management, and the bishop of New Orleans, Antoine Blanc, had sought a religious community to staff it. See Catta, *Moreau*, 1:934.

6. Arrival of Mother Mary of the Saviour

Fr. Superior goes to Canada, sees Frs. Vérité and Rézé; Sr. M. of the Savior with two Sisters; Aug. 6th

Some days after the close of the annual retreat of the Priests, Fr. Superior started for Saint-Laurent where he was expected by Frs. Vérité and Rézé[5], the latter being a recent arrival from the Mother House, who was to replace the former and allow him to return to France. They spent about a week pleasantly together, after which Fr. Sorin took the road back to Notre Dame du Lac with the new superior, who had been expected for fifteen months, and two other French Sisters.[6] The journey was fortunate and rapid, although made amidst the dying and the dead, whom the cholera was then mowing down in most parts of the United States as well as in Europe.

General Retreat, seven take the habit; Aug. 15th; House finished, 160 ft. across; Nov.1st

The general retreat followed soon after his arrival. Seven postulants received the holy habit and the Society of the Sisters appeared once more to become filled with life, order, peace and happiness. Soon afterwards, their house was finished, that is to say, it was lengthened at one end and raised one story in the center, so that it presented a pretty front of ninety-two feet with two wings, less high, of forty feet each.

7. Consecration of the Church

Church of the Sacred Heart of Jesus consecrated by two bishops, Nov. 11th. Ninety confirmed, Nov. 11th

Four months previously, this august ceremony had been fixed for the third Sunday of November, the first after the octave of All Saints, as it is marked in the Constitutions of the Institution[7] for the dedication and the foundation

5. Joseph-Pierre Rézé, born Feb. 23, 1814, at Sablé (Sarthe), was already a priest of the diocese of Le Mans when he entered the congregation in 1840. He arrived in Canada July 17, 1849. M.g.

6. The superior was Mother Mary of the Savior and the two other Sisters were Mary of the Desert and Mary Bon Secours. Mary of the Desert (Angelique Godeaux) was born May 8, 1825, in Mayenne, received the habit in 1846 at Ste-Croix, and professed vows there in 1847. Mary Bon Secours (Esther LeDuc) was born Nov. 26, 1826, in Montreal, received the habit Aug. 13, 1848, at St-Laurent, and professed vows Nov. 16, 1849, at Bertrand. ASHC.

7. The institution in question is the Congregation of Holy Cross.

of the Mother House. Bp. Van de Velde of Chicago was present with the bishop of Vincennes, the consecrator; Mr. Shawe of Detroit preached.[8] The solemnity had as much pomp as could be had. It lasted seven hours, including confirmation, which was administered to ninety persons.

The new church was dedicated to the Sacred Heart of Jesus, probably the first of this title enriched by the privileges attached to consecration. It is small but very pretty, being altogether, sacristy included, only ninety-two feet long by thirty-eight wide and twenty high. It has three altars on which the holy mass can be celebrated at one and the same time.

On the following Tuesday the bishop gave confirmation to seven persons at Goshen and on Wednesday to twenty-one at Mishawaka. On Thursday he ordained two of our novices as subdeacons, Messrs. Shilling (a German) and Shortis (Irish).[9] On Friday, at Bertrand, he received the profession (of vows) of two Sisters, Mary of Bon Secours and Mary of St. Dosithea. On Saturday morning, he departed, well pleased, for Michigan City with two of our Fathers, administered confirmation there the next day, and on Monday at LaPorte, another of our congregations.

Two novices ordained subdeacons, Nov. 15th. Two Sisters admitted to vows, Nov. 16th

8. James O. Van de Velde, S.J., was born Apr. 3, 1795, at Lebbeke, near Termonde in the archdiocese of Mechlin, Belgium. Educated in Belgium and at Georgetown College in the District of Columbia, he had served on the faculty and then as president of St. Louis University from 1831 to 1843. Appointed the second bishop of Chicago in 1848, he was transferred to the diocese of Natchez, Mississippi, in 1853. The bishop of Vincennes was James Mary Maurice Landes d'Aussac de St-Palais, born Nov. 15, 1811, at La Salvetat in the diocese of Montpelier, France. Educated at the Sulpician Seminary in Paris, he had engaged in pastoral work in the diocese of Vincennes from 1836 to 1848, when he was named the fourth bishop of Vincennes. See Code, 66, 288. Rev. Michael Shawe had served as vicar general of the diocese of Vincennes and then on the faculty at Notre Dame before moving to Detroit. See Hope, 57, 68.

9. Christian Shilling was born Feb. 2, 1816, in Füth, Germany, entered the congregation in 1848, and did not profess vows until 1850. Richard Shortis was born Mar. 21, 1815, in Ireland, entered on Mar. 19, 1849, and professed vows on Mar. 19, 1850. M.g.

In this same visit, the first made to the house by our bishop, he added four new counties to our mission and the bishop of Chicago also wished to make us a present of a large congregation of Germans. Besides, His Lordship wished to make of the establishment of orphans at Notre Dame du Lac his diocesan establishment, as he had begun in regard to his seminary by sending there the only seminarian that he had.

8. Burning of the Apprentices' Shops

Burning of the workshops, kitchen, bakery and workroom of the Sister Sacristan; 16,000 fr.; Nov. 18th

On the night between Saturday and Sunday, 18 November, fire started in the workshops, it is not known how, and, in spite of all the efforts of the Brothers, Seminarians and of everybody, a line of buildings one hundred and thirty feet long and two stories high was wiped away by the flames in two hours. Such was the fury of the fire that it devoured nearly everything in the shops, in the kitchen and in the bakery together with their provisions, and the workroom of the Sister Sacristan, where the chapel lost in vestments and linen about three thousand francs. The total loss was at least sixteen thousand francs. Most of the beds of the orphans and their best clothes were a prey of the flames.

New kitchen and bakery in brick, 44 x 20 ft., begun Nov. 22, 1849

Mrs. Coquillard and Mrs. Woodworth of South Bend began a collection the day after the accident and in three days they raised about seven hundred francs in merchandise in South Bend, Niles and Mishawaka. It was necessary to rebuild at once the bakery and the kitchen, that is to say a brick building of forty-four feet by twenty, two stories high; that is, to begin, because the cold did not permit the finishing of even the first story.

Addition

It was not until the month of September 1850, that the work was resumed with an addition which made it seventy-seven feet long, having below a kitchen and cellar, with a room for the cooks, a bakery and an infirmary; upstairs were three bedrooms for the Priests, Brothers and pupils, a common refectory, a pharmacy and a cabinet for the infirmary.

The departure of Fr. Baroux for France took place before this time. About the middle of December he left his savages of Pokagon, whom he was not to see till nearly a year later. His collection was successful and contributed greatly to relieve the house from the embarrassment in which the fire of November had left it. Fr. Baroux devoted himself with zeal and earnestness to the work, and on his return in May 1851, he had the consolation of seeing all the shops springing up again which had been consumed by fire, forming an edifice 190 feet long by twenty-four wide, one and a half and two stories in height, no longer behind the college, but alongside the Grand Avenue, four hundred feet from the college.

Departure of Fr. Baroux for France

Rebuilding of the workshops

The expenses of this building were covered by the returns from several collections made for this purpose.

Result of the collections

1. That of Mmes. Coquillard and
   Woodworth in South Bend and Niles $ 75
2. That of Bro. Stephen in Illinois 125
3. That of Mrs. Woodworth in Detroit 40
4. That of Mrs. Woodworth in Cincinnati 140
5. That of the Propagation 1,150
6. That of Fr. Baroux 2,400
7. From various individuals 40

$3,970.

CHAPTER 9

1850

---

1. Expedition to California. Its Motives

For a long time the pecuniary embarrassments of the establishment had caused the administration an interminable series of disappointments and misery. The ravages of fire seemed at first destined to crown all the rest. Reflection begot the hope that God, who had thus far done everything at Notre Dame du Lac, would not permit his work to perish but would rather make this new trial serve for the accomplishment of his merciful designs.

An extraordinary event almost compelled the members of the chapter to take a step in whose success none of them would have placed any confidence, had it not been, in their unanimous opinion, justified before God by two powerful motives, namely: 1. that of preventing a terrible scandal which might ruin the work; 2. that of trying a means of paying arrears of indebtedness—and justified in the eyes of the public by the consequences of a fire which were to be repaired.

On these grounds the expedition to California was decided upon. Br. Gatien[1] was going to leave the Society to marry and to settle down near the college. He consented

---

1. The translator, Toohey, mistakenly rendered the name Stephen (Etienne in French) instead of Gatien. Cf. p. 94 of the original ms. with p. 140 of the Toohey ms.

to depart for those distant regions. Three other Brothers who could be relied on and three companions besides were given him, and all set out towards the end of March with the purpose of devoting themselves to the re-establishment of the orphans' house.[2]

2. Father Gouesse Is Sent to New Orleans, January 28, 1850

Towards the end of January, Fr. Gouesse was sent as Visitor to the orphans' establishment of New Orleans where he was to remain as spiritual director of the members of the house, already seven in number. Two Sisters went with him.[3]

3. Defection of Brothers Basil and Joseph

Some months afterwards, Br. Basil, who taught the first class, a man of a gloomy and variable character, threw off

2. A full account of the California expedition is given in Franklin Cullen, *Holy Cross on the Gold Dust Trail* (Notre Dame, Ind.: Indiana Province Archives Center, 1989), 1–32. In addition to Br. Gatien, who had come to America with Sorin in 1841, were Brs. Lawrence, another member of the original colony, Justin (Louis Gautier), 49, and Placidus (Urban Allard), 38, both of whom had joined the congregation in France in 1839. Justin had come to America in 1844 and Placidus in 1846. George B. Woodworth, a resident of South Bend, was the leader of the expedition, which included two other young men, Gregory Campau, a student at Notre Dame, and Michael Dowling, who may have been either an apprentice or a hired farm worker at Notre Dame. The seven drew up an agreement and organized themselves as the St. Joseph Company. The company found no gold to speak of. Br. Gatien left the community in California and Br. Placidus died there. Brs. Lawrence and Justin returned to Notre Dame in 1851.

3. The two Sisters were Mary of the Angels and Mary of St. Agnes (Leocadia Hogan). See Mary of the Angels to Sorin, Apr. 21, 1850, Sorin Papers, IPA. While information about the former is not available, she had made her profession of vows only on Jan. 27, 1850. See below, section 13. The latter was born in Ireland on Feb. 1, 1822, and received the habit at Notre Dame on Aug. 15, 1849. She was still a novice when she went to New Orleans. ASHC.

the yoke of his profession and departed incognito, no one knows whither.[4] His example was soon followed by another professed Brother, Br. Joseph, the Master of Novices, in fact, who, having been sent in confidence to collect in the diocese of Vincennes for the orphans, stopped at the bishop's house whence he sent his renunciation that he was not any longer a member of the association.[5] This was a scandal rather than a loss.

This Brother, whose imagination had every year given serious trouble to the community, was not without talent nor even devotedness to the Society; but his haughty temper soon made him unbearable to all those with whom he lived.

4. Brother Emmanuel Obtains a Dispensation of Some Months from His Vows

This same year was marked by a third defection, that of Br. Emmanuel who taught the German class at Fort Wayne.[6] He, however, retired like a religious, having first obtained a dispensation of some months to which he was still obliged. The cause of his departure seems to have been no other than the needs of an aged mother who had no support but him.

5. A Successful Scholastic Year

Discourse of D. Gregg, Secretary of the United States

The Scholastic Year was more successful and with a better attendance than any previous year. The average number of pupils was fifty-eight. The year was terminated by a brilliant discourse by the Honorable D. Gregg, Sec-

4. Br. Basil (Timothy O'Neil), born in Ireland in 1810, had entered the congregation at St. Peter's in November 1842 and had taught for a year at the Assumption parish school in Brooklyn. M.g.

5. Br. Joseph was the first recruit for the Brothers in the United States. See above, chapters 1, 4:4 and 5:3.

6. Br. Emmanuel (Antoine Wopermann) was born in Germany in 1820, entered the congregation in 1844, and withdrew Aug. 1, 1850. M.g.

retary of the United States in Illinois.[7] This speech was printed and circulated to the great benefit of the college.

6. St. Mary's Academy

Equal success seems to have crowned the labors of the Sisters at Bertrand, although the number of boarders there is thus far only fifteen to twenty.

7. The Missions

The missions being oftener and more regularly visited, are assuming a more consoling and encouraging appearance. Two new churches were blessed this year, one at Michigan City and the other at Niles, and the cornerstone of a third church has also been blessed at Kalamazoo.

8. Journey of Father Sorin to New Orleans, July 4, 1850

The day after the Distribution of Prizes, a letter more urgent than any of its predecessors having come from New Orleans, the Minor Chapter, thinking that the existence of our members was seriously threatened in Louisiana unless instant means were taken to check the evils that turbulent and ambitious individual was causing to grow in proportion day by day,[8] recognized the necessity of a visit by the Fr. Superior himself, and on the evening of the same day he started for the South.

Summary of the trouble caused this. year by Fr. Gouesse

He remained eight days at New Orleans, gave the Brothers and Sisters a retreat, arranged everything in a satisfactory manner for those two branches, but could not

7. David L. Gregg later served in the U.S. diplomatic service. It is uncertain what position he might have held when he gave the commencement address in 1850. See Joseph A. Lyons, *Silver Jubilee of the University of Notre Dame, June 23rd, 1869* (Chicago: E. B. Myers & Company, 1869), 155. See also Wack, 219–220, note 41.

8. The individual in question, Rev. François Gouesse, appears to have been an alcoholic. See Granger to Moreau, Sept. 1, 1852, and Jahan to Moreau, Sept. 1, 1852, in GA. Also, see above, chapter 2, note 14.

make any impression on the haughty dispositions of the man who ought to have given all the others the example of submission and who, far from doing so, told all that would listen to him that he was to be named Local Superior of New Orleans by the Mother House in spite of Fr. Sorin. The latter, however, had already received from Fr. Rector, several months before, authorization to dismiss the individual in question from the Association.

Nevertheless, having no one to put in this man's place just then, he preferred to restrict himself to making his report to Sainte-Croix, persuaded that justice would be done without making a stir by the prompt recall to Europe of so dangerous a subject. What was his surprise to learn from the man in October that he had at last received from France the document naming him Local Superior of New Orleans.

Such a mysterious proceeding deeply afflicted the Minor Chapter of the Priests and the best members of the Association in New Orleans. To all the representations that were addressed to Rev. Fr. Rector, not a line came for more than six months to check an evil that was growing in a frightening manner.

The absence of Fr. Rector, who was at this time in Rome,[9] favored its progress. Moreover, heaven had permitted, as we discovered later, a word (to be) overheard which would soon bring about the total ruin of the work of Sainte-Croix in the United States.

It appears that the Rev. Fr. Rector had concluded from the fact of sending Fr. Gouesse to New Orleans that Notre Dame du Lac placed confidence in him and that consequently he could be named Local Superior, since the mere fact that he was at the head of some Brothers gave him a right to this title according to the Constitutions; finally, that it was the one means of bringing about a general reconciliation, and that to please Notre Dame du Lac they

9. Basil Moreau was away from the motherhouse at Ste-Croix in Rome from Oct. 31, 1850, until Mar. 27, 1851. See Catta, *Moreau*, 1:801–830.

left him under the jurisdiction of Fr. Sorin, to whom he should send his account every year.

The truth is, however, that he had been sent to New Orleans merely to rid the house of the Lake of his presence, without any intention of leaving him there for long, still less of ever giving him any other title but that of Spiritual Director of the Asylum.

It is still a mystery at Notre Dame du Lac how the Mother House could be so mistaken in a matter that had been so often set before the eyes of the people there. Be this as it may, having in vain used all the means suggested by prudence and charity during about a year, the Minor Chapter felt compelled to inform Archbishop Blanc that the nomination of this Father should not hold, that it was probably the result of a surprise; and some months later the Minor Chapter informed His Grace of the positive dismissal of this same Father from the Association in the United States. This, however, was only done in the month of June of the following year.

In order not to have to come back again on this sad chapter and to relate at least what is most important in the year 1850, it is necessary to add that of all the trials of the Association in this country, there was none that brought it nearer to its fall.

Whilst heaven was blessing the work at Rome, the devil was sifting it here. If human ambition had no other examples to bring forward in proof of the unfortunate effects that result from it, ours would suffice to inspire every sensible man with disgust. And if we were only at the end!

9. State of the College

The reopening in September 1850, was attended by a larger number of students, but the number did not continue to increase as in the past, so that the average attendance was less than in the previous year.

The interior pain that paralyzed the devotedness of the members of the Minor Chapter of the priests so as to cause serious fears for the continuance of the house naturally checked all external activity. Now, to preserve its existence in this country, a college needs to arouse the attention of the public, to fix it and thus to secure pupils. If the number was not as encouraging, there was at least more peace in all the branches of the work at Notre Dame du Lac. It was (misery) enough to have to fight at the same time with the Mother House and with the wrong-headed man in the South.

10. Growth of St. Mary's Academy at Bertrand

On the other hand, St. Mary's Academy this year begins to fly with its own wings. Miss Shea withdraws, and all things improve. A wrong-headed person amongst the Sisters can do so much, and the peace that follows her departure shows that she is not to be regretted. The pupils are almost double in number, their spirit improves perceptibly and the looks of the institution improve daily.

In the month of January the State of Michigan recognized St. Mary's Academy and bestowed a liberal charter on it.[10] In a word, the future of this house was assured and the public had confidence in it.

Two Sisters, having been sent to Loretto, Kentucky, to learn music and drawing, returned towards the end of this year and at once made themselves useful to the institution.[11]

11. Ordination of Fathers Shortis and Schilling

On 17 March, Rev. Mr. R. Shortis and Rev. Mr. C. Schilling[12] were ordained deacons by the Bishop of Detroit,

10. Creek, 16, states that the act of incorporation was recorded Apr. 2, 1850.

11. The two Sisters were Emily (Julia Rivard), born in Canada on Nov. 23, 1824, and Cenacle (Clotile Joanneault), born in Le Mans on Apr. 28, 1823. Both received the habit at Notre Dame on Aug. 15, 1849. ASHC. They studied at the academy conducted by the Sisters of Loretto, then in Loretto, Marion County, Kentucky. See M. Eleanore Brosnahan, *On the King's Highway* (New York: D. Appleton and Company, 1931), 158.

12. His name was previously given as Shilling; see above, chapter 8:7.

and on the nineteenth, the feast of St. Joseph, they were promoted to the sacred order of the Priesthood. The same day each of them made his perpetual profession (of vows). They were both ordained for the missions.

12. Foundation of St. John

The former was reserved for the railroad, and the latter was sent to St. John with the promise of a Brother and two Sisters, who were to join him in the month of April following. This foundation, made in the midst of a German population already numbering from five to six hundred inhabitants, could at the start be only a burden, but there are hopes that it will in time repay the expenses. It is eighty miles from Notre Dame,[13] but is to be on the line of a new railroad which it is expected will be built to connect the Mississippi with the East.

13. Professions

On 20 March, the bishop of Detroit received the profession of Sisters Mary of the Compassion, of St. Catherine, of St. Cecilia, of St. John, and of St. Aloysius Gonzaga at Bertrand. On 27 January, Father Sorin received that of Sr. Mary of the Angels at Notre Dame du Lac, and on 26 May that of Sr. Mary of St. Francis at Bertrand.[14]

13. St. John is west of Notre Dame, in Lake County, Indiana.

14. Of the seven Sisters mentioned here, no information is available in the community records about three of them, Srs. St. Alyosius Gonzaga, St. Cecilia, and Mary of the Angels. Sr. St. John Baptist (Elizabeth Koch) was born in Germany on Oct. 1, 1816, entered the congregation Dec. 1, 1846, and received the habit at Bertrand Dec. 14, 1847. The other three Sisters were born in Ireland: Compassion (Margaret Gleeson) on Oct. 27, 1827; St. Catharine (Catharine Shandly) on Sept. 8, 1816; and St. Francis (Anne Molloy) on Jan. 14, 1823. All three had entered and received the habit at Bertrand—Sr. St. Francis only the previous year, on Feb. 2, 1849, and the other two on Dec. 25, 1845, and Nov. 21, 1846, respectively. ASHC.

CHAPTER 10

1851

---

1. Another Railroad Line to
Pass through South Bend

The year 1851 opened, as one might say, with a loud burst of joy from all northern Indiana. A question vital to the region had been decided in its favor by the legislature at Indianapolis; a railroad had been secured through the St. Joseph Valley, passing through South Bend, Mishawaka, Elkhart, etc. This joy was all the more lively because the enormous wealth of the Michigan Central Railroad Company had long been considered as an insurmountable obstacle to the realization of this project, no matter how advantageous it might be to the area.

The prayers of the Association had been frequently offered up for the success of this enterprise. Finally, in the early part of January, the news was communicated everywhere by the noise of the cannon as an event of extraordinary importance. The joy was as great at Notre Dame du Lac as elsewhere.

Besides the common advantages to the area of a railroad line securing to the borders of Michigan and Indiana the great commercial route between the East and the West[1]

---

1. The new line, the Michigan Southern and Northern Indiana Railway Company, ran from Toledo, Ohio, via Hillsdale, Michigan,

and thus determining a number of other branches which would all strike the main line at some point or other, besides those advantages and such as would necessarily arise from competition between two powerful companies, Notre Dame du Lac, which, like St. Mary's Academy, was between the two lines, felt that two ways of communication of the most useful kind were secured to her for attending her many missions, for the journeys and visits of the Brothers and Sisters assigned to teach and, finally, for the pupils of the College and of the Academy. Moreover, this new railroad would bring European emigration in this direction and would thus facilitate what had been so painfully organized for Catholicism.

Notre Dame du Lac did not, like so many others, offer superfluous thanks to the able senators who had secured a triumph for the rights of the region, and to whose efforts all the credit for this happy consummation was attributed; it was, in the eyes of the children of Holy Cross, a great blessing for which heaven was above all to receive their thanksgiving.

It would be difficult to set a money value on the benefit of this railroad to an establishment like Notre Dame du Lac which finds itself placed beside a line that may be called one of the first of the United States. Before the end of this year, Notre Dame du Lac will be, by means of it, within two days of New York, twenty hours from Cincinnati, eight hours from Chicago and a few hours from even its most distant missions.

The length of this article must find its justification in the absorbing interest which this railroad has been exciting for six months all along its course. The cars are promised and expected at South Bend by next September first.

---

and Mishawaka, South Bend, and La Porte, Indiana to Chicago. It was later part of the New York Central System. The first through train from the East arrived in South Bend on the evening of Oct. 4, 1851, where it was greeted by a joyous celebration. Howard, 1:236–237.

2. Post Office: Father Sorin Postmaster and
Inspector of Public Roads

Another advantage of a private nature followed closely that mentioned above, namely, the establishment of a Post Office at Notre Dame du Lac with the name of Notre Dame. This had been attempted already, in 1850, but had failed on the pretext that South Bend was too near.

Recourse was again had to prayer. The Blessed Virgin and St. Joseph were alternately importuned by all the house, until finally H. Clay,[2] one of the men most likely to mark an epoch in the United States, obtained this favor for Notre Dame du Lac to the great satisfaction of the whole Association and of the entire mission in general.

The profit is merely a sparing of money and of inconvenience, but there is another very valuable circumstance connected herewith: the passing of the stage coach regularly under the windows of the college. The house is daily becoming better known and the roads leading to it will have to be better cared for.

This consideration of the roads in this region had sufficient importance in the mind of Fr. Sorin to cause him to have himself named *Inspector of Public Roads*. In virtue of this office, he hopes to serve the interests of Notre Dame du Lac in the district confided to his care.

The office, however, as well as that of Postmaster gives him only as much trouble as he may feel inclined to take, since most of the work can be put in the hands of one or more Brothers as assistants, he himself remaining in charge.

3. Election to Public Offices

It has just been stated that the superior of Notre Dame du Lac considered it advantageous to have himself named

2. Senator Henry Clay of Kentucky had a long and distinguished career in government, serving as Speaker of the House of Representatives, secretary of state, and United States senator, the office that he held in 1851. He was the unsuccessful candidate for president of the Whig Party in 1828, 1832, and 1844. He died

Postmaster and Inspector of Public Roads. Here it may not be out of place to remark that it is important for an Institution like Notre Dame du Lac, generally looked upon by Americans with all the prejudice of the public against convents, to come into close contact with neighbors and to take an interest in all that concerns the general good of the area, to show zeal in those matters and to convince everyone that we are citizens in heart as well as in name.

A new means, and often the most efficacious of all, of proving one's honesty is by keeping exact accounts and by doing justice to all concerned and thus to surround the house with the confidence of the people, sometimes even to place them under obligations which will make friends of them. *Consideration of what the House gains by voting*

For these reasons, Fr. Sorin recently judged it advisable to present himself with some Brothers at the elections for the offices of the area. He has done it only once, but the results only make him regret that he did not begin to do it sooner. From this time, even the most insignificant offices brought him some candidates, honest men who are always disposed to act fairly toward the Institution and toward Catholics in general.

Perhaps there is no people that nourishes a greater desire for offices. Hence, it is easy to guess what consideration an Institution will have in their eyes which can decide two-thirds of all the local elections. The Presbyterians in particular are galled at seeing this power with all its consequences in the hands of a Catholic priest. In fact, if it is only used prudently, it is a precious resource both for the House and for the locality because of the good choice that can be made of public officers.

4. Return of Father Baroux

Finally, about 24 May, Fr. Baroux arrived from France with one Brother and two Sisters for his mission among the

---

June 29, 1853. It is uncertain how Clay came to be instrumental in making Notre Dame the site of a post office. See Wack, 224.

savages at Pokagon.[3] His return caused great joy, especially among his dear flock, left for nearly eighteen months without a resident pastor. Everybody knows that the Indians remain all their lives like children who must always be led by the hand or they will fall.

During this time they did what they would never venture to do if he had been present, namely, they separated into two villages eighteen miles apart. This separation can have favorable results only in the event it should become a cause of the reunion of all the savages of the region in the same neighborhood. As long as they are thus scattered in little bands, it is impossible to make them draw any fruit from the habitual residence of a priest nor from a school amongst them.

Poor Indians! They are fast disappearing from the land which not long ago was covered by numbers of their warriors. Before two centuries (shall have passed), they will be spoken of in history as of a nation completely destroyed. The Catholic Church alone is able to preserve them from an otherwise inevitable ruin, and most frequently there is a lack of the personnel as well as of the funds to take such care of them as their weakness requires.

It is just as hard to keep them from drinking as it is to make them work. This tells plainly that religion alone can oppose a sufficiently strong check to their violent passions, and that without it, the savages will only furnish a disgusting spectacle of corruption, debauchery and cruelty, and of destruction everywhere. With frequent religious exercises,

3. One of the Sisters was Mary of the Redemption (Pauline Rajot), born May 24, 1823, in Rennes, France. She had entered the congregation at Le Mans in March 1847 and received the habit there July 5, 1847. She served as superior at Bertrand, Michigan, in 1848–49 and was at St-Laurent, Canada, from May to August 1849 before returning to France. She came back to the U.S. in 1851 and worked with Baroux's Indians for a year before moving to Canada, where she made professional of perpetual vows at St-Laurent, Mar. 25, 1855. ASHC. The identity of the other Sister and of the Brother is uncertain.

sermons, confessions, they may be good; without them, it is pitiful.

5. Misunderstandings and the Consequences

The house of the Lake had cherished the hope that Fr. Baroux would return bearing conciliatory documents from the Mother House. It was quite the contrary.

It seems that at Sainte-Croix the complaints that had been received from America had not been understood, and that they were rather looked upon as lies, or at least as exaggerations. The personal and official remarks, both as regards certain individuals and on some serious principles, were put entirely to one side and left unanswered, and discontent, instead of diminishing with time which smooths and destroys all things, was only on the increase.

How it could happen that for years men whose intentions on both sides were certainly pure not only did not understand each other but evidently caused much pain of spirit and of heart is one of those mysteries whose explanation will doubtless be found in the development of the plan of the divine economy.

However, to be just in these memoirs, it must be stated what appears evident in the eyes of all the members that have had a knowledge of this deadly misunderstanding, that nothing was more pernicious to the work. St. Teresa somewhere calls these miseries "the war of the saints." The author of these remarks, who has followed things closely, would be more inclined to call them "the triumph of Beelzebub on his marauding excursions." Much precious time is thus wasted in a correspondence unworthy of Religious, and the remaining time is spent without energy, without courage and without devotedness. A sad existence, which renders the yoke of the religious life almost insupportable, and which would make one regret that he was not a solitary, rather than to be compelled to feel so painfully the bonds of society even in a community.

CHAPTER 11

1852

---

1. Father Sorin Visits Europe Again

Tired of representing in vain by letter all those subjects of complaint, the Minor Chapter of Notre Dame du Lac at last determined to have them carried to Sainte-Croix by Fr. Sorin in person. Leaving on December second, he arrived at the Mother House about the end of the month.

Great was the surprise of the Very Reverend Fr. Rector at the unexpected arrival of this Father. He himself had been absent more than six months in Rome, and during all that time had followed the affairs of his houses in America only from a distance. Most of the letters relating to the difficulties of the Lake had not even been read by him.

His Chapter was convened and the grievances of Fr. Sorin were discussed for four hours. The erection of the House of New Orleans into a Local Superiorship was maintained but left entirely, as to the revenues and charges, under the jurisdiction of the Lake whose superior had just been named Provincial for the United States.[1]

Fr. Cointet, named by Fr. Sorin for the Asylum, was recognized as Local Superior, although Fr. Gouesse had

---

1. See Basil Moreau, "Circular Letter 47 (Dec. 8, 1851)," in Heston, trans. *Circular Letters of Moreau*, 1:259. A provincial superior is in charge of a large geographical area, e.g., a whole country or a part thereof.

been sent back there to put himself at the disposal of the archbishop rather than to fulfill any religious obedience of the Society.

Thus ended, in a meeting of some hours, the serious and pernicious differences which the inattention of the Mother House had unfortunately allowed to grow out of all proportion. Affection did not seem to be lacking, but it became evident to Fr. Sorin that for the future, little assistance could be expected from the Mother House, which was hardly able to meet its own necessities, being drained by the new foundations of Rome and of Orléans.[2]

2. Father Sorin in Rome

Having settled matters satisfactorily at Sainte-Croix, Fr. Sorin took only a few weeks to visit the acquaintances and the Protectors of his Mission. He was fortunate in these visits and believed that he had gained valuable friends for the Work.

Having afterwards obtained the sanction of the Very Reverend Fr. Rector to visit Rome, he started for Italy toward the end of February. During the seven weeks spent by him in the Eternal City, he had the consolation to be twice admitted into the presence of His Holiness and to obtain from him precious privileges. During most of this time he lived with Monsignor Merode, Chamberlain of the Pope, and during the rest with his confrère, Fr. Drouelle, Superior at Vigna Pia.

The great point that almost solely occupied the attention of those two Fathers was the approbation of the Association by the Holy See. The matter was examined but could not be settled on account of the recent difficulties of

2. In March 1850, a contingent of Holy Cross priests, Brothers and Sisters had taken over the direction and staffing of the preparatory seminary of the diocese of Orléans, France, located at La Chapelle, St-Mesmin. In November of that same year, Moreau himself, together with four Brothers, had gone to Rome, where the congregation had taken responsibility for two institutions for abandoned children, Santa Prisca, a trade school, and Vigna Pia, an agricultural school. See Catta, *Moreau*, 1:798–829.

Picpus and the opposition of a French prelate.[3] Nevertheless, all things were left on a good footing, and Fr. Sorin
carried with him from Rome, amongst other consolations,
the assurance of the good will of His Holiness towards
Sainte-Croix and its foundations in other lands.

On his return to France, he received letters from Notre
Dame du Lac pressing him urgently to hasten his return.
He therefore departed at once with three ecclesiastics and
four young postulants for the Sisters. Besides, he took with
him a number of objects valuable for the mission.

Since the departure of Fr. Sorin for France, the work
had developed beyond his expectations. At the time of
his return, there were sixty boarders at the university and
thirty at the academy, fifteen postulants for the Brothers,
eight for the Priests and eight for the Sisters.

3. New Novitiate

One of the first resolutions made after the return of
Fr. Superior was to build a new novitiate for the Priests,
and to restore to its first purpose that of the Brothers. The
cornerstone was blessed. The spot chosen was on the island,
opposite the Brothers' novitiate.[4] The plan was on a larger
scale, eighty feet by thirty, with fourteen private rooms.

4. Foundation of Mackinac

At this same time it was resolved to establish a Sisters'
school and a Brothers' school at Mackinac. Sr. Mary of the

3. The religious community whose headquarters was in the
rue de Picpus in Paris, the Congregation of the Sacred Hearts of
Jesus and Mary and of Perpetual Adoration, which had won Roman
approbation in 1817, combined men and women in a single congregation as did the Congregation of Holy Cross. Difficulties had arisen
because of the alleged lack of freedom for the Ladies of Adoration,
the women's branch of the Picpus community, and the Vatican was
opposed to approving another congregation with a similar structure.
The French prelate who opposed approbation for Holy Cross was
Bp. Bouvier of Le Mans. See Catta, *Moreau,* 1:846–852.

4. The priests' novitiate is elsewhere described as being "in the
peninsula facing the old church." See Minor Chapter Book, July 6,
1852, IPA.

Cenacle was taken there by the Mother Superior, together with Sr. Mary of St. Frederick.[5] This establishment was founded at the urgent request of the Rev. Mr. Peril, the pastor of the place. Some weeks later, Brother John Baptist[6] was also sent to open a school for boys.

5. Father Baroux Starts for Bengal

In the beginning of September of this same year, an order came to have Fr. Baroux, pastor of Pokagon, along with a Brother and a Sister who could speak English, get ready immediately to become part of the colony of fifteen Religious who were soon to start for Calcutta in Bengal where the Propaganda had just assigned a mission to the Association.

In a week, all the preparations for departure had been completed. Br. Benedict and Sr. Victor were the two on whom the choice fell to accompany the dearly beloved Father Missioner.[7]

The immediate result of this departure was the abandonment for the time being of the mission amongst the savages at Pokagon, which was taken up again, however, at the end of a month by the Reverend Mr. Fourmond, a novice.[8]

5. On the second Sr. Mary of the Cenacle, see chapter 9, note 11. Sr. Mary of St. Frederick (Frances O'Reilly) was born Apr. 27, 1834, in Delaware and received the habit July 16, 1852. ASHC. Costin, 63–64, mentions a third Sister as part of this foundation, a postulant, Brigid O'Brien, who died nineteen years later as Sr. Angelica: born Aug. 30, 1812, in Ireland, she received the habit July 23, 1854. ASHC. Mackinac is an island in the strait between the two peninsulas which constitute the state of Michigan.

6. Br. John the Baptist (John O'Brien) was born in Ireland, Oct. 8, 1824, entered the congregation from Madison, Indiana, in January 1850, and received the habit in March 1850. He withdrew from the community in August 1852. M.g.

7. Br. Benedict (Patrick Fitzpatrick), born in Ireland May 10, 1803, had received the habit at Notre Dame on Aug. 21, 1845, and professed vows on Oct. 22, 1848. He died at Chittagong, East Bengal, India in 1855. M.g. Sr. Mary of St. Victor was born in Ireland and had taken the habit at Notre Dame. ASHC.

8. Almire Fourmont was born Feb. 11, 1819, at Sable (Sarthe),

Some weeks after the departure of this gentleman for Pokagon, there seemed to be reason to doubt his loyalty toward Notre Dame du Lac. In fact, a month had not yet passed before he left the Society and had himself recognized as one of his priests by the bishop of Detroit with charge of the Indians of Pokagon and Silver Creek and of the Mission of St. Joseph.[9] The manner of this little transaction was disagreeable, but in itself was a great relief to Notre Dame du Lac for which those missions were becoming every year a greater burden.

6. Father Sorin Is Named for Bengal

In the month of August of this same year, the Rev. Fr. Rector wrote to Fr. Sorin that if he did not find someone to put at the head of the new mission of Bengal, he would be obliged to impose this burden on him. At the same time, he wrote to Fathers Granger and Cointet, whose answers showed only repugnance for the superiorship in this southern foundation.

Hardly had he received (the responses) than he took his measures definitively and sent his orders to the Chapters of Notre Dame du Lac and of Bertrand to accede at once to the departure of Fr. Sorin for Dacca in the month of May following and to the return of Fr. Cointet from New Orleans where he was to be replaced by Fr. Gouesse.

This latter had been in Canada for several months, having been obliged to leave Louisiana due to the representations of Fr. Sorin whilst he was in Le Mans. According to the tenor of the documents that determined his change, he was never even to stay in the United States. The sole

---

France, and was already a priest when he entered the congregation in France on May 11, 1852, the same day that he left for America with Fr. Sorin. He withdrew on Oct. 1, 1853. M.g.

9. Pokagon and Silver Creek are, respectively, five miles southwest and two miles northwest of Dowagiac, Michigan. St. Joseph is on Lake Michigan, at the mouth of the St. Joseph River, twenty-three miles west of Dowagiac and thirty-seven miles north of Notre Dame.

fact of his unexpected recall to the same post, which he had been compelled to vacate in spite of himself six months before, appeared inexplicable to the Chapters of the Lake and of Bertrand. It was thought that there was reason to fear everything from this turbulent spirit who was the declared enemy of the Lake. Independently of the question of changing Fr. Sorin, everybody had been shocked at his return.

Fr. Sorin, seeing that the Chapters were fully convinced of the impossibility of his removal from Notre Dame du Lac, and himself fearing the results which all declared to be inevitable, thought it his duty to telegraph Fathers Cointet and Gouesse to remain at their respective posts until it had been decided whether he himself could leave his post, the other changes depending on this one.

7. Father Gouesse Back at the Asylum

On the other hand, while the Chapters of the Lake and of Bertrand were respectfully formulating their representations to the Mother House, the orders issued by Sainte-Croix met with the same opposition in New Orleans. The announcement of the arrival of Fr. Gouesse had greatly annoyed Archbishop Blanc. To calm the fears of the Asylum on this matter, he summoned Fr. Sorin by telegraph, and the latter considered it a duty to obey this call. Fr. Gouesse had arrived some weeks before him.

Weary of these endless changes and annoyances on the part of the Mother House in regard to this Father, who for six years past has been a general cause of disturbance in the Society, Fr. Sorin was determined to be done with him and to send him back to Sainte-Croix.

But Archbishop Blanc, who had at first approved of this plan, thought it more prudent to wait. Not having anything better to do, Fr. Sorin, whose only aim was to secure peace at the Asylum, appeared to believe willingly in the promises of the good archbishop, who, rather than make up his mind to proceed energetically, the only thing that could possibly save the Society, preferred to take upon himself, so to say, to answer for Fr. Gouesse for the future.

Fr. Gouesse was therefore left to him, and Fr. Sorin started back with Fr. Cointet on January 3, 1853, for Notre Dame du Lac, apparently satisfied with the written promises of Fr. Gouesse, but in his heart pitying the saintly prelate and the members of the community on account of the troubles which he foresaw would result from this act of weakness, however it might be dignified by the name of prudence.

His fears were in reality only too well-founded; they were soon realized in their full extent. The first of his acts was to represent to Sainte-Croix the inconveniences of the correspondence between the members of the Asylum and the Provincial of the Lake. All were forbidden to continue it and to receive any obedience from Fr. Sorin. Some weeks later, they were also forbidden to send any money from the next semester from the month of May to the Lake, and all this without giving Fr. Sorin the least intimation that his powers of Provincial had been at all curtailed.

Such was Fr. Gouesse's obstinacy in maintaining silence vis-à-vis the Lake that when the good Brother Theodulus died before his eyes, he did not even think it proper to recommend him to the prayers of his associates at the Provincial House.[10]

If he had made only his confrères at the Lake suffer, but it was known from a reliable source that he was far from rendering happy those who had been left under his orders at the Asylum.

10. Br. Theodulus died of yellow fever in New Orleans, June 25, 1853. M.g.

Rev. Stephen Theodore Badin: first
priest ordained in the United States;
missionary to the Potawatomi;
purchased the land on which Notre
Dame was founded

Rev. Edward F. Sorin C.S.C., ca.
1857

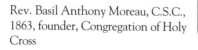

Rev. Basil Anthony Moreau, C.S.C.,
1863, founder, Congregation of Holy
Cross

The dying Deseille receives viaticum, 1837: painting by John Worden

Sorin's arrival at Notre Dame: Luigi Gregori's 1883 mural.

Brother Lawrence Ménage, C.S.C.,
member of first Holy Cross colony in
1841

Celestine de la Hailandiere,
second bishop of Vincennes,
1839–1847

The Old College, ca.1892

Brother Benoit, C.S.C.:
served at Notre Dame,1846–
1873

Rev. Alexis Granger, C.S.C.: served at
Notre Dame, 1844–1893

Brother Vincent, C.S.C., member of first Holy
Cross colony in 1841

Earliest extant panorama of Notre Dame, ca. 1848: copperplate engraving by John Manz of
Chicago

First St. Mary's Convent at
Bertrand, Michigan, 1844

Sister Mary of the Ascension, C.S.C., served at Notre Dame, 1846–
1901

Church at Bertrand, Michigan

Sister Mary of St. Angela, C.S.C., served at
Notre Dame and at St. Mary's, 1853–1887

St. Mary's Academy, Bertrand, ca. 1850

Students on steps of Bertrand Hall, St. Mary's Academy, 1866

CHAPTER 12

1853

---

1. Let the Majority Rule

St. Teresa somewhere speaks of "the war of the saints," intending to show that even with good and pure intentions men of God do not always agree as to the means to be employed to procure his glory, whether it be that God designs thereby to show to men that their lights are quite feeble or to offer them the occasion to gain some merits or, finally, to reach his ends by making use of human passions even when men least suspect it.

The year 1853 was an epoch-making year in the annals of Notre Dame du Lac and, whether for the advancement of the Association or for its humiliation, it was marked by events in which one could not fail to recognize a Providential intervention. But the better to grasp the chain of events that follow, it is well to take it up a little farther back.[1]

It has already been said in the preceding pages that in spite of the desire of Notre Dame du Lac to live in peace with Sainte-Croix, it never could enjoy that boon except at distant intervals and for a few months at a time. During the last six years, especially, it was not so much a religious life as an almost unbroken series of explanations, altercations,

---

1. For an account of the events recounted in this chapter that is much less sympathetic to Sorin, see Catta, *Moreau*, 1:952–983; 2:3–25.

prohibitions under pain of disobedience, reproaches full of threats, etc. In short, the most devoted and the most up-right souls had become the object of accusations and even the center of anxiety, vexations and troubles. Moreover, there was no more love for the duties of the community nor of the ministry; life itself was at times a burden.

Father Gouesse has been designated as one of the principal causes of this sad state of affairs. The journey of Fr. Sorin to France in 1852 had for its primary object to put an end to these sufferings, as injurious to the good of the mission as to that of the individual members of the Association.

People were so harassed that a change was desired at any price. Convinced that heaven could not approve of dispositions so contrary to the religious spirit which is essentially a spirit of peace and of charity, the Chapters of the Lake and of Bertrand had given Fr. Sorin all power on his departure for France, even to break off from Sainte-Croix if he saw no other means of securing peace for the work.

Once at Sainte-Croix, this Father soon found in the bundle of letters of Fr. Gouesse against him which were placed in his hands, in the long debates of the first council which assembled soon after his arrival, in the refusal of Fr. Rector to give him any subject from the Mother House, as well as in all that he saw and heard for himself, that he had little to expect for his mission from that quarter. In a word, the dispositions of Sainte-Croix toward the Lake were less than favorable in his eyes.

Nevertheless, the fear of falling from Charybdis into Scylla by attempting to enlarge his proper sphere and secure the independence of his mission, the daily and general expectation, on the other hand, of the approbation of Sainte-Croix by the Holy Father, and finally, the old love that bound this Father to Sainte-Croix and his first associates, all this, joined to the hopes which strained to force him to conceive that peace was finally established on a solid basis, determined him, after the lapse of some weeks, to write to the Chapters of the Lake and of Bertrand that all things were settled and that peace had been made.

Although he could not altogether believe it himself, for his part he acted on every occasion as if fully persuaded that such was the case.

During the two months that he afterwards spent in Rome, he did not open his lips in regard to the difficulties that had brought him once more from the Lake to Le Mans. He even had the goodness to devote nearly all his time to laboring, by means of visits and memorials in repeated instances, to push forward the approbation so earnestly desired at Sainte-Croix. And when he learned that the Brief of Approbation which had been spoken of as a certainty would have to be waited for much longer than was believed at Sainte-Croix, he was the first to be grieved at this as at a privation that affected him personally in the deepest manner.

In these same sentiments he returned to his adopted country towards the beginning of July and he was certainly not disposed to expose himself anew and by lightheartedness to lose the treasure that he had come so far to seek, peace. On the contrary, he would have willingly sacrificed all for the preservation of peace. How it came to pass that with such dispositions, which were shared in the same proportion by all the members of his Chapters, peace was of such short duration at Notre Dame du Lac will now be explained.

To the representations that Sainte-Croix itself had incited by its new arrangements and especially by the nomination of Fr. Gouesse as Local Superior of the Asylum at New Orleans, the members of the Chapters at the Lake and at Bertrand had received no other answer but offensive repetitions that maintained the right of the Mother House in what had been decided and that the nomination (of the superior) of the Asylum would by no means be recalled; that sooner than do so, all those that remained faithful to their vows would be recalled; in other words, that no credence was given to what had been said and written against (the nomination) by Fathers Sorin, Granger and Cointet; and that (Fr. Gouesse) would be sustained at Sainte-Croix against the unanimous voice of the two Chapters, which would not suffer the promotion to this office of a man who had publicly declared that he would be superior in spite of his Provincial and who by his conduct since his ordination had only too well shown the justice of his expulsion from the seminary of Le Mans, afterwards repeated by the Chapter of the Lake and by the Rector himself.[2]

It would be hard to believe that Sainte-Croix had not seen the danger of applying to such a man a principle just in itself, but which in the present case had become unjust, both in regard to the subject and to the application. For in his quality of Provincial, Fr. Sorin ought certainly to have the power to provide for the actual wants of the work in the United States; even after the nomination of the said Father by the Rector himself, it was possible that reasons unforeseen by the Rector might arise sufficient to justify a suspension of the orders of Sainte-Croix. The Provincial, being the representative of the Rector in his Province, is the judge of these reasons.

Fr. Sorin might be deceived in this examination, but he had right on his side in judging whether it was or was not expedient to put a Father in charge immediately who in his eyes was unworthy of the office. Yet this was the great reproach of Sainte-Croix, that Fr. Sorin had opposed the arrangements of the Rector. This was trying to shift the question and thus to put to one side the best-founded remonstrances of three men, who of all the members of the Association were perhaps the most unequivocally devoted, and from whom one word ought in justice to have been enough to silence the complaints of a brainless and ambitious man.

2. On the expulsion of Gouesse by the Chapter of the Lake, see chapter 9:1; also Catta, *Moreau*, 1:939–940. In December 1854, Gouesse returned to Le Mans where he lived and worked at the motherhouse. He was dismissed from the congregation by Moreau in April 1855. See the minutes of the general council, Apr. 18, 1855, wherein Moreau states that Fr. Gouesse had been dismissed because he had disgraced himself in front of the Sisters at the motherhouse. GA.

Here, however, the patience of the administration of the Lake came to an end. When it was clearly demonstrated that Sainte-Croix had no confidence in those that had given proofs of fidelity for many years, it became evident that Notre Dame du Lac no longer had anything to expect from Sainte-Croix, and that sooner or later it would be sacrificed with all its future to the caprice of the Mother House, which, moreover, had never sought to administer it, but rather to keep it in perpetual agitation.

In the painful circumstances in which the Lake was placed, which was asked to sacrifice its founder without being shown anyone who could take his place, to insist on reconciliation with a man who was considered, with good reason, its most mortal enemy, was to drive patience, even the most tried, to the last extremity. Good sense and the most ordinary prudence would have yielded in the presence of fears so natural and would have got rid of them by regarding them. Sainte-Croix wanted to demolish everything without regard for anybody.

For men less attached to their first engagements and their religious affections, a great deal less would have sufficed, no doubt, to make them regret that they had placed themselves under such a heavy yoke. As long as they had any solid hopes of improvement, they had suffered, if not without interior murmuring, at least without making it publicly manifest.

At the time of these events, they began to see that their patience in suffering everything did not in the least disarm Sainte-Croix, and that soon the ruin of their mission would be the inevitable result of the measures unless they were checked.

A proper memorial was prepared by the Secretary of the Minor Chapter of Notre Dame du Lac and signed by all the members, Father Superior alone excepted, to be sent to the Pope with a view of obtaining a separation from Sainte-Croix. A little later, the fear of inflicting too much harm on the Association caused a change of opinion and the memorial was sent to the Reverend Mr. Heurtibize[3] at Le Mans to be presented to Sainte-Croix for ratification for five years, without publicity, at the end of which time it could be seen what was best to do in agreement with the Reverend Fr. Rector.

The answer of the Rev. Mr. Heurtibize was such as might be expected from a prudent and pious man, who was the friend of Sainte-Croix and of the Fathers of the Lake. He advised patience and to expect from time, which changes all things, a remedy for our present miseries; adding that he did not wish to take it upon himself to decide whether our reasons were sufficient to justify the separation, but that if the decision was final, he advised us to petition the Ordinary for a dispensation from obedience to the Rector of Sainte-Croix.

Thus far, His Lordship of Vincennes knew nothing of the difficulties in question. It fell to the administration of the Lake to let him into such secrets; but the urgency of the difficulties made them go forward and ask for the dispensation but without stating in detail the reasons that led to this step. His Lordship, Bishop de St. Palais, granted the dispensation, but expressed the desire that the coming of the Visitor, who was to be sent from Sainte-Croix to settle everything, should be awaited.

The Chapter accordingly waited until the end of April. But as there was no more talk of a Visitor and the time fixed for the departure of Fr. Sorin had arrived, the bishop of Vincennes was informed of the embarrassment in which the latter was placed and he sent a second dispensation. On the same day, letters were sent to the Rev. Mr. Heurtibize, the Rev. Fr. Rector and the Rev. Fathers Champeau and Drouelle,[4] informing them of the declaration made for five

3. Heurtibize was a canon of the cathedral of Le Mans and, as a member of the faculty of St. Vincent's Seminary in Le Mans, had taught Moreau, Sorin, Granger, and, probably, Cointet. Catta, *Moreau*, 1:83, 977–978.

4. Louis-Dominique Champeau was born Dec. 5, 1817, at Le Breil (Sarthe), France. He was already a priest when he entered the Congregation of Holy Cross in 1840. He had served for eight years

years. The step was a bold one, but it seemed to be more than justified by the circumstances that had provoked it.

Once the step had been taken, peace seemed to reign in all hearts. People were so tired of the cruel state through which they had just passed that any change would have been considered an improvement. Without losing any more time, the Chapters went to work to profit by what they considered their deliverance from a yoke that, if not odious, was at least painful. Three novice Brothers were admitted to profession and soon afterward six ecclesiastical novices, two of whom were ordained priests, one a deacon, and the three others subdeacons.

About the beginning of August, a malignant epidemic, the yellow fever, broke out fiercely in New Orleans. Three Brothers and one Sister of the Asylum were carried off in a few weeks. Who would believe it? Fr. Gouesse had not the heart to write a word about it to Notre Dame du Lac! A prohibition had been issued to the members of the Asylum against correspondence with the Lake and with Bertrand. In the actual condition of things, this pharisaical spirit of the poor Father was little calculated to do away with the bitter feelings.

Archbishop Blanc himself was indignant. This saintly prelate, who up to this time had kept Fr. Gouesse as the representative of authority, finally recognizing that such a head would never guide things to any but an unfortunate end and that Sainte-Croix itself without the Lake could offer no guarantee to provide the Asylum with the necessary subjects, thought seriously of removing the primary cause of the miseries in question and demanded his recall from New Orleans.

Meanwhile, the Visitor from Sainte-Croix arrived unexpectedly at Notre Dame du Lac. Fr. Sorin, who had

---

as head of the community's school in Le Mans and then had been appointed head of the minor seminary of the diocese of Orléans when Holy Cross assumed the direction of that institution. Catta, *Moreau*, 1:633–634, 800. Drouelle, at this time, was superior of the congregation's houses in Rome. Catta, *Moreau*, 1:852–853.

learned, although only indirectly, the probable time of his visit, had written to him at Saint-Laurent, Lower Canada, not to come. But on arriving, he declared that he was not a man to be discouraged until he had tried everything in his power. However, it was clearly intimated to him that he was received as a friend, as Fr. Chappé,[5] but by no means in the capacity of Visitor.

He asked for no more, and pretty soon he was surprised at not finding things as bad as he had expected. He had come to take with him those that wished to return to France, but to his great surprise he discovered that nobody appeared even to suspect the real object of his visit. The difficulties were known only by the Minor Chapter; outside of it, all was peace and silence. Hence his mission had no object, unless he should take upon himself to publish matters thus far kept secret.

He was satisfied to see in private the individual members of the Chapter, and he left no means untried to bring them to other sentiments, but all was in vain; not one seemed ready to adopt his views, which appeared to surprise him not a little. He could not help recognizing in those souls, who in his opinion were deceived by the evil spirit, a real desire of what was right and, especially, an immense longing for peace.

Although the separation was thus far known only by the members of the Chapter, Fr. Chappé did not fail to see the difficulties in bringing back the Lake and Bertrand to the conditions of submission required by Sainte-Croix.

He saw in all the members perfect unity of views, convictions and determination and, at the same time, individual liberty. The administration, which he had never suspected to be any other than Fr. Sorin's, presented to him, in spite of his old prejudices, the evidence of a council

5. Pierre Chappé, born Nov. 3, 1809, at Brûlon (Sarthe), France, had entered the congregation as a seminarian in 1837 and had been, along with Sorin, one of the group of four who were the first priests after Moreau to make vows in the community on Aug. 15, 1840. M.g.

of administration acting according to rule by the majority of votes. It was no longer, consequently, a single man that had to be taken into consideration, since up to this time it was the Chapter that had discussed and adopted every serious measure in the government of the Work.

On the other hand, all that he had learned of Notre Dame du Lac seemed to him to fall short of what he, himself, saw with his own eyes. The College had just received a considerable increase. A written promise of one of the young Fathers of the house to pay ten thousand dollars in a year had permitted the adding of two wings to the main building, and thus there would be room for two hundred and fifty boarders. At the same time, behind the infirmary, a large house was going up for the Sisters that were needed for the work of the College.

The magnificent novitiate of the priests as well as that of the Brothers was evidently full of promise for the future. St. Mary's Academy and that recently opened at Mishawaka,[6] as well as the postulate at Bertrand, which could scarcely hold half the subjects that asked for the habit of the Society, could leave no doubts on his mind as to the beautiful prospects that had been rightly established in America.

2. Father Sorin Submits

Here a new era is about to begin, founded not on the shifting sands of human passions but on the immolation of these same passions, even when all hope seemed to have disappeared of reconciling men so thoroughly convinced of the wrong-doing of the other party. God permitted that, contrary to all the anticipations of the Lake, Fr. Rector

6. Holy Angels Academy was opened in Mishawaka, Indiana, on Dec. 8, 1854, when the orphans and other dependent children along with several Sisters were transferred from Bertrand, Michigan, to a house in that town. In May 1855 these children and the Sisters moved to the Rush property along the St. Joseph River, the present site of St. Mary's College. Brosnahan, 174–175.

appeared ready to push matters to extremities, carrying the affair even to Rome, if necessary.

Fr. Sorin, who from the first had been held back by the fear of injuring the Association which he had not ceased to love, was restrained by the thought of the consequences of a dispute wherein every evil passion would be brought into play to the great scandal of the faithful and to the injury of both the belligerent parties.

Up to this time, Fr. Sorin had been sincere and honest in his opposition. He had wished to save the Association in the United States. But when he saw the direction that things were going to take, he yielded, and sooner than publicly raise the standard of revolt against the Mother House, he asked himself, whilst reciting his beads, if now that Sainte-Croix knew everything, it would not be more religious to surrender at discretion and to leave to God the consequences of a step that he could no longer defer without involving the whole Work in an atmosphere of scandal that would not be easily dissipated. Doubtless, He that changes the hearts of men of His own accord disposed that of the Father in question to give a favorable reception to this participation.

At nine in the evening, at an hour when perhaps he was farthest from expecting any results from his long efforts, Fr. Chappé was requested to come down to Fr. Sorin's room. What must have been his surprise and joy when he heard the latter read, tears in his eyes, two pages which he had just written to the Very Rev. Fr. Rector, begging him to forget the past, and placing himself at his disposal, without condition and without reserve.

The reading was followed by truly fraternal embraces. Peace was already consummated; the conditions were left entirely to the good will of the conqueror, Fr. Sorin being ready to accept them all, even if it should cost him his expulsion from the Society. The only favor that he took the liberty of asking was that his councillors should not be troubled, who, in his opinion, did not deserve the censure of Sainte-Croix.

The very next morning, Fr. Chappé left Notre Dame du Lac to bear to the Mother House the joyful tidings of the submission of the Lake. Five months later, Fr. Sorin, in writing these pages, could hardly refrain from weeping at the thought of the miraculous change of which he had been the object.

To proceed to the Mother House the following month, to subscribe cheerfully to all that the Rev. Fr. Rector required of him, to have his Chapter dissolved, the professions made in the meantime declared null, and he himself named the Assistant to Fr. Rézé, with all the privileges of his house withdrawn,[7] to return then to the Lake by obedience after three months, there to drink to the dregs the chalice of humiliation that awaited him, to seek in future only the merit of blind obedience, even if the ruin of the house were to follow, such were the dispositions that were to accompany the sacrifice made by Fr. Sorin of all his vanity and all his pride. Whether through self-love or a more noble motive, he would not have wished that in anything this sacrifice should be incomplete.

On his return to the United States in the beginning of February, Fr. Sorin's first care was to carry out all the prescriptions of the Very Rev. Fr. Rector, however severe they were, and to conform his views in all things, having no other desire than that of repairing his errors by a religious and irreproachable life. God did not abandon him in this trial, and soon, in the joy and the peace that filled his soul, he could say with the prophet: *Bonum mihi quia humiliasti me, Domine.*

There is nothing more deceptive than the human heart. Amid ordinary temptations Fr. Sorin would not have been able to answer for himself; but when the circumstances are called to mind in which he was placed, it will be easy to understand how he allowed himself to be surprised by the spirit of falsehood, and that he had let

7. Rev. Joseph Rézé, the superior of the Holy Cross religious in Canada, was put in charge of all the members of the congregation in North America for several years. Catta, *Moreau*, 2:23.

himself be blinded in a manner that he discovered only by degrees and that he deplored bitterly for the rest of his life. If he sums it up here, it is not to palliate his fault, but rather for the instruction of those who will come after him.

He was called to Bengal, to a dignity of which he does not think himself worthy. His entire house, even bishops, tell him that if he leaves his post the house will be ruined. A member of the Society promises in writing that if he stays he will give him his fortune (more than a million), and at the same time he thinks he sees in the nomination of a Father to the superiorship a formal act of contempt by the Mother House in return for the information supplied. He persuades himself that to remain at his post is not only allowed him but is to the advantage of the whole Association. To guard against remorse of conscience, he has recourse to his bishop to obtain a dispensation from his vow of obedience.

Is it surprising that he fell under the weight of so many and such specious considerations? Hardly! But that the hand of God did not abandon him in his fall and that he was able to rise again, that is what surprises him far more and fills him with the most lively and the most humble gratitude. God grant that he may never lose sight of the fact that for a religious there is no peace nor safety save in blind obedience, and that after having grieved the Association by a scandal heretofore unheard of in her bosom, he should do everything to make up for it by his exemplary submission on every occasion.

Such are, at least now, his dispositions, and since by the grace of God he now recognizes that all the motives of justification which he rashly brought forward some months ago for his disobedience were a source of the devil and nothing more, it seems to him impossible that he can ever hesitate to obey in the future.

CHAPTER 13

1854

1. Return of Father Sorin to Notre Dame du Lac

Fr. Sorin had started for Sainte-Croix in the month of November with the idea, indeed the conviction, that he would be sent to Bengal. Obedience, contrary to his anticipations, sent him back some months later to his former post where trials awaited him such as he had never experienced heretofore.

The passage was most distressing and most dangerous; it was made in the month of January and lasted twenty-five days. Fr. Sorin had with him four Sisters, one of whom was charged by the Mother House to make the regular visit, and another, Sr. Mary of St. Angela, a young American Sister who had just made her profession at Sainte-Croix and who was returning to the United States with the obedience of directress of St. Mary's Academy at Bertrand.[1]

1. Sr. Mary of St. Angela (Eliza Gillespie) was born Feb. 21, 1824, in Brownsville, Pennsylvania, the second generation in her family to be born in America. En route to Chicago in April 1853, she stopped at Notre Dame to visit her brother, Neal, who had entered the Congregation of Holy Cross there and was preparing for ordination. On being introduced to Sorin, he told her that she "was the one I have been praying for to direct our Sisters." She received the habit on Apr. 17, 1853, and was then sent by Sorin to the Sisters of the Good Shepherd in Caen, France, to make her novitiate. Sorin was, at this time, arranging the secession of the Holy Cross community in America from the motherhouse. She professed

Their return to Notre Dame du Lac on 2 February was a holiday for everybody, but especially for the five travellers whom Providence had saved from more than one danger and who had hardly dared to believe in the hope of ever again seeing the land which they had already watered with their sweat and those walls that enclosed their dearest affections.

To publish and put in force all the new decisions of the Mother House was the first concern of Fr. Sorin on his return. The Minor Chapter was done away with for the time being and Fr. Gastineau,[2] named Local Superior at the Asylum in New Orleans, was to act for some months as assistant and Counsellor to the Superior of the Lake until the Rev. Fr. Rézé and Mother Mary of the Seven Dolors[3] could come down from Canada to visit Notre Dame du Lac and New Orleans.

Fr. Gastineau betakes himself to the Asylum

Meanwhile, the needs of the Asylum became too pressing to wait for spring and orders were given to (Fr. Gastineau) at the beginning of the following month to proceed at once to his post with the Sister Superior,[4] whom he had brought from Sainte-Croix to take the management of

her vows on Dec. 24, 1853, before Fr. Moreau at the motherhouse in Ste-Croix. Sorin was present, having come to France to make his submission. See Anna Shannon McAllister, *Flame in the Wilderness* (Notre Dame, Ind.: The Sisters of the Holy Cross, 1944), 5, 88, 96–101.

2. Julien-Pierre Gastineau, born June 6, 1820, at La Brulette (Mayenne), France, was already a priest in the diocese of Le Mans when he entered the Congregation of Holy Cross at Ste-Croix in 1846. After a year spent in testing his vocation among the Trappists, he left for North America on Dec. 31, 1853. M.g.

3. On Fr. Rézé, see chapter 8, note 5, and chapter 12, note 7. Mother Mary of the Seven Dolors (Léocadie Gascoin), born Mar. 1, 1818, at Montenay (Mayenne), France, was one of the first four women to receive the habit as Marianite Sisters of Holy Cross on Aug. 4, 1841. Fr. Moreau made her his assistant for the governance of the Sisters and sent her to Canada in 1849. See Catta, *Mother Mary*, 4, 68, 109ff.

4. One source identifies this Sister as Marie de la Passion. See M.g., #593.

that house where the Association already counted fourteen Sisters in two establishments.

But he had hardly reached his destination when he *He disappears* was seized with fear at the difficulties that arose before his mind, and after some days he disappeared without informing anyone of his intentions or of his place of retreat. This unexpected and mysterious flight was, they say, a great sensation and even caused alarm at the Asylum.

Two weeks afterwards, the dear Father wrote from Rochester, in the State of New York, to Fr. Sorin, informing him of what had happened to him and of his intention to return at once to Notre Dame du Lac. Without wishing to constitute himself judge in a matter that he could not help looking upon as a rather ridiculous escapade, Fr. Sorin *He goes to* advised him rather to go to the Provincial in Canada, *Canada* which he did at once.

This circumstance had to be mentioned here as an explanation of what is to follow. It greatly embarrassed the administration of the Very Reverend Father (Moreau). There were not yet any supernumeraries in the Society of the Salvatorists.[5] After having looked around for someone to send to the Asylum, His Reverence was obliged to fall back on Fr. Cointet, who had already spent about eighteen months there and who had been compelled to return to the Lake on account of his health, almost totally ruined. Over about sixteen months, during which he was once more *Fr. Cointet* attending to his missions in the North, the dear Father had *named to the* regained by degrees his strength and his former energy. *Asylum*

Great was his surprise on learning that he was once more named for New Orleans, but equally great was his resignation. He would have started at once for the post

5. Editor's note: At this point, page 129 in the original ms., a page headed "Chap. 13e Anée 1854" is bound which does not connect either with what precedes or with what follows. As it summarizes the same sad story that is told at length in the following pages, it does not seem to have been intended as part of the narrative of events in 1854. It may have been a note on the epidemic for the chronicler's use and it is not included here.

He awaits the colony from France

to which he was recalled, had he not at the same time received orders to wait for two Brothers whom the Mother House was sending him for the Asylum. Some weeks between the arrival of this letter and that of the expected travellers were useful in making the necessary preparations and in putting on a good footing his many and important functions at Notre Dame du Lac: for he was Vice-President and Director of all the missions depending on the Lake.

We have just said "some weeks"; Providence willed that it should be some months. Our two Brothers were sixty-five days on the ocean. When they landed in New York without money and without resources of any kind, their first act was to telegraph and to write to the Lake for the funds necessary to continue their journey. The two Sisters who accompanied them only added to their embarrassment.

Their telegram and letter were both so badly addressed that they were not answered, never having found their way to the Lake. Br. Dominic[6] believed that he was making good use of some pennies that remained to him out of a loan of two hundred francs from the treasury of a very charitable Redemptorist Father by spending them in making his way to the Lake. Of his three travelling companions, whom he had left behind, not one could speak a word of English. It was necessary to send money by express to pay the expenses of those three brave soldiers of the Cross and save them from being sold at auction to pay their personal debts.

Finally, God permitted that they arrived; but during all those mysterious mishaps, events of grave importance were rapidly succeeding one upon another at Notre Dame du Lac.

Epidemic at Notre Dame; a postulant dies

During the Annual Retreat of the Sisters in their new house, three hundred paces from the College, one of their postulants was suddenly seized with pains in the chest so violent that in some hours she succumbed, having hardly

6. Br. Dominic (Michael Wolf), born Aug. 28, 1821, in Ingenheim, Germany, entered the Congregation of Holy Cross in October 1844, and professed vows in 1848. He died at New Orleans, Sept. 16, 1854. M.g.

been able to make her confession and to receive extreme unction.

On the following night, one of the apprentices of the Brothers, thirteen years old, a child full of spirit and of favor, was found dead in his bed by his own father, who had come to see him and who had himself been watching over him for several days. *A child*

This was enough to spread terror through the house, and especially in the minds of those who had charge of it; but the hour of trial had come, and the cup of bitterness which was to be emptied even to the dregs had only let some drops fall from its overflow on the poor children of Notre Dame du Lac.

Two pupils of the College were in succession carried away noiselessly and without causing much surprise as their passage to a better life had been long expected. *Two pupils*

The Annual Retreat of the Brothers arrived. On the third day, at eight o'clock in the morning, word was brought to the poor superior that Br. Alexis, one of the best members of the Society, had drowned in the lake during the night.[7] Oh, what sad days there are in the life of man here below! Such a thunder-clap was calculated to stupefy any man interested in this sad event. For some time it shook and agitated the soul of the sad director of a house so severely tried for some weeks. Soon, however, resignation to the will of heaven came and restored calm, although traces of sadness remained which only time could by degrees efface. *Br. Alexis drowns*

The retreat of the Priests followed closely on that of the Brothers. Like the two previous Retreats, it was made in recollection and with all the signs of a retreat in which the grace of God has free play.

Thus regenerated in all its parts, the Work presented to the eyes of faith a well-founded hope that heaven would

7. Br. Alexis (Patrick Day), born in 1819 in Ireland, entered the Congregation of Holy Cross at Notre Dame on Sept. 11, 1848, and professed vows on Feb. 2, 1851. His death occurred on Aug. 9, 1854. M.g.

bless it for its efforts to please God and for the afflictions that had weighed upon it. Every one rejoiced and sought in the peace and innocence that follow a general retreat pledges of new blessings. Alas, how different are the thoughts of man's heart from the thoughts of God!

Hardly had the last retreat ended when sicknesses broke out, multiplied, and became day by day more serious and alarming, and they were almost general in the three Societies. Sr. Mary of St. Aloysius Gonzaga died at Bertrand on Assumption day itself; Sr. Mary of St. Anastasia[8] soon followed her from the same room. Two places were thus made vacant in the ranks of the professed; but evidently two of the elect had gone to heaven.

Two novices,
one postulant

Then followed two novice Sisters and one postulant, falling one after the other to the terrible scourge which was nothing less than an epidemic, resulting from the combination of the two most terrible maladies of the country: dysentery and typhus. It was as if two of the most powerful enemies of human life had challenged each other to the death in order to crush a young family hardly out of its swaddling-clothes.

The society of the Sisters was not alone the object of heaven's wrath, if it can be said that a Father is angry when he calls home to himself his children, after having left them for a time in exile, to dry their tears and to set on their brow the royal and immortal crown promised to their fidelity.

Five Broth-
ers: Dominic,
Clement, Joseph,
Cesaire, Daniel

Whatever may have been the designs of heaven, which it is not given us to penetrate but which we should adore in silence and perfect submission, the Brothers offered at the same time their victims. Five of them and three postulants were carried off, one by one, in spite of all the efforts of the house to save them. Of the five, only one was professed, Br. Dominic; the four others were novices,

8. On Sr. M. of St. Aloysius Gonzaga, see chapter 9:13. Sr. Mary of St. Anastasia (Mary Julia Byrnes) was born in Ireland in 1825 and received the habit in Bertrand on May 26, 1853. She died Sept. 5, 1854. ASHC.

Brothers Clement, Joseph, Cesaire and Daniel.[9] They all offered up their lives in a most edifying manner. If the number of deaths was calculated to spread terror amongst the survivors, their last moments, on the other hand, were so pious and consoling that only one impression seemed to remain in the depth of the souls of those who were witnesses: "May my last moments be like those of these just ones," may my soul thus leave her prison.

Their piety

But what rendered painful to the last degree those ravages of death amongst the Brothers and the Sisters was to see that his blows fell indiscriminately on all sides and that the society of the Salvatorists, whose numbers were still so few, especially considering the wants of the country, was not spared any more than the other two societies.

Father Curley, a young Irish missioner ordained only one year, was the first of the Priests of Holy Cross called to bear the standard of the Society to heaven.[10] He was taken with dysentery during the retreat and continued to languish and grow weaker and weaker until the end, which came on 4 September. His death made a profound but happy sensation. It left nothing to be desired, nothing to be feared.

Father Curley

But alas! it was only the forerunner of the dreadful stroke that was soon to fall like a thunder-clap on Notre Dame du Lac. Ten days after the burial of Fr. Curley,

9. On Br. Dominic, see above, note 6. The M.g. states that he died in New Orleans. Br. Clement (John Lonergan) was born in either 1799 or 1808 in Ireland, entered the community on Oct. 15, 1851, at Notre Dame, professed vows Sept. 15, 1854, and died the same day. Br. Joseph (Patrick Carroll) was born Feb. 1, 1832, in Ireland, entered the community at Notre Dame on Jan. 9, 1853, and died Sept. 21, 1854. Br. Cesaire (John McNulty) was born July 12, 1821, in Ireland, entered the community at Notre Dame on Feb. 19, 1854 and died Sept. 21, 1854. Br. Daniel (Patrick William Kelly) was born Mar. 17, 1813, in Ireland, entered the community on Dec. 22, 1852, and died Oct. 21, 1854. M.g.

10. John Curley, born Feb. 26, 1822, in Ireland, entered the community at Notre Dame on Nov 8, 1851. He professed vows Aug. 15, 1853, and died Sept. 7, 1854. M.g.

Fr. Cointet himself fell sick on his return from a mission. It would be useless to attempt here to describe the fears, the terrors and anguish of the whole house during the eight days of his illness.

For eleven years he had been the ornament, the light, the joy and the life of the Community and of the Mission. His piety, zeal and devotedness had never for a moment flagged. Gifted with prodigious activity and with rare talents, he had employed each day, since his arrival in the New World, for the salvation of souls and the glory of God.

Of him could be said, although in a far inferior manner, what is written of the Saviour of men: "He went about doing good." To preserve such a precious life, each one in the house had considered it a duty to offer his own life; but God willed this great sacrifice, and under his all-powerful hand one must curb his own will and seek consolation in the words of Our Savior: "*Fiat voluntas tua*."

The death of this dear Father caused universal mourning among all the Catholics of the area. Ah! his was one of the purest names that the history of the Church in America can offer to the piety of the faithful. In losing him, the Association suffered, according to human judgement, one of those losses that cannot be repaired; a gain for him, without doubt, for in the short time that he had lived, he accomplished much.

He was one of those men of solid merit, without the least ostentation, a man of God who saw only God in all things. Each one thought that they appreciated him well during his life, and all now see, after he has disappeared, that the void left by him in descending into the tomb is every day becoming more immense. No one knew him better nor loved him more sincerely than the poor Superior of the Lake. One need not be astonished to learn here that on the night when he was obliged to announce to this other self that he was going to die, to administer to him (the last sacraments) and, finally, to receive his last breath, his soul was crushed, his mind bewildered and near to a state of disorganization as sad as death itself. . . .

Eighteen members of the desolate family of Notre Dame du Lac had just disappeared, almost one out of every five. Two only had not been attacked, and the survivors looked more like skeletons or the walking dead than living men. Employments even the most indispensable had daily to be abandoned, and yet it was of the utmost importance to keep this state of affairs from being known and that the ordinary routine be strictly maintained. *Eighteen dead in the Community*

Seventy pupils had entered and an exact knowledge of the condition of the community's health would have sufficed to empty the college in twenty-four hours. Happily, good health reigned amongst them; only three or four were attacked and saved, with one exception. But if a panicky fear did not seize upon them, it was unquestionably due to the intervention of a special Providence. At times there was only a single professor on his feet whilst four were incapacitated and out of action. Half of the deaths were unknown to them; the sacraments were administered and burials took place in the evening and in the shadows of the night. *Sad state*

Oh, what mournful days were those of the months of August and September 1854! Oh, may God grant that such days never return to Notre Dame du Lac! A second trial of such a nature would be more than enough to ruin it from top to bottom.

Finally, towards the month of November, health began to return and with strength the hope of better days began to dawn. Only one death, that of the good Sr. Mary of Bethlehem[11] at age fifty-four, came to afflict the house again. She was the last of the four who had first come with Fr. Cointet in 1843. She died at the Academy of the Holy Angels in Mishawaka, full of merits and virtues rather than of years. *Sr. Mary of Bethlehem*

She had been employed for three years in the laundry, which she managed almost alone. The last eight years of her life were devoted to an employment that seemed to daily grow dearer to her, doubtless because of the simplicity *Her work*

11. See chapter 2, note 16.

Her ways

and the good nature of this innocent soul; we refer to the care of the cows, the calves, the lambs and the hens, etc. Being endowed with a robust constitution, she could endure much fatigue. She did not lie down to rest in summer before eleven o'clock, although she rose at four in the morning. She found her joys in providing for the daily needs of the numerous and interesting family confided to her care. She would sooner have deprived herself of the necessaries than allow one of those little animals to suffer. Hence, she was known and loved by all those innocent creatures, who gave her little rest.

We dare not assert here that she had succeeded in making herself understood by her calves or her sheep, but one might imagine that she herself believed it when one noticed the affectionate manner in which she was continually speaking to them. Dear good Sister, whose pure and tender heart had compassion even for brute (creation), obtain for us from heaven, where you now doubtless are rejoicing this day, the same simplicity, the same innocent way so that after your example we may also merit to be placed amongst the blessed who are simple and pure of heart.

But since it was the sovereign will, let us return once more to this history of trials and crosses. The chalice was not yet drained and those who had to continue to hold it to their lips were called to something even more bitter than all that had been presented to them up till then.

2. March 1855

Mr. Devos falls ill and dies

For some months, the sicknesses had diminished but not disappeared. Such was the exhaustion of the personnel at the end of autumn that the least fatigue or the first unforeseen change sent back to the infirmary even those that were thought to have entirely recovered. But at the beginning of the month of March several cases of bilious fever assumed such a malignant character that a return of the previous September and October was feared.

Mr. Devos,[12] one of the professors of the college, a novice of the Society of Priests, a young Belgian of great talents and of much promise, was among the first to be attacked. For several months, the Institution had, at great expense, secured the services of a distinguished physician, Dr. McKinnis, a graduate of Paris and of Glasgow, who at the same time filled two of the most important chairs at the university.

Under the care of this doctor, Mr. Devos, like everybody else, thought himself comparatively safe during the first ten days of his illness. But it soon became only too evident that he was in danger and that he was going to die, as indeed happened on the thirteenth day of his sickness.

It is true that the sentiments of faith and of piety which he displayed contributed not a little to console the community for the new loss that they had just suffered. Apprehension as to the impression that would be made by the death of a professor of the college so soon after the plague that had devastated it, were only too well founded. Mr. Devos was highly esteemed and loved by all the pupils, who keenly felt his loss.

To make matters worse, he had hardly expired when one of the best Brothers, John of the Cross,[13] the head of the workshop and a bootmaker, one of the most able, most exemplary and best known (religious) in the area, himself became critical and followed closely in the footsteps of the deceased. It was the same malady with all the same symptoms. The result was not long in doubt and eight days later the good Brother died, carrying with him the sincerest regrets of the whole house but especially of the apprentices, whose chief director he had been for several years.

Br. John of the Cross dies

12. Louis Devos, born Jan. 21, 1830, at Moorsledge, Belgium, entered the community at Notre Dame on June 1, 1852. He died Mar. 15, 1855. M.g.

13. Br. John of the Cross (James King), born in May 1815, in Ireland, entered the community at Notre Dame on July 26, 1849. He died Mar. 30, 1855. M.g.

To give a correct even though incomplete view of the impressions made by this unexpected death, it is necessary to bring together here several considerations which, examined in their mutual relations, gave this trial a weight so heavy that, in the eyes of the members of the Chapter of Notre Dame, the total ruin of the Institution of the Lake must inevitably follow unless a very special intervention of Providence made itself felt.

The place is un-healthy

The immediate tangible effect of the death of Br. John of the Cross was to awaken in all minds the memory of the numerous losses of the previous summer and autumn. But instead of attributing them as formerly to an epidemic that might visit even the most healthy localities, people now wished to find the cause in the place itself. The greater number, and they were the people of most sense, attributed to the marsh between the two lakes to the west of the college the first cause of all the illnesses. Others attributed it to a certain herb, others to a fish of which the Indians had always been very much afraid and which was rather numerous in the lake. Still others maintained that it was the water of our wells, although it was just as cool and agreeable to drink as possible. The opinions did not agree but each one had one and all were unanimous in declaring that under actual conditions the place was unhealthy. No one said authoritatively, "This is the cause," or, "That is the cause." But all kept repeating, "There is a cause, it is quite unfortunate, quite sad." Such was public opinion.

Is it not a remarkable fact that out of three hundred persons who were then connected, directly or indirectly, with Notre Dame, not even one took occasion to desert his post? Each one had reason to fear for his own days, yet there was neither desertion nor retreat. We will presently state the reason.

It was at the beginning of the reign of the Know Nothings, sworn enemies of Catholics. Notre Dame could not but appear to them as sovereignly bold. It was almost the only stronghold of Catholicism in northern Indiana. It was quite natural that they should avail themselves of such

favorable circumstances to hasten its fall, without taking
on themselves the odium.

On the other hand, by a series of coincidences more   *Alarming crisis*
or less unfortunate, besides what we have already men-
tioned, the establishment was quite heavily in debt. A
miserable imposter had just been discovered, who had deceived the administration in the sum of $15,000, which
he had solemnly promised in writing the year before. It
turned out that instead of having a big fortune which he
would sign over to the house, he had nothing and he took
away with him funds of the community ($100 besides $250
for board).

Moreover, prices were exorbitantly high, wheat and
corn being double the ordinary price. A financial crisis
had just upset the commerce of the United States. Banks
were collapsing by the dozens; no one knew which notes
to accept. The payment of the students' bills was either
deferred or no answer returned; meanwhile, creditors were
never more in need of their money.

Judge what must have been the feelings of the administrators of the Lake in such threatening circumstances. After
so much labor, fatigue and expense, public opinion, at the
rate at which it was going, would in some weeks destroy
forever the rich future of Notre Dame. It was unfortunately
only too evident that matters were rapidly reaching that
point and that on any day the most insignificant incident
might cause alarm in such critical circumstances and create
a panicky terror amongst creditors, boarders and novices,
and that would be the last of Notre Dame.

The only human hope that could have given any encouragement could no longer be held on to, that of seeing
the fall of the mill-dam, this being looked upon as the most
likely cause of all the trouble. The proprietor demanded
$9000, of which $3000 was to be paid in cash, and the
institution was too poor to buy the property. Besides, it   *Continuation*
had nothing to expect from New Orleans, where it had
advanced a good deal both in funds and its best subjects.
The academies of Bertrand and of Mishawaka had, up to

this time, given no surplus; their constant need of development and the difficulty of supporting so many persons at
a distance of six miles from the house must necessarily for
some time not only absorb all profit but be a drag on the
treasury of Notre Dame.

Judging according to reason, the establishment of the
Lake would soon be spoken of as a ruin, a ruin whose
fall would be heard across the mountains and the valleys
and would even reach the ears of the Mother House. All
the elements seemed to have conspired to make this catastrophe inevitable. Death had just carried away one fifth of
the community; sickness paralyzed a good half of those still
surviving; men were needed for the works and they had to
be secured at great expense.

Ah! When the earth no longer gives any hope, then
the Christian heart naturally turns to heaven in search of
consolation and encouragement. There only does one pour
out his soul. The best friends avoided one another and
when they did meet, each sought to read in the eyes of the
other the fears that were in his own heart. All the beauty
and all the joy of Notre Dame had departed by degrees. The
people were prepared at any day for the last extremities.

Everyone prays   Meanwhile, everyone, in silence and as far as his
strength permitted, attended to his work. Neither complaints nor murmurs nor regrets were heard. All seemed to
be resigned to the will of God, whatever that will might
be. Not only was there resignation, but there was prayer,
and in prayer one dared yet to hope. One likes to think
that God is infinitely rich in mercy, that he sometimes
calls us back even from the gates of the tomb. Each knew
that one never trusts in the Lord in vain; the more serious
and desperate affairs seemed to be, the more did they take
pleasure in saying to our merciful Lord that it was worthy
of him to extend his mighty hand and save the Lake where
all was going to ruin. *De Lacu miseria et ex tuto facis.*

O my God, through what agonies it pleased you then
to make us pass! Only some weeks before, a bishop had departed from Notre Dame enchanted, like ourselves, by the
beautiful future of our little family, and he made public his

favorable impressions of our Society in the United States. And behold us suddenly plunged in darkness deeper than ever, in the very shadow of death. We were certainly "like those destined for death." Our enemies had encompassed us on all sides and there was no escape for us; this at a time when we thought we were entering on an era of success and prosperity.

Happily, O my God, this state of affairs did not last long. Everybody had learned the lesson that there was no hope but in the mercy of heaven and in a Providential intervention, if the mission of the Lake was not to be at an end. Prayers, signs and groans were day and night appealing to the throne of mercy. Heaven was doubtless touched and some rays of hope came to scatter the dark clouds which had been enveloping Notre Dame for some time.

The very day after the funeral of the pious Brother John of the Cross, the proprietor of the farm in question came of his own accord to offer his land on terms that were so surprising that we scarcely dared to believe them.[14] Heretofore, he had demanded $9000, to be paid in very short installments. Now he was willing to take $8000, payable $1000 down and the rest in installments over four years. In a word, the purchase of this land by the House was made, if not as easy as desirable, at least reasonable and possible. *A change in things*

Fortunately, the long winter of 1854-55 was not yet over. The ice was not gone and thus the lake might be lowered before the hot weather and the marsh, which the public voice declared to be the cause of our sicknesses, might be dried without danger. Fortunately also, the Mother House had long before permitted the purchase of this property on condition that it not be obligated in the matter. *The Rush property purchased for $8,000*

Four days were spent in negotiation and in drawing up the titles, mortgages, etc. Finally, on the evening of the fourth day, when all the papers had been signed by both parties and nothing remained but to exchange them, our

14. The owner of the dam and of the property surrounding it has been identified as a Mr. Rush. See Hope, 85.

man left town without saying a word and went home, thus leaving hardly any doubt that he withdrew his offer and would not sell at this price and on these conditions.

We, in common with the whole town, had a very unfavorable opinion of him. It was quite evident that he had imposed on us and that his intention from the start was only to make sure of our desire to obtain his land at any price. This was on the Wednesday of Holy Week.

The fall of the dam

There are occasions when, by adopting vigorous measures, the enemy is surprised and frightened and we thus elude his snares. On Thursday morning, before mass, Fr. Sorin sent five or six of his stoutest men with strict orders to listen to no one and to tear down the dam; they were especially charged to answer anyone who might attempt to stop them that they received no orders from anybody except their master and that the land was his. Never was an order more promptly carried out.

Our man could not hold out against this bold stroke, tearing down under his eyes a dam from which he could have still earned some thousand of dollars more.

The fall of the dam changed his position vis-à-vis the College. We had a quasi-title to justify us. Public indignation, which was ready to prosecute him for this new piece of trickery, frightened him. One hour afterwards, he went to town and handed over the papers to the Brother commissioner.

The joy of the community

It is impossible to describe the joy that filled the community when it was learned that the dam was torn down. All returned thanks to Heaven as for a most important event. Everyone looked upon it as a special blessing and as a promise of health, even if progress did not immediately result.

Thus, my God, did you call us back from the gates of the tomb. Thus, did you revive in us hopes of better days. Be thou blessed therefore, O Lord, and make us worthy.

Advantages from the purchase of the Rush farm

The treasury of Notre Dame was not enriched by the purchase spoken of but from more than one point of view it was a good transaction. It secured the monopoly of the lime for all the neighborhood and the next day the privilege of stopping all competition on this land was purchased for five hundred dollars per year on a lease of three years.

A second privilege perhaps no less valuable was the fall of water of fifty or sixty feet between the Lake and the River, the control of which was secured to the house and which might some day serve to put in motion a flour mill, a saw mill or some other machinery for manufacturing.

Besides, it was a piece of land of 185 acres with a new house and a fine barn. It was resolved to establish on it at once the infirmary for the Institution. The distance of half a mile was suitable and the location on the very bank of the St. Joseph River was, it was said, one of the prettiest and most healthy in the whole area.

Finally, this famous piece of ground offered one last advantage which, though it necessitated another outlay which it might be desirable to defer, became in reality an economy and a matter of prime importance. The novitiate of the Sisters at Notre Dame was the spot that had suffered most from sickness. The establishment at Bertrand had been kept up and developed only with fear and great hesitation in view of the sentiments of the bishop of Detroit, which were not growing more favorable; the foundation in Mishawaka was amounting to nothing since it had been found insufficient to remove St. Mary's thither.

Nevertheless, these three houses were increasing and by their distance the one from the other they daily necessitated greater expenses of transportation and more travelling by Priests, Brothers and Sisters. To gather them together at a convenient distance from Notre Dame would be clearly a great benefit for the Society of the Sisters as well as for the College, which could then obtain from the Sisters all the services they were capable of rendering without having and without imposing on them the inconvenience of too close a proximity or too great a distance.

Fr. Granger, in his walks with his novices, had noticed an admirable site on this piece of ground, on an elevation seventy-five feet above the river and at a distance of a mile and a quarter from the college. He had from the very first desired it for the Sisters. Examined by the Superior and by the Sisters themselves, there was found to be such a combination of advantages that it was resolved to establish there, sooner or later, the residence of the aforesaid Society and their headquarters.

It is decided to move the two academies

Tuesday after *Quasimodo* it was resolved, in an extraordinary meeting of the Chapter of Administration, that any further expenditures at St. Mary's, Holy Angels and even Notre Dame would be stopped and that steps were to be taken at once to remove to the new property such of the old buildings as were worth the trouble and were not actually needed; this with the view of removing thither by degrees the orphan girls, the postulants, the novices and finally the boarders, without waiting till there were means to put up new buildings for all those purposes and to abandon the old buildings. Three thousand dollars were considered sufficient

Principal reasons for this change

to effect this move and before two years this whole debt would be fully repaid by the savings that would naturally result from it, not to speak of the satisfaction and the real advantages that would be secured to the Society of the Marianites and indirectly to the two other (Societies).

There was still another reason for this resolve. The question of the approbation of our Association was soon to be taken up again in Rome after the death of Bp. Bouvier.[15] The bishop of Detroit, who more than once had expressed his disapproval of a house of Sisters under the windows of the College, might well have carried this accusation to Rome and it was important to be prepared to escape its consequences. Now the beginning of a principal house where it was evidently the intention to establish the Sisters' Society, showed that they were near the college only for some days whilst awaiting for everything to be ready to receive them (at the new site) to which no one could object.

It is perhaps not out of place to mention that the Superior had just learned from a reliable source that the Propaganda had recently ordered the Jesuits in America to

15. Bp. Jean-Baptiste Bouvier of Le Mans, France, died in Rome on Dec. 26, 1854. See Catta, *Moreau*, 1:876.

dismiss all women whom they had in their employ, both in their colleges and in their missions.

However that may be, the transfer, as we have said, was to take place only gradually and according as the resources would permit. This dear house shall be called St. Mary of the Immaculate Conception.[16] On this very day at five o'clock, *Deo volente,* we are going to bless the first stone according to the rites of the Church under this august title.

Blessing of the first stone; to be called St. Mary of the Immaculate Conception

April 24, 1855

---

16. The dogma of the Immaculate Conception had been proclaimed in Rome only five months before, on Dec. 8, 1854.

CHAPTER 14
1855

What caused us to carry the history of 1854 as far
as the end of April of this year cannot have escaped the
attention of whoever read the sad story contained therein.
It was one whole which could hardly admit of division. As
the long trials of the Hebrews in Egypt ended only with
the passage of the angel, so also this long series of crosses
and sufferings of all kinds extended over the family of
Holy Cross in America until the new Passover, the day for
eating the paschal lamb. On that day there came a change
almost miraculous, a passage from the deepest sorrow to
rejoicing; one could say, morally speaking, a passage from
death to life.

The purchase of the 185 acres from Rush secured to
Notre Dame advantages whose value the future alone will
make known and appreciated. The health of the Congregation, the cultivation of some thirty of the richest acres
around the College, the monopoly of the chalk and marl,
a most valuable water privilege, and finally a beautiful site
for the Society of the Marianites, with novitiate, academy,
workshop, etc., with all desirable conveniences and with
hardly any inconvenience, for the Congregation itself. One
of the principal objects of the administration was to secure
them those advantages as soon as possible.

It was therefore decided, as already mentioned, that the
two houses of Mishawaka and Bertrand should be removed
to the new location. The former was almost rebuilt when an

unexpected event led to the conclusion that the immediate transfer of the other should be begun.

For several years the stepfather of one of our Fathers and one of our Sisters (Fr. Gillespie and Mary of St. Angela), Mr. Phelan of Lancaster, Ohio, had been speaking of bequeathing a valuable farm to the Congregation of Holy Cross with the view of having a branch of the Society established in that place.[1] More than once, he had been urged by his estimable and pious wife to make the donation and to give possession of it without delay, during his lifetime, but to all solicitations of this kind he answered in such a manner as to give only the weakest of hopes that he could ever make up his mind to this.

Important donation of Mr. and Mrs. Phelan

It was therefore a surprise to Fr. Sorin when, some days before the distribution of prizes in 1855, he received through the hands of Mrs. Phelan a letter from Mr. Phelan announcing that after mature deliberation, he thought it better to give his farm immediately to the Congregation of Holy Cross, provided that the Congregation assumed a mortgage of seven thousand dollars due in two and a half years. The farm that he was offering was, according to him, worth at least thirty thousand dollars.

Fr. Sorin considered the matter too serious for merely secondary attention. He went to Lancaster the following week with Mrs. Phelan herself, and Sr. Mary of St. Angela. God blessed this journey; after a sojourn of eight days with Mr. Phelan, they separated, mutually bound by the following contract:

1. On Sr. M. of St. Angela, see chapter 13, note 1. Rev. Neal H. Gillespie was born Jan. 17, 1831, in Brownsville, Pennsylvania, and received a bachelor's degree from Notre Dame in 1849. After two years with his mother and stepfather in Lancaster, Ohio, he returned to enter the Congregation of Holy Cross in 1851 and professed vows Aug. 15, 1853. M.g. After her first husband, John Purcell Gillespie, died on Jan, 28, 1836, Gillespie's mother, Mary Madeleine Miers, returned to her hometown of Lancaster, Ohio, with her three children, Eliza, Mary Rebecca, and Neal. In February 1840, she married William Phelan, a prosperous widower, in Lancaster. McAllister, 4–23.

Mr. and Mrs. Phelan gave to the Congregation of Holy Cross, established at Notre Dame, Indiana, property valued at $89,650 in real estate and mortgages on which was due $22,500, for which Fr. Sorin assumed the responsibility. He, moreover, bound himself to pay Mr. and Mrs. Phelan an annuity of three thousand dollars and during their lifetime to receive two boarders gratis, one at the College and the other at St. Mary's. Fr. Sorin and his successors were left free to dispose of all this property as they saw fit, Mr. Phelan merely expressing the desire that his beautiful farm should be kept by the Congregation with the view of some day establishing itself there, but without making this an obligation. Finally, Fr. Sorin gave Mr. Phelan a mortgage on the property and on Notre Dame in the amount of fifty thousand dollars as a security for the payment of the annuity of three thousand dollars.

Such were the conditions of this contract by which the Congregation of Holy Cross in the United States secured possession of a solid property worth at least three times the indebtedness on it.

That this gift must appear Providential, especially under the circumstances in which it was made, everybody at Notre Dame understood. They saw in it the fulfillment of the words: "In the evening weeping shall have place, and in the morning gladness."[2]

$4,000 from Rev. Mr. Philip Foley of Toledo

Some months before, Notre Dame had acquired a property in the City of Toledo valued at four thousand dollars which sum was due by the Rev. Mr. Foley.[3] He had purchased two scholarships at the College for twenty years for three thousand dollars, and the rest was due for the board of some young men previously kept by him at Notre Dame.

$6,000 from Mr. W. Corby of Detroit

Finally, about this same time, a seminarian gave Fr. Sorin the absolute title to a little piece of property that he owned near Detroit and which was valued at six thousand dollars. Thus, Providence repaired the losses sustained by Notre Dame the previous year.

2. Psalm 30:5
3. On these scholarships, see Foley to Sorin, June 10, 1854, IPA.

Moreover, several new foundations were made since the beginning of this year: one at Louisville amongst Germans, where two Brothers taught 150 children, receiving two hundred dollars each; another at Toledo on nearly the same conditions for English-speaking children; a third at Michigan City and a fourth at Laporte, within the limits of our mission, with about fifty children in each place. Finally, there was a Sisters' school one mile and a half from Notre Dame in the new town called New Lowell, bearing the name School of the Immaculate Conception, and having already an attendance of sixty or seventy children, Irish, Canadian and American.

Foundations at Louisville, Toledo, Michigan City, Laporte and New Lowell

The new Institution of St. Mary's of the Immaculate Conception appeared to excite the interest of the best residents of South Bend. Judge Stanfield[4] himself very graciously answered the different questions addressed to him on this subject by the Sister Secretary in the name of the Sisters' Council. He even offered his services to draw up the plan of incorporation of the new academy. Consequently, all the necessary papers for this undertaking were soon prepared by him in a Council meeting of six Sisters and Fr. Sorin.

Formation of the new charter of incorporation of St. Mary's

Those six Sisters, having declared in writing and under oath, in the presence of Judge Stanfield, their intention of forming a corporation, according to the laws of the State of Indiana, for the erection and the conduct of an academy which they wished to name St. Mary's, and having then elected their president and secretary, as well as the six administrators of the Institution, Fr. Sorin executed a deed to fifty acres of land in favor of the academy thus formed, on which ground the Institution was to develop, and he endowed it with five thousand dollars to be immediately employed in putting up buildings.

4. Thomas S. Stanfield had settled in South Bend in 1831 and was a prominent citizen and attorney. Prior to being selected judge of the Circuit Court in 1852, he had served three terms in the Indiana Legislature and had been a candidate for lieutenant-governor in 1849. He was an active member of the Presbyterian Church. *South Bend and the Men Who Made It* (South Bend, Ind.: The Tribune Printing Co., 1901), 87–88.

All these documents were at once taken by the judge himself to the St. Joseph County Court to be registered and to have from that moment the force of law. Thus, the Academy of St. Mary of the Immaculate Conception had a legal existence and was recognized by the State more than a month before the completion of the first house.

The work was pushed forward vigorously; it was necessary to have things in readiness by the first of September. The two houses of Mishawaka and Bertrand were now destroyed.

Episcopal visit

The mission of Notre Dame had not been visited by its bishop since 1849. Toward the end of July, Bp. de St. Palais, bishop of Vincennes, came for the second time to make the regular visit. He remained nearly a month, and appeared to be well pleased with the progress that religion had made through the work of Holy Cross in this part of the North where (the Congregation) is established. In the interval since his first visit, the congregations, churches, buildings and the personnel of Notre Dame had almost doubled. The letter that His Lordship wrote to the Superior some weeks after his departure from Notre Dame shows his satisfaction and what an interest he takes in the establishment.

Distribution of prizes, 1855; Bp. Young, Mr. P. Ewing

The distribution of prizes at the College this year was honored by the presence of Bishop Young of Erie and Mr. Ph. Ewing,[5] brother-in-law of Sr. Mary of St. Angela, the directress of St. Mary's Academy at Bertrand. Mr. Ewing, a devoted friend of the house, delivered a very remarkable oration. On the following day, Bishop Young gave the customary discourse at the distribution at

5. Bp. Joshua M. Young was born Oct. 29, 1808, in Shapleigh, Maine, and was received into the Catholic Church, Oct. 10, 1828, in Portland, Maine. Ordained for the diocese of Cincinnati, Apr. 1, 1838, he had been the Gillespies' pastor in Lancaster, Ohio, in the 1840s. On Apr. 23, 1854, he was ordained bishop of Erie, Pennsylvania. Code, 300; McAllister, 23–25. Philemon Ewing was a cousin of the Gillespies and the eldest son of Thomas Ewing, a prominent Whig politician who had served as U.S. senator from Ohio and as secretary of the treasury in the administration of President William Henry Harrison. The younger Ewing married Mary Rebecca Gillespie in 1848. McAllister, 26, 32, 45.

St. Mary's. On both occasions, large numbers were present, and the plays and the speeches prepared by the scholars did them honor whilst pleasing the large audiences.

This year was marked by abundant rainfall. The harvest, which promised to be very large, right up to the last day, was surprised, after having been cut, by rains lasting for several weeks, which threatened the almost total ruin of the wheat of the countryside. The sheaves were not only sprouting in the field, but had actually turned green on the outside. The consequence was the loss of at least a quarter of the wheat throughout the area and for Notre Dame, in particular, an expense for flour which it was estimated would reach two thousand dollars. *Harvest spoiled*

We have already mentioned the new Academy of the Sisters of Holy Cross. Let us return to it for a moment. *New St. Mary's of the Immaculate Conception; advantages of the new site*

It lies a mile and a quarter west of the College, on the right bank of the St. Joseph River. It would perhaps be impossible, apart from all personal advantages to the Society, to find another site all the length of the St. Joseph, so well suited and so charming as that occupied today by this Institution. It covers a magnificent plateau bounded on the south by the river at a depth of seventy-five feet, and on the west by a rich prairie almost at the ordinary level of the waters of the St. Joseph. Fr. Sorin had at first given twenty acres, and somewhat later he added thirty more.

The general plan of the present buildings is to be seen in the lines traced at the top of this page.[6] It is to be three hundred and sixty feet in length. Before the end of this year, the central part was entirely finished and afforded room for sixty boarders and some thirty Sisters. Towards the beginning of December, the postulants' house, with twenty-two subjects, was added, and there was room for all.

6. This drawing appears at the tip of p. 158 of the original ms.

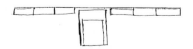

Towards the end of the same month, the northern portion was sufficiently advanced to accommodate the entire Immaculate Conception workers' school of thirty girls and three Sisters. The central portion, which was to jut out 120 feet in the front and which is to include a fine, large chapel of eighty by forty feet with the community house in the rear between the first two buildings, was deferred till the following spring.

From this time, the new Institution became the headquarters of the Sisters of Holy Cross in the United States, no longer in a transient way, but fixed and permanent. They enjoyed all the advantages they could desire as religious attached to a congregation to which they could render all the services to be expected from this third branch, and from which in return they could obtain all those that they were entitled to by reason of the spiritual and fundamental alliance which the Vicar of Christ was soon to consecrate.[7]

The Academy was neither too near the College nor too far from it, but at just such a distance as to secure the mutual and daily services of the two houses, without giving rise to any inconveniences, not even that of keeping other Sisters at the College, except those needed in the kitchen and the infirmary. A commissioner with a suitable wagon could carry provisions, laundry, etc., from one house to the other, and he could easily do this in one hour. The visits of the Superiors did not require more time and could easily be made on foot, and a priest from the College or from one of the novitiates easily went to St. Mary's every day to say mass, unless he was called elsewhere. All letters were sent and received at the same post office of Notre Dame, a new convenience.

The three Societies established and recognized by the State

Thus, before the end of 1855, Fr. Sorin had the consolation of seeing with his own eyes what he had so earnestly

7. In fact, Pope Pius IX demanded and Fr. Moreau agreed to the separation of the Sisters from the Brothers and Priests of Holy Cross before he approved the latter in 1856 and 1857. The Marianite Sisters of Holy Cross were organized as a separate and autonomous congregation in 1858. See Catta, *Moreau,* 2:167–188.

desired: the three branches of the Congregation established in a permanent and most desirable manner, recognized by the State, and each secured by a charter of incorporation, the Fathers at the university, the Brothers in the St. Joseph's workshops, and the Sisters in the Academy.

Towards the beginning of the month of October, Fr. Sorin received some letters from the Very Rev. Fr. Rector, which grieved more than they surprised him. They had to do with sending immediately to the Mother House the sum of fifteen thousand francs in order to save it from inevitable ruin. Food was then so dear in France that Sainte-Croix was obliged to send away all useless mouths and to reduce everything to what was strictly necessary. Two other letters followed the first in quick succession to hurry the loan and to send the money.

Financial embarrassment of Ste-Croix; Fr. Sorin sends $3,000 to Very Rev. Father

Fortunately, Providence had permitted that Fr. Sorin, a few weeks before, had succeeded in obtaining a loan of ten thousand dollars. An express was sent that very day to New York to arrange matters, and the funds arrived in time to save the Mother House from embarrassment.

The unexpected disbursement of such a considerable sum just at the time when the arrangements made for this same money had been put into effect could not fail to cause the administration of Notre Dame difficulties, which if not of the gravest kind, were very serious. Fr. Sorin could not but see this; but, even if they were to be still greater, he would have unhesitatingly sent all that was actually at his disposal. Besides, in addition to the devotedness of his heart to Sainte-Croix, which he found the occasion of satisfying, he was glad to be able to prove this sincere devotedness as a reply to all the suspicions and accusations of which circumstances rather than his actions had made him the object for some years in the Congregation.

It was with this view and on the same principles that, ten days later, he sent another ten thousand francs to the Very Rev. Fr. Rector to help him to send hither a colony of Sisters who could no longer get their living at Sainte-Croix. Twelve were sent without delay and arrived at Notre Dame about the middle of January of the following year. But, before they landed in America, Fr. Sorin felt all the

Second dispatch of $2,000 to Ste-Croix

Loss of $1,000

consequences of this double transfer of funds, while he, himself, was hard put to meet the expenses of his house. One of the immediate consequences was a loss of a thousand dollars to have notes amounting to eight thousand dollars discounted, not to mention the journey to Montreal and to New York.

New troubles in New Orleans

Naturally, after having given these proofs of attachment to the Mother House, the house of the Lake might have expected and rejoiced in the hope that all memory of past miseries would be buried. Heaven had ordered it otherwise. Unequivocal expressions of gratitude were not slow in coming from the Very Rev. Father, it is true; but, whilst Fr. Sorin gladly received the assurance of the joy and gratitude of Sainte-Croix for the service, which was magnified rather than understated, other letters reached him from New Orleans which pierced him to the heart.

At the request of Sainte-Croix, Fr. Sorin had just resumed charge of the three houses in that city, which had recently lost their Superior, the Rev. Fr. Guesdon,[8] and a Brother in September last, and had sent a Brother as Visitor along with the Mother Superior and two Sisters to make the regular visit of that foundation.[9] Although they were

8. It seems that there were four houses in New Orleans: St. Mary's Asylum (1849), St. Mary's Workshop (1851), Sisters' novitiate and Brothers' novitiate. See below, p. 153. Rev. Isidore Jean-Baptiste Guesdon was born Apr. 22, 1825, at Desertines (Mayenne), France, and entered the Congregation of Holy Cross at Ste-Croix on Feb. 8, 1847. He withdrew in Sept. 1847, but re-entered Aug. 8, 1852, professed vows on Sept. 4, 1852, was ordained and left for New Orleans on Feb. 16, 1855, with an appointment as provincial and local superior. He died in New Orleans of yellow fever on Sept. 18, 1855. M.g. Fr. Moreau had decided to place the New Orleans houses under Sorin again in late 1855 because he had no one in France to send there as superior. Catta, *Moreau*, 2:51ff.

9. On this visitation of the New Orleans houses, see M. Georgia Costin, "The Disastrous Visit: 1855," presented at the annual Conference on the History of the Congregations of Holy Cross (hereafter CHCHC), 1990, pp. 7–8. Costin identifies the three Sisters as Mary of the Ascension (Mathurin Salou), who had been in America since 1846 (see chapter 5, note 2); Mary of the Immaculate Conception (Prevert), who had been sent by Fr. Moreau to visit the American

the bearers of express letters from the Rev. Fr. Rector, and
although Fr. Sorin had taken all imaginable precautions to
avoid wounding any susceptibilities, the Sisters and Brothers of the Asylum would listen to nothing that came from
the Lake; and, shielding their conduct under the fair name
of attachment to Sainte-Croix, they trampled under foot
even the arrangements of Sainte-Croix and insulted the
envoys from the Lake in the most outrageous manner, so
far even as to compel the Mother Superior to return to the
Lake amidst the ice and snow, although they knew that
she had gone to New Orleans by order of the doctors to
pass the winter there as well as to fulfill an obedience most
painful in itself. She, accordingly, returned, to the great
surprise and mortification of the whole Chapter, which was
informed of the strange proceedings of the Sisters of New
Orleans.

This was the last act of this year 1855, so fruitful in *Resumé of the*
grave events for the work of Sainte-Croix in the United *year 1855*
States. This year, which posterity will doubtless call the
year of the Immaculate Conception, will always remain
one of the most remarkable in the annals of this mission.
More than any other since the commencement of Notre
Dame du Lac, it was a mixture of blessings and trials, of
joys and crosses. The death of Br. John of the Cross and of
Mr. Devos renewing all the agonies of the previous autumn;
the pecuniary embarrassments of Notre Dame and the continuance of the fatal epidemic; the well-founded fear that
soon the place would be judged unhealthy, which would
have meant certain destruction; the compulsory acquisition
of the Rush property in order to lower the lakes and dry the
surroundings; the necessity of either building at Mishawaka
and Bertrand or of removing the two academies to the

---

houses in 1854 and had stayed on to help in the face of the cholera
epidemic at Notre Dame; and Mary of St. Ligouri (Chretien), who
had come to America in 1853 and had been serving at the manual
labor school in Mishawaka, Indiana. All three Sisters were French-
born and French-speaking. Arriving on the evening of Nov. 27,
1855, the visitors were given a cold reception and their authority
was questioned.

new property, which had every advantage for the Sisters' establishment in connection with the Priests and Brothers; the additional expenses arising from this unavoidable resolution; the donation, meanwhile, by Mr. and Mrs. Phelan which, whilst not immediately filling the treasury, supplied a fund to meet claims such as the house had not previously had; the sale of a portion of this donation to the archbishop of St. Louis when no one else would buy; the affairs of New Orleans; the foundation of the house of New York; the distress of Sainte-Croix; the sending of a dozen Sisters to the United States; the foundation of three Brothers' schools at Toledo, Louisville and Mishawaka, and three other Sisters' schools at Lowell, Laporte and Michigan City; the dismissal of two Brothers and one novice priest which, although diminishing the number, was really a gain by reason of the peace and regularity that prevailed after their departure; two large brick churches begun at St. John's and at Lowell. Here are facts each of which would require a chapter to itself, but which it is enough to sum up here in a few lines in order to show that this year has placed the Institution on a footing almost entirely new, and that it now appears under forms that it never before had.

Before closing the chapter of this year, 1855, which cannot fail to be epoch-making in the annals of the Congregation, and from which will probably date a new phase in the standing of the Province of Notre Dame in the United States, we give here a list of the Establishments composing this Province at the end of 1855.

1.	New Orleans	Asylum and Workshop
2.	Cincinnati	Brothers' School
3.	Louisville	Brothers' School
4.	Toledo	Brothers' School
5.	Hamilton	Brothers' School
6.	Milwaukee	Brothers' School
7.	New York	Workshop and Postulate
8.	Mishawaka	Church and Sisters' School
9.	St. John's	Church and Sisters' School
10.	Lowell	Church and Sisters' School

| 11. Laporte | Church and Sisters' School |
| 12. Michigan City | Church and Sisters' School |

The statistics of these different foundations are briefly summed up as follows.

1. New Orleans

That of New Orleans, properly speaking, dates from the passage of the Visitor from Sainte-Croix to the United States in 1848. As he was proceeding from Notre Dame to Guadeloupe, where he was to arrive towards the end of autumn, Fr. Drouelle was requested by Fr. Sorin to stop in this city and to try to obtain a footing there for the Society of the Brothers by introducing them into an orphan asylum (for the teaching) of arts and trades.

He succeeded in this, and put in writing the conditions that he thought would be acceptable to Notre Dame du Lac, which he first proposed to Archbishop Blanc and the twelve lay members who formed the council of administration of the asylum. They were accepted without difficulty and were then forwarded to the Chapter of the Lake, which had to accept or reject them. The Society agreed to furnish four Brothers at the start and to increase the number as it should be judged necessary by the administration, on the payment of $125 for each member, and $150 for the director. There were at the time only seventy-five orphans in the house which until this time had been in charge of a Catholic family.

The conditions were signed by both contracting parties, and, accordingly, four Brothers were got ready to proceed thither in the month of May 1849. Br. Vincent was named director, to be assisted by Brothers Basil, Theodulus, de Sales, and Aloysius Gonzaga.[10] The distance of New

10. Br. Vincent (Jean Pieau) was a member of the original colony that came from France in 1841. See Editor's Preface. On Br. Basil (Timothy O'Neil), see: chapter 2, note 1; chapter 9, note 4. Br. Theodulus (François Barbé) was born Feb. 20, 1818, in Jublains (Mayenne), France. He entered the Congregation of Holy Cross

Orleans from Notre Dame is nearly 1500 miles. The journey at that time took from twelve to fifteen days; that is
to say, about three times as long as it now requires.

The city has about 180,000 inhabitants from all the
nations of the globe, but especially natives of France and
Creoles. The French, Irish, and German Catholics form
one-third of the population. Everyone knows the opulence
of Louisiana of which New Orleans is the principal point,
but what is no less notorious is the unhealthiness of the
area, which is ravaged almost every year by yellow fever or
cholera. Another thing that is no secret is the depravity of
morals of a great number of the inhabitants of a region in
which the evil passions are more strongly favored than in
any other part of the Union. Imagine to yourself a large city
in which abound luxury and the products of all the world,
where the heat of the climate enervates all energy, where
in general Faith exercises little influence, and you will have
an idea of the level of morals of New Orleans. There are,
however, numerous and very consoling exceptions.

The five Brothers whom we have just named had been
only a few months at their new post when they perceived
that they might find a place for some Sisters in caring for
several dozens of little children under six or seven years of
age. The archbishop himself understood what services Sisters could render, and he wrote on the matter to Fr. Sorin,
more by way of seeing whether the matter had entered into
his views than to make a positive request. The affair was
new for the archbishop and for the community.

---

at Ste-Croix on July 2, 1838, and professed vows Aug. 22, 1843.
He accompanied Fr. Sorin on the latter's return to America in
1846 and was serving as the commissioner of St. Mary's Asylum in
New Orleans when he died there of yellow fever, June 25, 1853.
Br. Francis de Sales (Pierre Berel) was born Dec. 31, 1805, at
Monthault (Ille-et-Vilaine), France, entered the Congregation at
Ste-Croix in August 1842, began his novitiate Aug. 27, 1843, at
Notre Dame, and professed vows there Oct. 22, 1848. Br. Aloysius
Gonzaga (Robert Sidley) was born in 1830 at Stone Hall, County
Clare, Ireland, entered the congregation Nov. 7, 1847, at Notre
Dame, and withdrew Aug. 27, 1852. M.g.

Some letters having been exchanged on the subject, it was resolved to make a trial of it, and Sisters Mary of the Five Wounds, of the Nativity and of Calvary went from Kentucky to the asylum of New Orleans at the end of the scholastic year.[11] They were each to receive a hundred dollars, and they were to be increased in number as needed. For them as well as for the Brothers, the asylum paid the first expenses for travelling.

It was natural that they experienced the need of having a resident priest in an establishment which already contained nearly one hundred persons under the charge of religious. Hence, letters were sent to the Lake asking for one of the Fathers of the Society.

There was then at Notre Dame a young professed priest, difficult of spirit, fickle and whose judgment was not very sound. He had been sent by Sainte-Croix and during the few years that he spent at Notre Dame, he was successively tried in almost all the jobs. He soon tired of everything, and he took advantage of the small number of priests in the mission, which could not afford to deprive itself of the services of a missioner unless he showed himself notoriously unworthy. This young priest had been dismissed once before prior to his ordination; but, far from stirring any gratitude in him, the favor done him in taking him back only provoked resentment which one day would have deplorable effects.

For the sake of peace, the house should have dismissed him a second time and for good; but, he had become formidable, and the question for the administration of the Lake was not so much whether it should finally get rid of him, as how to get rid of him. On the other hand, he had to repeat to all who would listen to him that it was the

11. On Sr. Mary of the Five Wounds, see chapter 3, note 2. On Sr. Mary of Calvary, see chapter 2, note 16. Sr. Mary of the Nativity (Elisabeth Daly) was born Apr. 13, 1808, at Cullycorbert, County Monaghan, Ireland, entered the Congregation of Holy Cross at Notre Dame, Oct. 28, 1843, and professed vows Sept. 10, 1846. AMS. Chapter 8:3 indicates that the Sisters arrived at the same time as the Brothers in New Orleans.

fault of his two confreres, Fr. Granger and Fr. Cointet, if he caused so much embarrassment. He could not abide either of them; generally, the Superior himself fared no better with him.

Still, this constantly repeated excuse gave rise to the idea of offering him a chance to prove its truth by sending him to a place at a distance where neither of them could trouble him. He gladly consented to go to New Orleans; but, when the day fixed for his departure arrived, he declared positively that he would not go to this new post except with the title and all the powers of Local Superior. Disgusting as was this conduct, it was only the beginning of a career of six long years of similar proceedings, more or less shocking. Not only did he declare his resolution, but he held to it. The next day, the Priests' Chapter sent the Mother House a formal petition for the dismissal of this sorry subject.

In the interim it was thought that if he were sent as Visitor he would be satisfied, because this obedience would really give him all the powers of a Superior de facto. And he was, in reality, content with the title, and he went off, removing from the shoulders of those that knew him best an enormous load; but it soon became apparent that he was only removed from the Lake the better to study his revenge. The first chapter held by him at the asylum was marked by a veritable diatribe against Notre Dame du Lac, of which he would not long permit the asylum to be a dependent, etc., etc.[12]

He thus showed how full of bitterness and lacking in judgment he was. In a few days he involved himself in difficulties with his best subjects, and he kept the others by flattering their evil inclinations to vanity, ambition and independence.

Heaven could not bless a house in which God did not reign. There was neither peace nor happiness for anybody.

12. Fr. Gouesse first arrived in New Orleans in February 1850. See James T. Connelly, "Holy Cross in New Orleans: The Crisis of 1850–54," CHCHC, 1988, pp. 6–7.

One of the first Brothers (Basil) escaped in disguise and went to die miserably some hundreds of miles away. Soon, miseries were accumulating to an alarming degree. Letters followed letters to the Lake, urging Fr. Sorin to come and visit the asylum. Finally, he went there by the decision of the Chapter, gave a retreat to the Brothers and to the Sisters, who all seemed to return to their former sentiments towards him and towards the Lake.

But Fr. Sorin was deeply pained to hear him who ought to have given everyone an example proclaim in open chapter that he would be Local Superior in spite of Fr. Sorin. Meanwhile, the latter had among his papers the act of Fr. Gouesse's dismissal pronounced by Sainte-Croix; but, seeing no one to take his place, he thought it better to let some months pass and to make his report to His Reverence.

But it would be too painful to go over again the details of this lamentable history. It is already set down in Section Eight of Chapter Nine of these Chronicles. For this page on New Orleans let it suffice to say that at the end of six months, which is incomprehensible even five years afterwards, this same Father did actually obtain his appointment, and he, himself, was the first to proclaim his triumph.

This state of affairs continued until the journey of Fr. Sorin to France in 1852. It took him some hours to make the Chapter understand the nature of the events that were so lamentably succeeding one another in New Orleans. He obtained the ratification of his appointment of Fr. Cointet to the asylum, and he returned with well-founded hope of seeing peace restored in the Province.

Unfortunately, the stay of this worthy Father was not of long duration. He was hardly two years at the asylum when the great disturbance at the Lake occurred on the occasion of the recall of Fr. Sorin. At the same time, Fr. Cointet received orders to proceed to Notre Dame and to deliver up his place to Fr. Gouesse, who was ordered and who came immediately from Canada. Therefore, he was again in charge in January 1853, and remained there until he was recalled to the Mother House in 1854.

Toward the end of the year 1853, Father Gouesse was replaced by Fr. Salmon, who did not last one year, dying at the beginning of the following autumn in the current epidemic.[13] The year 1853 had been marked by an epidemic of the same kind which carried off three Brothers and one Sister. The year following was also memorable for the death of the Father who succeeded Fr. Salmon and who came in the spring of 1855, dying in September of the same year and of the same yellow fever along with Br. Martial, who had come from France in 1854.[14]

After the death of Fr. Guesdon, the establishment of New Orleans was more than ever in misery. There was neither rule nor discipline. Everyone did just about as he pleased, except that Br. Elias seemed to maintain some pretense of being director or superior.[15]

Towards the month of November, the Rev. Fr. Rector having requested Fr. Sorin to take charge once more, the Mother Superior and Brother Stephen were sent from the Lake as Visitors, but could not win recognition from either the Brothers or the Sisters.

Amidst all these trials the asylum had grown considerably. The two epidemics of 1853 and 1854 had claimed a number of victims amongst the orphans, but a still greater

13. Fr. Pierre–François Salmon was born Jan. 20, 1818, at Beaulieu (Mayenne), France, entered the Congregation of Holy Cross at Ste-Croix, and began his novitiate on Aug. 22, 1839, as Br. Theotime. After ten years as a Brother, he entered the seminary, was ordained, and left France for America, Oct. 11, 1853. He died of yellow fever in New Orleans, Sept. 6, 1854. M.g.

14. The reference is to Fr. Guesdon. See above, note 8. Br. Martial (Adolphe Benion) was born May 1, 1830, at Chatelain (Mayenne), France, and was working as a tailor when he entered the Congregation of Holy Cross on Mar. 17, 1852, at Ste-Croix. He professed vows June 5, 1854, and left for America eleven days later. He died in New Orleans on Sept. 26, 1855. M.g.

15. Br. Elias (Auguste Perony) was born Oct. 23, 1815, at Treport (Seine Inf.), France, entered the Congregation of Holy Cross at Ste-Croix, Jan. 4, 1838, and professed vows Aug. 22, 1841. He left France for America with Fr. Salmon, Oct. 11, 1853, and returned to France in 1856. From 1857 until his death on June 21, 1867, he worked in the congregation's houses in the Papal States. M.g.

number of children in the city had lost their parents, and in 1853 the number of orphans increased to 250 and 275. Since 1852, there were usually at the asylum eight or nine Brothers and as many Sisters.

In 1852, the Sisters took possession of a fine house built for their use by the administration, and the year 1854 saw another house twice as large going up for the orphans.

In 1851, the Sisters of Holy Cross added to their work in the asylum a new establishment for young girls without means of subsistence who were old enough to learn a trade. It was called St. Mary's Workshop, and it soon caught the fancy of the public. But amidst the dissensions that continued to agitate the Society until 1856, little could be done towards its development, and up to that time it continued to be an excellent project awaiting its execution, rather than a real creation. There were never more than forty children and more often twenty-five to thirty.

From the beginning of 1852, the dream was entertained of opening a novitiate for the Sisters in the city and another at the asylum for the Brothers. To make the success more assured, petitions were sent again and again to Sainte-Croix, until the erection of this establishment into a Province had been secured; the letters patent reached the asylum on the very day of Fr. Guesdon's death.

Such, in brief, is the history of the sad annals of this foundation, which alone gave more trouble and vexation to Notre Dame and to Sainte-Croix than any other foundation since the beginning of the Congregation. God permitted this, no doubt, to open the eyes of everybody and to bring about, in his time, measures calculated to secure the peace and happiness of all the members for the future. It cost much to learn to understand the dangers and the needs of this country. Let us hope that such dear experience will be profitable to all.

The administration of the Lake had no desire to reappear in New Orleans, where it had been so grossly insulted and humiliated by the discourses of the Father referred to above and by the scandalous quarrels which he had provoked and continued to foment between Sainte-Croix and the Lake. It was remembered that when Fr. Gues-don had been sent thither from France, he said openly to Fr. Rooney,[16] whom the Lake had sent there some months before at the repeated request of Sainte-Croix as Local Superior, that the Mother House had never had such an intention.

However, His Reverence wrote twice to Fr. Sorin, ask-ing him to resume the direction of the establishments of New Orleans, which he wished to place on their original footing. Moreover, the Rev. Fr. Rector enclosed in his last (letter) a formal order to all the members of New Orleans to submit for the future to Fr. Sorin: for, he said, Providence manifests its will, and the death of Fr. Guesdon leaves no doubt that we must return to the former order of things.

On receipt of those documents, Fr. Sorin did not for a moment imagine that there could be the least difficulty. Moreover, as letters were constantly arriving from the asy-lum as before, asking for some Brothers to teach English, it was thought proper at Notre Dame to send a Visitor for the Brothers and one for the Sisters to acquaint them-selves with the state of affairs and to make a report to the Minor Chapter before formally accepting anew those establishments.

It was, therefore, resolved that besides Br. Stephen, who was appointed Visitor, another Brother should be sent who would be able at once to fill the void in teaching. To the Mother Superior and the travelling companion who was to go and return with her, it was also decided that a third Sister should be sent whom they might want to take charge of the house after the visit and the acceptance. No change was to be made in the obediences or the offices of the members. Nevertheless, the arrival of the Visitors

16. Fr. Michael Rooney was born Jan. 8, 1830, in Albany, New York. He entered the Congregation of Holy Cross, July 11, 1849, at Notre Dame, professed vows Aug. 15, 1852, and was ordained at Notre Dame on Feb. 2, 1853. Before going to New Orleans, he had served as pastor in Laporte, Indiana. He withdrew from the congregation Nov. 9, 1855. M.g. Costin, "The Disastrous Visit," 6, states that he left New Orleans in early May 1855.

was the signal for a revolt in which no respect was shown either to the arrangements of the Reverend Father or to the counsels of the Visitors. Not only did they not recognize them, but they obtained from Sainte-Croix approbation and support and the condemnation of the proceedings of the Lake. This success of ambition was disconcerting. The Mother Superior had already withdrawn; after these outrages, Brother Stephen was recalled.

2. Cincinnati

Cincinnati is not only the largest city of Ohio, but of all the West, of which it is called the Queen. It has about 150,000 inhabitants and stands on the left[17] bank of the beautiful river of the same name, nearly all of whose commerce it absorbs.

In 1851, the Society of Holy Cross founded there an establishment of four Brothers and one priest for the orphans of St. Joseph (an institution), already in existence for ten years for the German population. The difficulty of reaching an understanding with the temporal and lay administration of this asylum caused the foundation to be abandoned after eighteen months, and the Brothers who were there at the time moved to St. John's, a large parish where they soon had charge of three or four hundred children.[18] The conditions were and still are the same. The Brothers are paid a thousand dollars and they find their own board and lodging. At present, we have three Brothers there teaching German, one teaching English and another for the kitchen.

This establishment has always given full satisfaction, having always been the first parish school in Cincinnati

17. The chronicler wrote "left" bank although Cincinnati is on the northern or right-hand side of the Ohio River as one comes down river.

18. St. John the Baptist parish on Green Street in Cincinnati, founded in 1844, was the third German parish established in the city. The Holy Cross Brothers taught the boys in the parochial school from 1852 to 1861. See Lamott, file of parish histories, Archives of the Archdiocese of Cincinnati.

in the manner of conducting it, and in the progress and number of its pupils. It was founded in the hope that it would do much good in that place and that vocations would there be found amongst the Germans; presently, it serves as a postulate for Germans.

Everybody knows that this city is populated by Germans, and there is every reason to think that in time there will be amongst them a rich harvest of subjects for the Society. Moreover, it is a center of business and commerce, and Notre Dame cannot but derive great advantages from a house in this vast center. The Brothers own a brick residence facing St. John's Church. They have at this writing five hundred children divided into four classes.

3. Louisville

Louisville is situated on the right[19] bank of the Ohio one hundred and fifty (miles) below Cincinnati, is the first and oldest city of Kentucky, has about 50,000 inhabitants, is the seat of a bishop and has several Catholic churches.

The Brothers were established there in 1855 at St. Boniface's Church, amongst the Germans, by the request of the Franciscan Fathers, as was the case in Cincinnati. They are paid just about as at St. John's, and have about two hundred children with three Brothers, one of whom is occupied in cooking and in attending to the house and sacristy. This is a foundation of a certain importance for the Congregation as well as for the place itself.

In general, what is done amongst the Germans in this country offers more for the future than amongst the Irish and the French. The Germans are honest, if not generous; the others do not keep their promises; among the former there is order and system, amongst the latter great negligence and little perseverance. There is no doubt but that our German brethren will succeed better than any other nationality in America, and that the Community itself will find more resources in its German subjects than in

---

19. Although the chronicler wrote "right" bank, Louisville is on the southern or left bank of the Ohio River.

the others. Hence, the importance of making foundations amongst the Germans!

4. Toledo

Toledo is only six hours' ride from Notre Dame on the railroad of Northern Indiana. This city, which to date counts only some fifteen thousand inhabitants, is, nevertheless, one of the first and more important of Ohio. It lies at the head of Lake Erie where it monopolizes almost all the grain exports from the West. Up to this time, the Catholic population is nearly all Irish, although a German church has just been built.

The Brothers' school was established there in the month of May 1855, by two Irish Brothers, in consideration of a salary of two hundred dollars per year for each of them. They already have 150 children there.

Unfortunately, one notices here, as in all maritime or lake ports, that there is much drunkenness and, consequently, much misery and immorality. The children are not regular in their attendance as among the Germans. The parents neglect to send them to school or they imagine that they need them at home, most of them being poor. It is, perhaps, the place in all the environs where a school of this kind is most needed, but it affords neither the guarantees nor the future of the two former places.

5. Hamilton

Hamilton is a pretty little town of six thousand souls, ten miles from Cincinnati, whose Catholic population is almost exclusively German. The foundation of a Brothers' school was laid there toward the end of 1855, at the request of the Rev. Fr. Eberhard of the Order of St. Francis, on the same conditions as in Cincinnati. It was, however, begun by an Irish Brother, who was to be relieved as soon as the examinations at St. John's School permitted Br. Dominic from St. John's to go to Hamilton. This school is, therefore, too new to permit anything very precise to be said of it; from all appearances, it will be a success.

6. Milwaukee

Milwaukee is amongst the most important cities of the West, containing at the present day nearly forty thousand souls. For beauty and salubrity it has no equal beyond the lakes. It is situated on the western shore of Lake Michigan, five hours ride from Chicago and, consequently, eight hours from Notre Dame. The Germans predominate, although the English-speaking population there is numerous.

The Brothers' school was founded at the request as well as at the expense of Bp. Henni[20] himself in the basement of his former cathedral. It is for the Irish, the Germans being, for the moment, well served by excellent schools in charge of laymen. As yet, there are only two Brothers with some fifty children. Still, amongst all the foundations of the Society in this country, it is the one that offers the best prospects for the Society itself, since the diocese of Milwaukee is more exclusively Catholic and our holy religion is flourishing there more than anywhere else in the United States. It, therefore, appears to be beyond doubt that this school, if properly managed, will be a success, especially in procuring vocations.

7. New York

In 1854, Mother Mary of the Five Wounds, having gone to France to collect for her workshop in New Orleans, somehow or other obtained an obedience from the Rev. Fr. Rector to found a similar house in New York, and she had even collected funds for that purpose. The archbishop of New York, being in Rome at the time, could not be consulted, and on her return from France, Mother Five Wounds could not know for certain whether or not her

---

20. John Martin Henni was born June 15, 1805, in Misanenga, Switzerland, and was educated in Switzerland, Rome, and at St. Thomas Seminary, Bardstown, Kentucky. Ordained a priest for the diocese of Cincinnati in 1829, he was ordained as the first bishop of Milwaukee in 1844. Code, 131.

services were desired in New York. The archbishop had not yet returned; otherwise, it seems that she would not have gone back to New Orleans.

She went there, however, but after some months returned to New York at the invitation of the Rev. Fr. Madéore[21] of the Fathers of Mercy, who had communicated the project to His Grace and had obtained his approval. She had left New Orleans with the consent of her Superior, Fr. Guesdon, but not being able to procure either a location or furniture without binding herself to meet all the expenses and assume all the responsibilities of the enterprise, Fr. Guesdon sent her orders to leave New York and to return, declaring expressly that he would have nothing to do with this foundation.

Some months afterwards, Fr. Guesdon died and the Mother in question thought herself at liberty to reflect and to act for herself. She wrote to the Rev. Fr. Rézé in Canada and to Fr. Sorin at Notre Dame to get some Sisters to help her in starting this work, which she painted in the most alluring colors. She succeeded in obtaining two Sisters from each place, and in several weeks she found herself at the head of twenty-five postulants in a fine house on Twenty-Ninth Street in New York, rented for a thousand dollars a year.

Unfortunately, those that gather often scatter. The Sisters who joined her from Canada could not agree with her. Their misunderstandings were not long kept secret. Soon, Fr. Madéore and the archbishop were made acquainted with the miseries amidst which the work was beginning. After some weeks of quarreling and after some disagreeable and offensive letters had been exchanged between Fr. Madéore and the Superior of Canada, Sr. Mary of the Redemption was obliged to return to Saint-Laurent, but

21. Rev. Benedict Madéore of the Fathers of Mercy had been entrusted with the task of organizing an orphanage in conjunction with St. Vincent de Paul parish in New York City. The archbishop of New York was John Hughes. See Catta, *Moreau*, 2:280ff.

not before she had inflicted an almost irreparable injury by decrying the Superioress and the Society in the spirit of those very ones who should have esteemed it the most.

Whilst these things were going on, Fr. Sorin received a letter from His Reverence, promising him that this foundation, if it succeeded, would depend on Notre Dame. At the same time, Fr. Sorin came to Canada on business, and as the same business also took him to New York immediately afterwards, he thought it proper, being on the spot, to get some information about a foundation that was to depend on the Lake.

After having seen the house and consulting with Fr. Madéore and the archbishop, it seemed evident to him that neither the archbishop nor Fr. Madéore nor the Sisters themselves knew on whom the establishment depended and that everybody was tired of this uncertainty, which threatened everything with speedy and inevitable ruin. In this emergency, Fr. Sorin believed that he was authorized to take the house under his direction and to assume the responsibility for it. Everyone was gladdened by this. He spent three days there, and before departing, he promised to furnish the personnel necessary for the work.

Hardly had he arrived home when he learned of the revolt of the members at the asylum in New Orleans and of the presumed and proximate return of the Mother Superior. How those first difficulties were to end remained to be seen. Fifteen days afterwards, the Mother returned from New Orleans and made her report to the Chapter. It was at once decided that she should formally visit the new house in New York whither she was to take her report, forward it to Sainte-Croix, and await the answer whilst performing her duties as Visitor.

Once in New York, Mother Mary of the Ascension set to work, not only to open a novitiate according to the rules, but also to make herself acquainted with the views and the objective that had been proposed in establishing this new work as well as the means of attaining them. At the end of several weeks, she became more and more convinced that the good superioress and foundress of this house was not a person to properly manage it. Each day there were new projects, new journeys and nothing stable, but a constant state of endless changes. Then there were quarrels, dissensions and sullenness altogether unbecoming in a religious house.

This good Sister, who had not even the remotest notion that anyone could be right in not approving of her chimerical ideas, had made up her mind to go in person to Notre Dame in order to have an understanding with Fr. Sorin, when the latter, being already informed of all the annoyance that she was giving the Visitor, all of whose efforts were thus paralyzed, sent her an order by telegraph, being fully resolved to put an end to the troubles that she had been giving in New York.

But on the very next day, having received the famous answer of the Chapter of Sainte-Croix condemning all his proceedings in New Orleans, Fr. Sorin telegraphed a second time in the contrary sense. Unfortunately the two telegrams arrived in New York in the inverse order, and Sr. Mary of the Five Wounds left immediately for Notre Dame. Fr. Madéore was pleased at her departure, and he would assuredly have seen things moving in a consoling manner if the action of the Lake had continued firm and vigorous. It seems that heaven had other views on this work.

The documents with which Mother Mary of the Five Wounds had been supplied by the Reverend Father and by the Secretary General having been carefully examined; the new obedience of Superioress recently sent her from Sainte-Croix, with her two assistants, a Stewardess and a Mistress of Novices, and the messages with which they were charged, for instance, not to give the habit to anyone without the approbation of His Reverence, even if the postulants had already been admitted by the Lake; the positive declarations of the Foundress[22] that the Reverend Father would no more cede New York to the Lake than

22. "The Foundress" apparently refers to Mother Mary of the Seven Dolors. See chapter 13, note 3.

he would New Orleans: when everything was taken into consideration, Fr. Sorin saw clearly that he had gone too far in attempting to act as circumstances demanded in New York. To be under his direction was clearly to expose the new foundation to the same miseries that disgraced the Congregation in the South. If Sainte-Croix had at one time shown different intentions, it was no longer doubtful that it wished to retain this new house under its control.

Fr. Madéore and the archbishop, as well as the Sisters, had expected a firm and vigorous cooperation from Fr. Sorin, as has been said; he could no longer act, since even the permission to admit to the reception of the habit had been withdrawn. Moreover, the cruel deception and crushing troubles that he had just experienced at the asylum of New Orleans had so intimidated him or, rather, baffled him, that the very idea of exposing himself again made him shudder (the word may seem too strong, but considered in the light of the torches kindled on his way for some years by human passions, not only to give him light but to roast him by inches, it will be found to be the word that in our language precisely expresses what he felt) at sight of the danger and in his insatiable thirst for peace.

In any other circumstances and under any other influence, he would have taken the time to expose the state of affairs to the Mother House. Here it was necessary to act.

To withdraw from New York after the disgraceful retreat from the South would be to ruin himself entirely in the eyes of the public, not only of New York, but of the whole country. Nevertheless, it was necessary to resolve upon it, or to recommence, coolly, the same war in which the Congregation had just buried its honor under a crushing load of ignominy in Louisiana.

The members of the Chapters of the Lake were pained beyond measure by the conduct of the Mother House. The letters of Sainte-Croix said that the Brothers and the Sisters of the asylum had been reprimanded, while those that came from the asylum declared plainly that they had been approved and supported.

It is useless to write here of the suspicions that were entertained as to the causes why Sainte-Croix had offered New Orleans and New York to the Lake. Oh, there are in the lives of religious Societies, as well as in those of individuals, moments of trial which are akin to discouragement, not to mention despair!

In those same days, the ten Sisters arrived from France, from whom was expected the example of all the virtues, since, in the words of the Superioress of Sainte-Croix, they were amongst the best in the Mother House. Those very Sisters had hardly passed fifteen days at the Lake before they had grieved, almost disgusted, all the French Sisters who came in contact with them.

According to the report of their directress, they did not even preserve amongst themselves the appearance of charity. Jealousy, indiscretion, levity, and especially the itching to talk of the miseries of Sainte-Croix, which they made out to be contemptible, especially in the person of the Very Rev. Father, whom they represented as a man who wanted to do everything himself and who embroiled whatever he meddled with, who could hold on to no one and with whom it was enough to be intimate to be dismissed from the Society. (Amongst other things they spoke in a very flippant way of his temptation[23] as a proof of mental aberration rather joking about the effects than grieving for the cause.) Such were the dispositions of those good women on their arrival until Fr. Sorin, who had on the very first day warned them of their indiscretions on the journey from New York, put them all on absolute silence for an indefinite period.

Cruel deception! He had placed himself in a very serious financial embarrassment in order to relieve the Mother House, and he saw his efforts turned to the destruction of all respect for the Mother House. The two weeks spent by those ten persons at the Lake changed all the sympathies

23. From March to November of 1855, Fr. Moreau had undergone a kind of spiritual trial which has been likened to a dark night of the soul. See Catta, *Moreau*, 2:106–114.

and compassion for the Mother House in its distress into indifference and even disgust. In a word, the result of all that they said was the feeling that Sainte-Croix was on the point of falling, and that it would be hardly any wonder; that the money sent from here had not been used in paying a single debt, and that nevertheless there was a sum total of 240,000 francs to be paid. The lack of administration, the reckless expenditures of the Brothers, the strange means employed to raise funds, all was painted by them in such colors that the wonder was that Sainte-Croix was still in existence. But how is it that they were allowed to say all those things? In a half-day, ten tongues that were charged to say nothing, will say a great deal.

When Fr. Sorin learned of this strange conduct, he would have liked to send them all back to France. But besides the expense, that would have been a new cause of complaint and censure at Sainte-Croix. It was necessary to be resolved, although not without sighing, to keep them, such as they were.

In the meantime, the Chapter of the Lake had to take a definite stand as regards the foundation of New York. Everybody there was so tired of troubles and domestic dissensions that any means of restoring peace would have been welcomed as a blessing from heaven, unless it were evidently disfigured by sin. Now in the present case there was no question of sin nor of any obligation of justice, since we could even yet leave New York in the state in which we had found it. There was merely question of a great humiliation; but even in this humiliation there appeared the assurance of putting an end to all quarrels and disagreements; the recall of the Mother Superior was resolved upon, as well as that Mother Mary of the Five Wounds should be sent back to the post to which she had been recently elected, according to the latest documents from France.

To the interested, ecclesiastical authorities in New York, the truth was stated in the simplest and most inoffensive manner possible, which amounted to the declaration that in consequence of the perceived changes in the intentions of the Mother House, it appears that Sainte-Croix wished for the future to take charge of the foundation; that it was therefore to their interest to communicate directly with Sainte-Croix and our duty to withdraw; that Sainte-Croix showed thereby the importance that it attached to this establishment.

Such was the end of the intervention of the Lake in New York. The Mother Superior returned and it seems as if calm ought now to succeed the tempest, if, indeed, peace can ever become the lot of the poor children of Sainte-Croix.

Perhaps the people at Sainte-Croix had become convinced that the Lake had a great desire to establish itself in New Orleans and New York. Assuredly, for some years past, the advantages presented by those two establishments were more than counterbalanced by the quarrels in which the Lake was soon involved with the Mother House in regard to the one and the other of them. In all candor, the Lake had no desire of either the one or the other. Devotion to the honor of the Congregation alone made it deviate one last time from its modest reserve. It is today so vexed and so wounded that with the grace of God it hopes never again to fall into that grave error of sowing scandal instead of edification and that at the cost of its peace, its funds and its subjects.

Before ending the history of this memorable year, which God in his infinite mercy was pleased to enrich with several unexpected blessings and as many crosses equally unlooked for, let it be permitted us to humbly confess that, without omitting to do full justice to man by assigning him the part that belongs to him, we recognize and bless with all our heart the adorable hand of Providence which guides all things towards the welfare of the elect. Even in the latest contradictions, something so strangely unexpected happened that we recognize that Heaven doubtless willed our humiliation and confusion in order to detach us from human applause and to make us place all our confidence in it alone. In this sense, the more the conduct of the Mother House appeared to us to go against all the dictates of wisdom and prudence, so much the more did we endeavor to see that the blow was aimed from above to punish us for our sins and to make us better religious.

It would be a mistake to think that we harbor the least resentment against our Fathers. We have sincerely regretted the pain that we seem to have caused them and the impossibility in which they placed us of doing the good that we hoped and desired to do and to advance the interests of the Congregation. But in the eyes of God, merit is not always measured by success nor by the development of an enterprise. We have sincerely desired and sought the good; this is all that we can say or wish to say. May God be thanked even for this good desire with which he has inspired us.

When the Very Rev. Father requested Fr. Sorin to resume charge of the house of New Orleans, it was not a favor that he was granting but a burden he was imposing, and it called for devotedness rather than great eagerness on the part of the Lake. This is the origin of the great mistake of Sainte-Croix.

It was not Fr. Sorin's business to dictate to the Rector what arrangements he should make with the asylum to prepare them for the change that he wanted to make, especially as his opinion was not asked. Fr. Sorin ought to have supposed that that was all done beforehand and he had no reason to anticipate that a painful act of condescension and devotedness would be construed as ambition, nor that he himself should be insulted as he was; still less should he have had to see those rebels approved and supported in what, at bottom, was contempt for whatever placed a restraint on their spirit of independence and which threatened this one and that one with the loss of their offices and the liberty of doing as they pleased.

Be this as it may, it is certain that Sainte-Croix was grossly deceived by four or five members who were unworthy of their habits and of any confidence, aided by a certain priest,[24] not of ours, whose conduct in those matters

24. The priest referred to is probably Gilbert Raymond, a Sulpician from Angers, France, who was known to Fr. Moreau and who

reflects no credit on him. In spite of the pretended orders of Sainte-Croix to the asylum to pay its debts to the Lake, not a cent has ever been paid. In a word, to keep from feeling resentment it is necessary to call to mind each day that it is by many tribulations that we reach heaven and that those who will live piously in Christ Jesus must be prepared to suffer much. May Heaven therefore bless those dear associations so abundantly that they may do wonders, without ever again knocking at our doors and forgetting themselves. Amen.

8. Mishawaka, Indiana

Four miles southeast of Notre Dame is the pretty little town with this Indian name, containing about two thousand inhabitants, some fifty of whom are Catholics. Mishawaka, which is already thirty years old, has always been known for its iron works, which are its support and the basis of commerce of the neighborhood. It is one of the towns of the North that has best preserved the spirit of bigotry and hatred of everything Catholic.

In 1848 the Fathers of the Lake took every means to persuade the Catholics of Mishawaka to purchase a little frame building which would answer for a church until they could do better. The house was bought for six hundred dollars, and until 1856, it answered the purpose for the Irish and the Germans, who had meanwhile become much more numerous than they were before.

In 1854, Fr. Sorin had been seriously thinking of transferring thither the academy and the novitiate from Bertrand. A house and a very convenient location had been offered at a good price; the purchase was made and the house fitted up as a school. But the prejudices of the inhabitants, which, it was hoped, would be broken down

---

sent him several reports on the state of affairs in the Holy Cross houses in New Orleans. See Catta, *Moreau*, 2:44–49. Costin, "The Disastrous Visit," 9–10, states that Raymond was pastor of a parish in Opelousas, Louisiana, and that he was regarded by at least some of the religious in New Orleans as their superior, even though he was not a member of the Congregation of Holy Cross.

in time, remained the same, and in 1855, it was evident that Mishawaka did not offer all the advantages that were desirable before going to further expense.

The Rush property having been secured at this time, all thoughts of a permanent settlement for the Sisters were centered on this place, as has been already mentioned. In the month of May the Sisters' house at Mishawaka was placed in charge of a contractor to be removed to the Rush property, one mile west of Notre Dame.

However, the Mishawaka school was not destroyed, but simply transferred to another house less spacious but large enough, which had served as the priests' residence up to that time. Three Sisters took up their abode there after the General Retreat of 1855. They had the same number of pupils as before, thirty to forty. Three Sisters usually live there, and they are obliged to admit boys and girls, the congregation not being able to pay the salary of a Brother in addition to that of two or three Sisters.

Just now a pretty little frame church is going up on the Sisters' lot, together with a house for the priest. All this will cost from twelve to thirteen hundred dollars, and this will give the Catholics of this mission a Christian appearance, and all those advantages of which they had been heretofore deprived.

9. St. John's, Indiana

St. John's congregation, exclusively German, is eighty miles southwest of Notre Dame. There is neither town nor village, but merely a log church, to the end of which, at various intervals, additions have been made the full width of the building, giving four little rooms, two of them for the priest and the Brother, and two for the Sisters. For several years school was taught in the church. In 1852, a room was added, partitioned into two, where the little girls were taught separately. The St. John's mission is one of the most numerous of the Notre Dame district. It has at present at least one hundred and eighty families. It is the residence of a German Father, a Brother, and three Sisters.

There is serious talk of building a fine brick church to cost from eight to ten thousand dollars. The number of children attending the schools is from 140 to 180. Up to this time, the congregation, not having a suitable church, has done hardly anything for the priest or the Brother or Sisters. However, there can be no doubt that once the church is built and the pews rented, the Catholics of St. John's will be in a condition to support priest and schools without difficulty. Most of the people are in easy circumstances, and before long they will be rich farmers. In a few years, the care of this mission and of another little congregation, also German, seven miles farther, called Turkey Creek, will require two priests who will there find constantly increasing occupations, and will form one of the best secondary establishments of the Society.

The railroads at present bring us to within five miles of St. John's church.

10. Lowell, Indiana

The town of New Lowell, or simply Lowell, was so named after a celebrated city of Massachusetts, because of its excellent privilege of water on the St. Joseph River. It was recognized and marked on the cadastre of the towns of the State in 1849. Its founder was A. Coquillard,[25] who in 1836 had also begun the foundation of South Bend on the opposite bank, which at present contains at least three thousand souls.

The progress of this new town is indefinitely checked by the sudden death of Mr. Coquillard, who was killed by a fall at the beginning of the year. Be this as it may, this check cannot be of long duration, and, to judge from the

25. Alexis Coquillard, one of the founders of South Bend, was the first white man to settle permanently in St. Joseph County, Indiana. Born in Detroit, Sept. 28, 1795, Coquillard and a partner, Francis Comparet of Fort Wayne, purchased in 1822 the agency for the upper Great Lakes from John Jacob Astor's American Fur Company. Coquillard established a trading post on the St. Joseph River in 1823, thus becoming the first permanent resident of what would later be South Bend. Howard, 131–132.

ordinary causes that here determine the growth of cities, it must one day resume its growth. Now it cannot spread out without materially contributing to raise the value of the lands of Notre Dame, which it joins.

It has at present about two hundred souls, most of them Catholics. It has a house of Sisters who teach about one hundred children. The land was donated by the landowners of the town in 1849, and in 1853, Fr. Sorin built a brick school house, which has answered for a church up to the present. Adjoining the Sisters' house is another lot given for a church. Work was even begun on it last year; but the unexpected death of Mr. Coquillard caused it to be suspended. The walls are standing there five feet above the ground.

Up to the present, this school is a work of pure charity, most of the Catholics of Lowell being Canadians, who are poor everywhere in the United States. A priest goes to say mass there at nine o'clock every Sunday.

11. Laporte, Indiana

This mission has formed a station of the Notre Dame district since 1842. It is thirty miles distant, and the journey is now made by rail in one hour. In 1851, Fr. Sorin opened a subscription for building a brick church there which was to be called after the mystery of the day, the Nativity of the Blessed Virgin. But it was slow work. The Catholics were not numerous, and those best off lived at some distance, in the country, coming only occasionally to assist at the celebration of the holy mysteries in a private house.

It was not until 1854 that the Fathers of the College took upon themselves the responsibility of letting out the contract, built the church, and opened it for worship at the beginning of the following year. The congregation soon reassembled and all were astonished to see how numerous they were. Sisters were asked for, a house in front of the church was bought, and the school began in the month of May 1855.

The following winter, a young Father having taken the place of a priest at Laporte, who understood nothing of the handling of a congregation, things took a new shape. The Sisters had been somewhat languid. A fair was announced to procure them a more suitable house, by which they cleared five hundred dollars and made many friends. They soon exchanged their house for one immediately joining the church grounds.

From this time, their school became prosperous, and the Sisters continued to grow more popular day by day. Eighty children were soon entered in their register, one half Catholics, the others Protestants or infidels. The influence of the Sisters was felt throughout the entire congregation, and now everything leads to the belief that Laporte will be in every sense one of the most important missions of Notre Dame. It is a nice town of 4,500 souls located in the center of a vast and rich prairie, which cannot fail to grow rapidly.

12. Michigan City, Indiana

This town is situated about thirty miles to the northwest of Notre Dame, on the shore of the lake of the same name, and was provided with a Catholic church in 1841 by the Rev. Mr. de St. Palais, now our worthy bishop. He was then pastor of Chicago, whence he came three or four times a year to visit the different stations which at present form the mission of Notre Dame du Lac. It has about two thousand inhabitants of whom some two hundred are Catholics.

From time to time, one of the Fathers from Notre Dame took up his residence there, especially during the months of July, August, September and October, when there is most sickness. In 1852, the house sent a Brother there, who kept a school for a year. Towards the end of 1854, some Sisters were asked for and obtained. In a few months, they formed a class of from seventy-five to ninety children, most of them poor, and nearly all Catholics.

In 1854, a house had been built for the priest; before the close of the year, a house for the Sisters was added, which consisted of a prolongation of the church divided into four rooms, in which the Sisters reside and where they teach the little girls and the little boys of the Catholic population from 8:30 in the morning till 4:00 in the evening.

Michigan City will never grow large, although two railroads intersect there and keep up a noise that never ceases, by day or by night. Its future was more promising before the construction of those roads, when it was the only port of Indiana on Lake Michigan. Now that the lake commerce is taken away, Michigan City is like one of the little inland towns, but even less favored than they, since it is surrounded only by water and sand.[26]

26. On the Brothers' school in Michigan City, see Patricia Gruse Harris, *Centennial History of Catholic Education, Michigan City, Indiana, 1886–1986* (Michigan City, Ind.: St. Mary of the Immaculate Conception Church, 1986), 21–22.

CHAPTER 15

1856

Willy nilly, the work of Holy Cross in the United States will bear its own characteristic mark, its family escutcheon, the royal seal of the cross. This year more than any other has been a year of blessings; but they were all bestowed at the foot of the cross.

The approbation of the Priests and Brothers by the Holy See; the health of all in the institution, which lost only two in the whole year; the foundation in Chicago, consisting of one college, three Brothers' schools, three Sisters' schools, and an industrial school; that of Philadelphia, comprising, at the end of the year, fifteen Sisters, twenty-four boarders, and forty day scholars at the industrial school, not to mention a postulate for the Sisters and a parish school at St. Paul's with eight hundred children; that of Washington City comprising an orphan asylum and a day school under the direction of three Sisters; that of St. Joseph, Susquehanna County, where four Sisters of Holy Cross have just opened a young ladies' academy under the direction of the Very Rev. Mr. O'Reilly; that of Buffalo, whither four Brothers and three Sisters were sent about the middle of November to take charge of an orphan asylum under the patronage of the saintly Bishop Timon; finally that of Columbus, where it was thought more prudent to put only one Brother at the start, although everything is in readiness for an addition next year; the growth of the College, the number of whose students went up to

140 boarders; the development of the three novitiates, which at the end of the year had their full number, although there were more members than ever before admitted to the taking of the habit during the year.

On the other hand, the good spirit of the house; the perfect union, not only of the three communities, but of the individual members of each society amongst themselves; the consideration enjoyed by the house in the neighborhood; finally the erection, so much desired, of a monument to the dear Fr. Cointet in the shape of a lateral chapel added to the church of the Sacred Heart, followed by that of another chapel as a monument to Mr. Phelan,[1] and finally a third chapel in the form of a choir, or rather completing the cross of the original plan of the church; lastly, in the merely material point of view, a new impulse given to the manufacture of brick and lime on the Notre Dame grounds; besides, three or four missions completing their churches and reaching that stage when they will cease to be a burden to the community. Assuredly, there are here many joyful considerations (not to speak of the merry chimes, whose harmonics, however, are reserved for 1857) capable of inspiring the liveliest sentiments of gratitude to God, from whose hand come all the gifts that man receives here below.

On the reverse side of this long series of favors appears that deplorable misunderstanding of New York, which became a scandal to the initiated, and which resuscitated at the three angles of an old triangle of disputes, memories of a past that ought never to have come to life again; next, financial difficulties amounting almost to a crisis; and lastly, a fire that consumed the first buildings of Notre Dame du Lac and caused a loss of about three thousand dollars.

---

1. Having retired to St. Mary's with his wife, William Phelan died there in March 1856 and was buried in the Notre Dame cemetery. McAllister, 131–132. In 1857, the remains of Phelan as well as of Frs. Cointet and the Indian missionaries, DeSeille and Petit, were reinterred in the crypt of the church under the new choir. Wack, 312.

The blessings of 1856 more than counter-balanced the adversities. In the eyes of the public the institution grew more this year than in five other years together. Of course, all those blessings had to be joined to the cross and strengthened in the shadow of the Cross. And after all, there is where we learn useful lessons, and where we find, together with the hope of heaven, the love of those for which the enemy most envies us.

1. New York

To continue what we related of New York in 1855, and to conclude this article, let it suffice to say:

Fr. Sorin's letter had hardly reached Fr. Madéore and been communicated by him to the archbishop of New York when the Very Rev. Father again manifested intentions altogether contrary to those reported by the colony of Sisters from Sainte-Croix. His Reverence maintained that this establishment depended on the Lake, and letters in his own hand came pouring in in this sense. The contents of the third were submitted to the archbishop, who answered through Fr. Madéore that for the future he wanted to have no other intermediary between him and the superior general but the person that should be local superior of the establishment. A contract was drawn up in his name and sent to the Very Rev. Fr. Rector, then in Rome. All but the article in question was accepted, and to that His Reverence added: "Through the Lake as intermediary" (par l'intermédiation du Lac).

Fr. Sorin, being invited by the superioress to go to New York in the hope of coming to an understanding with the archbishop, proceeded thither in the month of May, found His Grace inflexible, wrote a full account of his interview to the Very Rev. Father strongly urging the establishment of a Province in New York, if it was considered desirable to retain the establishment there, and to send the Rev. Fr. Champeau, who would be given charge of the French church, etc. The proposal got no response; but the Very

Rev. Father insisted that the Sisters should rather be recalled to the Lake.

During this time, Fr. Madéore acted as superior, gave
the habit to thirteen postulants, several of whom had not
even been accepted by the chapter. On his side, the rector
reiterated his decisions.

In the month of August, the Mother Superior came
to the Lake, being fully persuaded that the archbishop,
whilst remaining firm, regretted to see the existence of
the establishment seriously threatened, and that he would
probably yield to the least overture. Just at this time the
Rev. Mr. Lafonte[2] wrote a confidential letter, giving assurance that the archbishop had changed. In consequence of
this letter, which was supposed to come indirectly from the
archbishop, a superior was provided. The Rev. Fr. Shortis
goes to New York, sees the misunderstanding, and is silent
about it for three weeks. Finally, it becomes evident that
the archbishop has not changed his mind, and that consequently, the formal orders of the rector must be carried out.

Sr. Mary of St. Angela was at this time in Philadelphia,
occupied in the foundation of a house of the same kind as
that of New York, undertaken, in reality, in the month of
August for the purpose of securing a certain independence
and consequently better terms for New York. This foundation caused a stir, and would at least answer as a refuge
for the Sisters of New York in case they should be obliged
to retire.

Sr. Mary of St. Angela, personally known and esteemed
by the archbishop, receives an obedience as visitor of the
house of New York with instructions to make a last effort
to save it in conformity with the constitutions; otherwise
to close it, and to arrange all things with the archbishop.
The latter alternative became her painful duty.

There were then seventeen Sisters, twenty-one postulants, and fifteen little orphan girls. The dowries of the

2. Rev. Lafond, a member of the Congregation of the Fathers
of Mercy, had founded St. Vincent de Paul parish in New York City.
Catta, *Moreau*, 2:280ff.

novices and the postulants, $2388, and the board-bills paid
in advance, $300, had been absorbed in the furnishing of
the house and the living expenses. One quarter's house
rent was due in some weeks, $425, five hundred dollars
advanced by Mr. Devlin and claimed by him, $155 to the
Empire City for provisions, seventy dollars to Mr. Devlin
on the one hand and thirty-six dollars on the other, one
hundred dollars claimed by the proprietor of the house for
changes and damages. Mr. Devlin consented to take the
furniture, estimated at cost and valued at $808 in payment
of the two sums mentioned above, $950; $150 which was
in the house was used to pay several little debts; Sr. Angela
gave four hundred dollars to defray the travelling expenses
of the personnel who were sent, some to Notre Dame, some
to Philadelphia and the rest to Susquehanna.

Here is a statement of receipts and expenditures:

Furniture of New York:

sent:	to Philadelphia	$ 100.00
	to Susquehanna	20.00
	to St. Mary's	50.00
left in the house		808.75
submitted to Mr. Devlin's estimate . .		60.00
in cash		130.00
in work		100.00
from relatives of the children		50.00

Total $1318.75

Paid travelling expenses of twenty-five persons going to
the Lake, $382; Frs. Granger and Shortis and Mother Su-
perior, $100; ten persons to Philadelphia, $40; four persons
to Susquehanna, $25; Sr. M. of Calvary to New Orleans,
$70; returned to pupils, $60; paid various accounts, $175;
to Mr. Devlin, $513; second quarter of the lease, $425;
different accounts at Mr. Devlin's, $70; Empire City, $155;
returned to postulants, $48 and $200. Brought down, $300
and $2388.31. In all $3632.56 advanced by Notre Dame
du Lac or for which it is responsible.

*Received
$1318.75; Paid
$4951.31*

Such was the end of this establishment in which the Lake, without having at all desired it, but merely in carrying out the orders of Sainte-Croix, was put to the expense of more than eight hundred dollars and made answerable for more than two thousand dollars to the postulants and three hundred dollars to the children who were boarders in the house of New York.

If we now take figures for our basis of examination and not mere probabilities, it will be seen that the house of New York at the time of its closure was not ahead. Its actual condition valued at the cash prices received from the merchants was hardly half of the dowries due the postulants; its treasury did not contain half of the money received for board, and, besides this, $950 was due to Mr. Devlin.

And yet there was no lack of industry and of economy, but the good Sisters were slaves in the hands of a man who, whilst protecting them, was ruining them. God grant that this lesson may serve to make the Congregation understand that strangers should never be admitted into the administration of its affairs.

2. Philadelphia

This house was opened in the beginning of August at the request of Bishop Neumann[3] of this city. Four Sisters were sent at first under the direction of Sr. St. Angela.

Philadelphia is the second city of the United States, and is in many points the rival of New York. The number of Catholics there is quite considerable, and the chances of success for a community are as favorable as any place.

The Sisters of Holy Cross were received by the holy bishop with all that goodness that characterizes him, and the clergy soon appeared to have only one sentiment towards the new religious house, whose object became

3. John N. Neumann, CSSR, was born Mar. 28, 1811, in Prachatitz, Bohemia, Austria. He emigrated to the United States and was ordained a priest in 1836 by Bp. Dubois of New York. He was made bishop of Philadelphia in 1852. See Code, 215.

popular amongst all classes, even of persons without any religion.

After residing for some time with the Sisters of the Good Shepherd, they rented a double house in a street not far from the new cathedral, and there opened a school for boarders and day scholars according to the new plan for industrial schools.[4] This house was soon full: twenty-nine boarders, forty-five day scholars, eleven postulants, twelve novices, and three professed Sisters formed the household towards the end of December, and arrangements were made for the beginning of January to put them in charge of a magnificent school at St. Paul's, one of the largest parishes of the city. Four hundred little girls were to be placed in the hands of four Sisters, and 250 little boys were to be under the charge of two Brothers of St. Joseph.

After their arrival in the large and beautiful city, the Sisters of Holy Cross continued to draw upon themselves the eyes of the public; the interest that had been shown in them from the beginning seemed to grow day by day, and the end of the year found them filled with a reasonable hope of soon being established solidly in a house of their own.

3. Washington City

It was also at the beginning of August that three Sisters of Holy Cross took possession of a new orphan asylum for little boys, which had only twelve for a beginning, in virtue of a contract which secured to each of them sixty dollars per year and the monthly fees of a certain number of day scholars.[5]

4. M. Campion Kuhn, "Philadelphia," in M. Georgia Costin, ed., *Fruits of the Tree*, 2:85, locates the house on Filbert St., between 17th and 18th Streets, and cites a contemporary flier referring to it as the House of the Immaculate Conception.

5. M. Campion Kuhn, "The Sisters Go East—And Stay," CHCHC, 1983, 1–3, identifies the institution as St. Joseph's Male Orphan Asylum, incorporated by act of Congress, Feb. 6, 1855.

The directors seem to be resolved to develop the establishment and are perfectly satisfied with the Sisters of Holy Cross. Next year, they intend to build for a much larger number of orphans. The Sisters of Charity terminate at fifteen [years] an orphanage of 125 little girls for the last twelve years. The directors are very desirous to obtain Brothers, not only for the teaching of their schools, but also to establish workshops.

Washington is eight hours from Philadelphia and three from Baltimore.

4. Susquehanna

This house was founded in the month of October with the surplus members of New York for whom there was scarcely lodging. Twelve little girls and three Sisters were sent there to continue an academy opened some years before by the Very Rev. Mr. O'Reilly, vicar general of Philadelphia. Having heard that the Sisters of Holy Cross were recently established at Philadelphia, he did not cease to make urgent demands for some of them until he had obtained the promise of two or three to take charge of his academy at Susquehanna, about a mile from the college also founded by him and offered unconditionally to the priests of Holy Cross.[6]

Susquehanna is in the northern part of Pennsylvania, in the midst of mountainous country well known for the salubrity of its climate. The place where the college and the

---

It began at the initiative of Rev. Timothy O'Toole, pastor of St. Patrick's Church in Washington, who was carrying on the work of his predecessor, Rev. William Matthews. The asylum's first location was at 13th and H Streets.

6. Rev. John Vincent Reilly was a priest of the diocese of Philadelphia who pastored the Catholics, mostly Irish immigrants, in that part of northeastern Pennsylvania that bordered on New York State. St. Joseph's Academy was opened in October 1856 by the Sisters of Holy Cross. Some accounts mention Rev. Richard Shortis, C.S.C., as having taught at St. Joseph's College in 1856–1858. See ASHC and G. A. Stearns, *The Schools of Susquehanna County, Pennsylvania, 1795–1945* (Montrose, Pa.: Susquehanna Historical Society, 1947), 41–42.

academy are situated is a center for the Catholics who form four parishes, for which priests of Holy Cross are sought. The bishop, especially, is extremely desirous to have this matter settled thus.

The only inconvenience that Fr. Sorin has thus far seen in the affair, besides the lack of priests to send thither, is the distance from all of the great highroads of transportation. The nearest point where the New York railroad touches is twenty miles off.

For the present, the occupation of this academy has been of advantage to the society of the Sisters for the reasons already mentioned, but unless there is an increase of subjects, it is doubtful if the establishment will be retained. Up to the present, the number of pupils has not gone over thirty-five.

Susquehanna is twenty-six hours from Notre Dame and eight hours from New York.

5. Chicago, Illinois

We now come to the most important of all the dependencies of the Province of Indiana. If heaven blesses this work, the house of Chicago will probably share in the destinies of the city in which it is located. Now it is the opinion of the public that Chicago will be one of the first cities of the Union. Its growth is unparalleled. Fifteen years ago, Chicago had only seven thousand inhabitants; today it has more than 100,000.

It was in last September that the Congregation established itself there, Priests, Brothers, and Sisters, in virtue of an agreement with the Ordinary for fifty years.

The principal points of this agreement are, on the one side:

> that for fifty years the Bishop gives to the Congregation of Holy Cross, for two thousand dollars per year, the use of the College of St. Mary of the Lake, with the ground on which it stands, three hundred feet by three hundred, to maintain there a select and very respectable school, with full liberty to add thereto any

other school for Brothers, Sisters, of trades, a Catholic bookstore, etc.;

in addition, all the Catholic schools of the city according as the Congregation could take charge of them or as school houses can be built;

finally, the German Congregation of St. Joseph, pertaining to the college.[7]

On the other side:

that the Congregation of Holy Cross pledges itself to observe these conditions during the time named;

the first years of this establishment cannot but be onerous to the Congregation; but afterwards it is more than probable that these advances will be fully refunded.

Chicago is the center of the West. A house of the society in this city was becoming daily of more importance. Some other religious community would infallibly establish itself there and would cut off from Notre Dame du Lac its principal resource in the West. Now Illinois seems especially destined, considering its proximity and its Catholic population, to become the granary of Notre Dame. There was therefore no recoiling from any sacrifice, no matter how great, to secure such an advantageous position.

Some months after their introduction into that big city, there were in the College of St. Mary of the Lake twenty-two members of the Congregation of Holy Cross, two priests, five Brothers, and fifteen Sisters teaching in the College, thirty-five day scholars, three boys' schools

7. The University of St. Mary of the Lake had been opened in 1846 by William Quarter, the first bishop of Chicago. The Congregation of Holy Cross contracted to operate the institution only as a preparatory school. See Marcellus James Monaco, "The Foundation of the University of St. Mary of the Lake Seminary," (M.A. thesis, St. Mary of the Lake Seminary, Mundelein, Ill., 1941), 17–18. St. Joseph Church was located at Rush St. and Chicago Ave. Organized in 1846, St. Joseph's was the second German parish established in Chicago. See Harry C. Koenig, A History of the Parishes of the Archdiocese of Chicago (Chicago: Catholic Bishop of Chicago, 1980), 506–508.

(580 children), three little girls' schools (340 children), and one industrial school kept by the Sisters. Moreover, the Congregation had charge of a magnificent German parish of about three thousand souls.

Chicago is four hours from Notre Dame by railroad. The Catholic population at the end of 1856 amounted to 35,000. Nearly fifty pupils of the College are from Illinois.

6. Columbus

This city, the capital of Ohio, has at present twenty thousand (inhabitants), three thousand of whom are Catholic. There are so far only two Catholic churches, one for Germans and the other for Irish. The former is very beautiful and very spacious. The number of German Catholics is at least two thousand.

Towards the end of the year 1856, a German Brother was sent there to open a school for little boys. The beginning seems most propitious; seventy-five children attend his school daily, and everything augurs a brilliant success for the coming year.

It is thirty hours from Notre Dame, five hours from Cincinnati.

7. Chimes

Almost four years ago a set of chimes had been ordered from Mr. Bollée of Le Mans, in virtue of a promise made by Rev. Mr. Joseph Biemans,[8] an ecclesiastical novice of the society, to pay all the expenses, provided the cost did not exceed 15,000 francs and that a clock accompanied it. Mr. Bollée having long delayed the manufacture of the chimes, and Mr. Biemans having left the society two years after giving his note for the fifteen thousand francs, it was

8. Ernest Bollée owned a foundry in Le Mans, France. See Wack, 317–320. Joseph Biemans was born Nov. 3, 1831, in Edeghem, Belgium, entered the Congregation of Holy Cross at Notre Dame on July 3, 1852, and professed vows Aug. 15, 1853. After being ordained a deacon, he withdrew from the community on June 6, 1854. M.g.

seriously thought to stop the work, but it was too late. The foundry operator had gone to considerable expense, and it seemed contrary to all principles of justice to leave all his preparations on his hands. The chimes were completed at the expense of the house, and they reached Notre Dame in good shape in September 1856, at a cost of eighteen thousand francs.

The blessing was fixed for 12 November following. Archbishop Purcell of Cincinnati himself performed the ceremony, assisted by Bp. Henni of Milwaukee and attended by a numerous concourse of priests and visitors. The ceremony was as solemn as it could be, and nothing would have been lacking had not a deplorable accident happened on the previous evening during the manifestations of joy caused by the presence of the archbishop.

One of the best students of the College, Mr. P. Hoye, a youth of twenty who was the leader in all the sports of the campus, lost his right arm, whilst too hastily loading the canon, which went off of itself, and which might have caused a still greater misfortune had not Providence kept special watch.

There is no doubt but that the effect of this magnificent carillon, the first of its kind in the United States, is a most favorable one for Notre Dame.

8. Fire

On 17 December, towards two o'clock in the morning, fire broke out in the stable, and in spite of all efforts, the building and all that belonged to it were swept away in several hours. Two horses were reduced to ashes, with a quantity of corn, oats, salt, meat, harness, farm implements, etc. Hardly anything could be saved, and the loss amounted to fifteen thousand francs. There was no insurance. It appears that the fire started in the room next to the horse stable, where candles were made.

The farmers' house, which was only twenty feet from the fire, was saved with difficulty. If the wind had been blowing in the direction of the granary, the loss would have been twice as great, and would have been inevitable.

The flames rose in a terrifying manner to more than fifty feet; the air was afire with sparks which the wind drove towards the College and the church. For nearly an hour a constant cloud of burning materials was passing over the church and the College, a rain of fire falling on the roofs. Fr. Sorin was not present where the first was raging. For nearly an hour he remained at the western tower, expecting every moment to see one or the other of the roofs to take fire, and then there would have been an end of Notre Dame du Lac. The severity of the cold would have left no hope of saving anything.

Doubtless, the Blessed Virgin did not permit that all those labors should be destroyed in a stroke, and Notre Dame du Lac continued to live.

CHAPTER 16

1857

*Growth of
the College*   This year was remarkable by the growth of the College. There were about two hundred entries during the ten months of school, a good number of the students belonging to a higher and more comfortable class. More order and greater respect for rules were seen, discipline was more vigorous, and the confraternities were never more regular. The university, taken as a whole, gained more than in any previous year.

and of St. Mary's   St. Mary's Academy kept pace in this movement, and although its numerical increase was not as great, the progress was equally real compared to previous years. It was only the second year of the institution of the Immaculate Conception. There was a lack of accommodations almost everywhere, and yet there were at least ten entries more than in the best years at Bertrand, more regular classes, and a more numerous and more remarkable distribution of premiums than in any year that had preceded. The mean proportion of students this year was 140 at the College and sixty at the Academy.

*Approbation of
the Congregation
by the Holy See*   But what made this year forever memorable in the annals of the Congregation was the twofold approbation by the Holy See: the first, dated [May 19, 1856] announcing the approbation of the Congregation of Holy Cross; and the second, dated [May 13, 1857[1]] that of the Rules and Constitutions.

---

1. Catta, *Moreau*, 2:197–240.

Thus was raised to the rank of the regular orders of the church a society which had only a few years of existence and for which such an early encouragement became a pledge of other special favors from heaven. Such was the surprise caused both within and without by this unexpected approbation of the Sovereign Pontiff, that many months after its promulgation, there were found unbelievers who denied it. Certain discontented spirits took occasion from this to come back again to the list of their grievances against the society and its venerable founder, thereby to justify their suspicions as to the fact of the approbation. But all were forced to give up by the shame of having made a last effort as fruitless and still more ridiculous than any they had heretofore made in the United States.

The approbation of the Congregation was not kept secret; it appeared in two entire columns of the Boston *Pilot*,[2] with the whole discourse of His Eminence, the Cardinal of Bordeaux, delivered at Sainte-Croix on the occasion of the consecration of the conventual church, and a portion of that of the Rev. Fr. Souillard on the Congregation of Holy Cross.[3]

Another event, which was only a consequence of the former, made this year the most extraordinary witnessed thus far by the children of Holy Cross in the United States. We refer to the visit of the Very Rev. Fr. Moreau, founder of the work, who had for many years been deferring from month to month the keeping of a promise, or rather, of a vow, which he had made to visit soon his establishments in America. The promulgation of the decree of approbation was the determining occasion for him, and on 27 August, His Reverence arrived at Notre Dame, where he was received with all the demonstrations of the most sincere and most enthusiastic joy.

Visit of Very Rev. Fr. Rector

2. A Catholic newspaper.

3. The conventual church of the Congregation of Holy Cross at Ste-Croix was consecrated by Cardinal Donnet, archbishop of Bordeau, on June 17, 1857. Rev. Souillard, a Dominican and a well-known preacher in France, gave an eight-day series of preparatory sermons in the church prior to its consecration. Catta, *Moreau*, 2:233–234.

He had a multitude of things to regulate in the three communities, and according to his itinerary, he could remain for only three weeks in the province. To the day he added two-thirds of the night, and when the time came for him to take his departure for France, it was found that he had done the work of several months. He had organized everything according to the new Constitutions, formed the chapters and the councils of Notre Dame and St. Mary's, presided at the elections of officers in both places, heard everyone in direction, admitted to the novitiate and to profession all that were prepared, and finally arranged the separation in temporals of the Sisters from the other two societies.

His last week was spent chiefly in visiting the houses of Chicago and Philadelphia. On Saturday, 19 September, he embarked on the Arago at New York for France where he arrived in due course, accompanied by Br. Vincent, the patriarch of the community of Josephites.

Financial crisis   Hardly had His Reverence left the coasts of America when there came that financial crisis which in a few months changed the face of commerce and business throughout the whole Union. Banks closed, not one by one, nor by dozens, but in whole states. The most solid houses declared bankruptcy, day after day, with millions of dollars of liabilities.

The crisis came so suddenly that no one had time to prepare for it. Notre Dame was less prepared than anyone else in the country. The society had, it is true, real estate more than sufficient to cover its indebtedness without touching on the grounds or the buildings of the university or the academy; but at that time there was hardly any sale except at a sacrifice of half the actual value of property.

There was a mortgage of thirty thousand francs on the College lands, a relic of the knavery of Mr. Biemans, which could be foreclosed any day. In fact, not only could the sum be demanded, but it actually was demanded as a result of the total ruin of the Messrs. Harper, who had accepted it in 1852. The property of St. Mary's was in like manner burdened by a mortgage of 25,000 francs, payable at five thousand a year.

Providence allowed the two sums to fall due at a time when there was nothing in the treasury to meet either one. Never had confidence in Divine Providence and in the protection of Our Lady of the Lake been more necessary. Nothing short of a miracle could prevent complete ruin. In ordinary times, the sum total of the debts would have been enough to alarm any administration acquainted with the business of the country; but in a panic like this, in which all branches of commerce in the United States had been plunged, human prudence was obviously insufficient.

Dangers for the institution

The opinion of one of the clearest heads of the Council of Administration favored a declaration of the institution's insolvency for four or five years; but the impression that such a measure must make on the ecclesiastical authorities, although it was perhaps the only means to save the Work from immediate ruin, caused it to be rejected, and there was no more question of it.

It is not without its advantages thus to pass sometimes through trials which, in a Christian point of view, recall communities as well as individuals to the center of all legitimate hopes and confidence. Then we feel the vanity of this world's riches, and the blindness of those that base their calculations on this foundation of moving sand.

In one of those critical moments in which we see only a large debt to be paid, and no human hope of being able to prevent a sale under the hammer of the property on which the creditors had a claim, Divine Providence calls into existence one of those circumstances in which Providence alone can deal with, and puts in the hands of the superiors the funds necessary to emerge from this first embarrassment. Although there still remains nine-tenths of the load, one feels in the depths of his heart a conviction that supports him in spite of all human fears; that is to say, that not only will Notre Dame weather this storm, but she will come forth from it more religious, more devoted to her sacred obligations and more solidly grounded on the basis of holy poverty, to continue fearlessly the edifice begun in the United States.

The crisis considered as a benefit

The crash of colossal ruins that was daily heard in the financial world around us, the shock we all felt during several months, made each one of us see how necessary it was to be deeply rooted in the earth, with the knife of economy and the lever of the spirit of poverty. Everyone could see that we were poised on the surface and seriously in danger from the approach of a storm which none had foreseen. Blessed forever, therefore, is the hand that chastises us to teach us, and that leads us to the gates of the tomb and leads us back to make us wiser.

The effects of the financial crisis were felt in all the houses of the work in the United States; but nowhere more severely than in Philadelphia and Chicago.

Straits of the house of Philadelphia

The house that had been purchased for the Sisters in West Philadelphia suited well in many respects,[4] but in contracting for a property of sixteen thousand dollars without even one penny to meet this expense, there had been no thought of a crisis which was to be more severe in Philadelphia than in any other city of the Union. The first payment of two thousand dollars was made, nevertheless, but there seems to be no other resource for the balance except the treasury of Providence.

As to the house of Chicago, far from being able to pay the third installment ($1000), it was necessary to try to escape from a contract which the bishop of that city made impossible to keep, refusing to abide by his own promises, on the faith of which it had been made. The school houses of the Brothers and of the Sisters were left in such a miserable state that there was no means of doing good. The promised collections and fairs had been restricted during the first year. The Jesuit Fathers had come to Chicago with the intention of building a church and a college, thus unintentionally destroying one of the principal objectives of the Congregation of Holy Cross when it settled in that city.

4. This house, purchased in February 1857, had three stories and was situated between Robin St., 39th St. (then called William St.), and Pine St. Kuhn, "Philadelphia," 86–87.

In all the great difficulties in which the work of Holy Cross at Notre Dame was involved since it came to the United States, Divine Providence always came to its aid in a manner so evident that it was impossible not to recognize its intervention. It is true that in all those critical moments the house was always earnest in seeking help where faith never fails to find it, and thus each trial made the community more confident and more religious than it had found it.

God holds the hearts of men in his hand and turns them as he pleases. The Congregation had a very striking proof of this in those days of panic. One of the neighbors, a rich German Catholic farmer, had at different times, by sales or deposits of money, obtained notes from Fr. Sorin amounting to sixty thousand francs. In the month of July and several times subsequently, he had declared positively that he wanted his money about the beginning of autumn. As he had no mortgage, and no security but the honesty of the house, the financial crisis naturally made him more uneasy and harder to be persuaded to consent to any delay. In the first days of November, he came to inquire if his money was ready for him, and he expressed himself rather forcibly on the subject.

Singular favor in the conduct of a creditor of Notre Dame. He refused payment of a debt of $12,000 just when he said that he would rigorously exact it

On 19 November, Fr. Sorin sent one of the principal Brothers to inform him that he had begun to the best of his ability to pay the debt, that he had deposited five thousand francs in the Bank of South Bend, and that he hoped to soon deposit twenty thousand francs and to give him the balance in notes, secured by mortgage, thus settling the matter.

What was the answer of the good man? That he did not want to be paid anything at all at the time; that he had no need of his money which he would have to put out at interest elsewhere or to deposit in a bank; that he had no confidence in any bank and that he would prefer to leave his money at Notre Dame rather than anywhere else, until he should need it.

This was not indeed making a present of the amount, but at a time when banks were failing by the dozen, because their frightened depositors made a run on them to claim their money, it was a real favor and a sign of great confidence for a naturally suspicious German to decline to accept his money when offered him, although he had only a signature without a mortgage on any property. This is not the ordinary way in which men act; but when God directs them for a special purpose, they do without knowing it what he wants them to do.

CHAPTER 17

1858

Never since the beginning of its existence in the New World had the Congregation entered upon a new year under more unfavorable auspices, nor yet with a more unbounded confidence in that Providence which had been thus far so merciful and so attentive. The financial crisis was not over, but the protection that had been vouchsafed during three months against the violence of a veritable hurricane gave hope of a similar protection until calm returned. Prayers, communions, thousands of Ave Marias, continued to be offered to heaven, and the constant joy that was depicted on each countenance showed that there was not even a shadow of fear.

Towards the end of 1857, the Rev. Fr. Léveque,[1] who had just made his profession, had been sent to France to canvass for subjects for the mission and for the Congregation in general. The idea pleased the venerable founder, who received the envoy from America with kindness and joy and recommended him to several bishops of Brittany, where in some weeks he succeeded in enlisting twenty-six young seminarians under the banner of Our Lady of Holy Cross. He was afterwards to visit Belgium and Germany.

Rev. Léveque sent to Europe to look for subjects

1. Zéphyrin Léveque was born Jan. 10, 1806, at La Riviere Ouelle, Kamouraska County, Quebec, Canada, entered the Congregation of Holy Cross at Notre Dame on Oct. 24, 1856, and professed vows Dec. 25, 1857. M.G.

Emigration of the Novitiate

Meanwhile, Providence was bringing to the novitiate of the Congregation so many subjects that there was not room for them. In the month of April every place was crowded, and it became necessary to find more spacious quarters. The novitiate of the Brothers had become not only too small, but also too unsafe to long continue with the crowd that was packed into it.

Immediately after Easter, it became necessary to re-move the larger portion of the little army, headed by their brave captain, to the western part of the Brothers' house, north of the College, until there should be on hand the means to build a new novitiate. However, it was resolved that about fifteen novices should continue to occupy their beds under the old roof, that they might watch over the precious treasures of St. Joseph's Island, and that more room might be left in the general quarters, which were also crowded.

New bishop of Fort Wayne; his visit to Notre Dame

Towards the beginning of this year, the diocese of Vin-cennes was at last divided, and Notre Dame became a part of the new diocese of Fort Wayne. The first bishop, J. H. Luers,[2] a German by birth, made his first visit to Notre Dame du Lac on the patronal feast of the Brothers, St. Joseph's Day. He ordained one and received one profes-sion. He spent nearly a week in the two houses, and went home, it was said, well pleased and edified.

New trials

The favorable impressions which the new and worthy bishop of Fort Wayne had carried away with him from Notre Dame were not of long duration, if we may credit a confidential letter written from Fort Wayne towards the end of the month of May.

2. John Henry Luers was born Sept. 29, 1819 at Lutten, West-phalia, near Münster, and had come to America with his parents when he was fourteen. Ordained for the diocese of Cincinnati in 1846, he had worked in the German parishes of that city, where he had come to know the Brothers of Holy Cross. See Code, 171; Alerding, *Fort Wayne*, 30–33; James Connelly, "Bishop Luers and the Autonomy of the Sisters of the Holy Cross," *Fruits of the Tree*, 2:12–33.

According to this letter, the sentiments of the young and pious prelate were the very contrary of what had been expected, that is to say that he was now well known as an enemy of all communities in general and of that of Notre Dame du Lac in particular. Two principal motives were stated as the cause of this unexpected change, namely, some complaints of the bishop of Vincennes at the provincial council which had just been held at Cincinnati,[3] and the declared hostility of an unfortunate priest, an ex-Jesuit of unsavory reputation, who, though everything was against him, had managed to have himself restored to the exercise of the sacred ministry by the good bishop of Fort Wayne. This man was said to be the sworn enemy of Notre Dame, though no cause was known for his malice.

Fr. Sorin, although he had received a gracious invitation from Archbishop Purcell to attend the council, was not able to be absent at the appointed time for several reasons, one of which took precedence over all the others. We were at the height of the financial crisis; Notre Dame had been caught unprepared for it, and although there was property enough last fall to pay off all debts, this property was daily less sufficient to meet the needs of the times, since it was impossible to make any sale.

The creditors in general were growing timid and were easily alarmed. The debts of the community were no secret to anyone; enemies profited by this to spread the rumor that the house would soon fall like so many others. Those that held mortgages against the College property, hearing it rumored that Fr. Sorin's titles were defective, were seized with panic and rushed to examine the records. Then it was found, not that Fr. Sorin had willfully deceived anyone, but that himself being deceived, all his creditors were involved with him in the same deception.

3. The second council of the ecclesiastical province of Cincinnati, held in that city in May 1858. See John Gilmary Shea, *History of the Catholic Church in the United States* (New York: D. H. McBride and Co., 1892), 4:546–547.

Two links were missing in the chain of titles, which Bp. de la Hailandiere had never had registered, and in the very title deed of Notre Dame given to Fr. Sorin by Bp. Bazin of happy memory, the word "west" had been repeated instead of "east." The effect was to twice confirm the possession of seventy-five acres of land of little value, and to leave Fr. Sorin without a title to the location on which buildings had now stood for fifteen years. The error was palpable. The lawyer who made the mistake, saw it at once, and advised that its correction be demanded of Bp. de St. Palais. That the matter was pressing and admitted of no delay was quite evident. Providence allowed that it should be otherwise.

The bishop of Vincennes hesitated, deferred the matter from week to week, and finally gave the new bishop of Fort Wayne a general title to whatever property he possessed in Northern Indiana, leaving Fr. Sorin without a title to the seventy-five acres in question. The South Bend lawyers saw in this something that it would not be becoming here to attribute to a bishop.

It became necessary to write to the new bishop who, on his visit in March, gave a deed to correct the famous error; but that this new document might be of any account, it was requisite that the deed from the bishop of Vincennes to the bishop of Fort Wayne should itself be recorded to prove that he was the rightful owner. The good bishop was humbly entreated twice to have the kindness to send his general title. Finally, on the week when he was starting for the council, he had his Vicar General write that he would not send it before his return from Cincinnati. The affair now looked mysterious to the administration of Notre Dame; it is now abandoned to Providence.

The immediate consequence of this failure of Fr. Sorin to prove his titles was to increase public distrust. On the week when he was to set out for the council, the South Bend court was in session. The house had to defend a suit growing chiefly out of this unfortunate matter of defective titles, and Fr. Sorin was politely informed that if, in the present state of affairs, he left or attempted to leave the State of Indiana, he would be arrested at the station. The idea of going to the council had therefore to be abandoned.

Perhaps it would have been better to give the archbishop a statement of affairs just as they stood, but this would have been a complaint; Fr. Sorin preferred to give as his excuse that he had engagements which prevented him from assisting at the council.

Here, as on many other occasions, Fr. Sorin made a mistake. His absence from the council was severely blamed, and the good bishop of Vincennes, who was the sole cause, was unsparing in his complaints. If the letter already mentioned is truthful, he brought charges which the sentiment of justice calls upon us to set down here, together with some facts in reply.

1. The only thing for which we had come, and the only important thing, the Brothers and their schools, had been neglected. 2. Immense sums had been collected from the railroad and had been sunk in establishing ourselves at Notre Dame, whilst nothing had been done for the missions. 3. All our resources and attention had been turned to the building of a college, whose utility was questionable, and to the multiplication of Sisters, who could be gotten everywhere, whilst nothing was done for the Brothers. 4. Fr. Sorin had commanded all his priests to take up collections for the orphans of Vincennes at Christmas, and had kept the money.

It was only natural that a bishop should be believed by all his colleagues, especially in matters which he ought to know well. The letter added that Bp. Luers, personally, had admitted all these facts, and that after the council the unfortunate priest who had already been referred to, did not fail to make things appears even worse.

To say that all these accusations were laid before Fr. Sorin, and that he did not feel moved, would be simply a falsehood. As a proof he was assured, in closing, that the bishop was going to take all his missions from him and to confine him strictly to the limits of the Notre Dame property and that without any pity whatsoever.

Fortunately, the month of Mary was not yet at an end; there still remained some hours before its close. It was one of the fruits of Calvary which the Blessed Virgin, in return for the canticles and the thirty-one joyful little feasts in her honor, presented for us to taste before we withdrew from her beloved knees.

Such a message was evidently a serious matter, and although the truth might be clear as day to those who know the facts themselves, it would be difficult to make it equally clear to prejudiced eyes. All was left in the hands of the divine Mother, and not a line was sent in response or justification for a whole week. Let us try here to establish the facts.

1. Is it true that we neglected the institute of the Brothers? Two simple facts will answer: 1. There are just now 107 members in their community here; 2. in twelve establishments they teach 2400 children. (In these figures we do not include their first foundation in Louisiana, which has just been made into a separate province, and which would considerably increase the above figures.) We know several communities of the same kind in the United States for which we feel great esteem, but we do not know that any of them has better succeeded in those two respects. (We do not here speak of the Brothers of the Christians Schools, who belong to Canada, and who from the beginning found resources there which are not at our command.)

Would it not be somewhat more just to acknowledge that until now, the clergy have generally taken but little interest in the matter of vocations, and just as little in the means of making them useful after they have been secured? We remember that the good bishop of Vincennes himself would have only one Brother, and could provide him with no other refectory but his kitchen amongst the servant girls; and as for the school, it was a miserable little cabin in which it was a mockery to attempt to keep a school. And yet such were the conditions in which this dear Brother was left until a certain feeling of pity caused his superior to recall him, regardless of consequences. It is hardly necessary to add that this was the end of our schools in the diocese. Sympathy was to be sought for elsewhere.

The Brothers' institute was in itself an enterprise full of difficulties and very doubtful in a country where there are nothing but obstacles in the way of a young man possessed of the necessary talents to perform his duty and to come up to what is expected of him. Bp. Hughes himself, being consulted on this subject by Fr. Sorin fifteen years ago, did not believe in the possibility of success. One of the reasons given by him was this: if you have subjects possessed of ability, they will want to become priests. All the difficulties pointed out by the illustrious bishop of New York have been met with in turn, and often all together.

Real vocations are rare and, so far from being encouraged, they are rather held in check, either because of the indifference of a great number of directors, or from their desire to keep in their own house or in their neighborhood the few young men of edifying lives that are to be found in the world.

When they have entered the novitiate, where they can no longer enjoy the liberty and the comforts of the people of the world in this country, they are ever haunted by the thought of the pleasures which they could enjoy and of the money which they could so easily earn.

If they persevere for some time and are sent out on the missions, dangers multiply and helps disappear; most frequently they are not provided with the half of what is necessary for the success of a school. Here it is a poor cabin with nothing whatsoever attractive about it; elsewhere, it is a damp and unhealthy basement; again it is desks or benches, maps or books, etc. that are wanting, and which are delayed whole months, until the patience of the teachers and of their students is exhausted.

If the Brothers live with the pastors, they are generally well treated, but they sometimes learn more than is good for them. If they have their own dwelling, they are often left too much to themselves and soon become disgusted with everything.

The Brothers' institute undertaken alone would probably have been a complete failure. It would not have been able to support itself, and would not have developed. Far from losing any of its chances of success, therefore, from

its union with the other branches which were added to it
here, as well as in France, it has therein a new element
of life for itself. It is in this union of the three branches
that we find the cause of the development of each, every member being equally interested in the welfare of the
three societies.

If the number of foundations is not greater, what we
have just written ought rather to show the protection from
on high over what has been done and the better founded
hopes of doing still more before long, since in only two
years the society of the Brothers has almost doubled itself,
and the novitiate is now better filled than it ever was.

The first thing to be thought of was to live, that is
to say, to create for the institute the means of subsistence
for the subjects and for the novitiate. Up to the present
time, the schools have made a very poor showing in the
column of the revenues of the community. It was found
necessary to fix the attention of a number of the Brothers
on things more certain in order to avoid expenses. Thus, it
was necessary to make farmers of the good Brothers, then
tailors, shoemakers, carpenters, blacksmiths, bakers, coop-
ers, gardeners. And when a college was started, wherein
all these branches of industry could be utilized, another
colony of Brothers had to be organized to do the work of
the college.

Meanwhile, the business of teaching was never lost
sight of. Whenever a candidate presented himself with the
intention and with the requisite talents for study, he was
put to study.

Once more we say, a work of this kind was very ticklish.
Time was required to lay the foundations before thinking
of building the edifice. This work is now founded, and if
heaven continues to bless it, it is ready for development.
God be blessed for the contradictions it has met with!

2. As to the immense sums collected on the railroad,
etc., there is reason to be surprised that this assertion was
seriously made, let alone complained of. Here again, figures
will answer for us. Fr. Sorin himself has taken the trouble
to make an abstract, page by page, of each dollar and cent

handed in by the missioners of the institute during fifteen years. This work has required time, but he feels no regret at having thus employed it, since it has thus furnished him with the sure means of putting in full light a truth which has become important—and of disabusing those that seek only the truth.

Let it be permitted us to remark here, that upon his arrival in South Bend in November 1842, in the thirteen counties entrusted to him by the bishops of Vincennes and Detroit, Fr. Sorin found only a handful of poor Catholics, scattered here and there over a tract of more than one hundred miles in diameter and containing scarcely 150 families in all, most of whom had been left entirely without spiritual aid for three years and more. For three years there had been no priest living at South Bend, the nearest being one in Chicago, who visited some places from time to time.

Add to this number about as many poor Catholic Indians scattered over the same territory, and you will have an idea of the mission of Notre Dame. Then it excited only pity; no one was envious of it. It was poor in all ways, with a poverty to make the heart bleed. There was a flock of three hundred families, dispersed, led astray, dissolute, destitute of almost every Catholic sentiment.

Fortunately, Fr. Sorin was yet fresh from his beloved France, rich in zeal and devotedness, and with a boundless confidence in the protection of the Queen of Heaven. His most ardent desires were gratified; he was at last a missioner, as he had so earnestly longed to be; and what is still more, half of his mission was composed of savages, and the other half of Catholics who could almost all be placed in the same category. He set to work with all his heart, and day and night all was consecrated to his beloved mission.

There was not a single church or chapel finished, except amongst the Indians at Pokagon, where the Rev. Mr. Deseille had succeeded, ten years before, in building a log chapel. Bertrand also possessed a little chapel, which was not finished, and in Michigan City was a store to be transformed into a church.

Nothing was therefore done, and, what is worse, there was nothing to be done for the present, considering the small number of Catholics at each settlement, and the scarcity of money. The only thing to do was to visit, as often as possible, those poor excuses of Catholicity, to gather them together in some private houses, and to save them, at least, from the misfortune of a sad shipwreck of the faith.

It need hardly be stated that the care of such a mission took up all the attention of the poor missioner of South Bend for the first year. He was almost always travelling, either on his regular rounds or to visit the sick and the dying.

He knew very well that his community was suffering from this divided attention, or rather that attention to the community had to be indefinitely postponed until he should receive some assistance; for, since neither the bishop of Vincennes nor the bishop of Detroit could do better for those poor missions and they had charged him with them, it was his first duty to watch over them.

Fr. Sorin had no sooner made himself acquainted with his field of labor than he wrote to every place in France whence he could expect help from men of prayer or of wealth. His endeavors were not fruitless. Amongst the rest, they secured for him a new missioner, one of his former fellow students, a most cherished friend, the Rev. Fr. Cointet, of such happy memory in all this vast district. He worked like an apostle for eleven years in the mission, which he watered with his sweat whilst edifying it by his great virtues and instructing it by his knowledge.

Three other missioners from France soon followed him, then a fourth, and they all went to work with love and devotedness in the vast field which the Father of the family had confided to the young Society of Holy Cross until they should themselves have formed new subjects on the spot who would afterwards enter into their labors and gather the fruits.

God saw the needs of this mission, and in his own time he provided the men and the means necessary. Fr. Sorin and his first associates had a great many acquaintances in

France, amongst the class of pious and charitable souls. They often received considerable alms from them. Frequently, also, the Propagation of the Faith came to their aid. Whatever they could obtain and add from their own patrimony also went to the foundation of the work.

Let it be remembered that this foundation of Notre Dame was carried on without the least local assistance, that the country where the foundation was laid was deeply imbued with prejudices and low bigotry, that the very name, "Catholic," was a proverb of reproach, that the very spot given by the bishop of Vincennes for this purpose was nothing but a forest of 524 acres, ten of which were cleared and worn out; that the Jesuits had refused to accept it, and that no one would have then been willing to pay the sum at which the property was appraised, namely, three thousand dollars.

Every cent had, therefore, to come first from outside; the labors of the members of the institute did the rest. Providence blessed their common devotedness beyond all their hopes. Fifteen years afterwards they had churches at Notre Dame, Bertrand, Niles, Kalamazoo, Mishawaka, Michigan City, Laporte, St. John, Calumet, South Bend, and Valparaiso.

They had, besides, prepared for holy orders fourteen priests whose names are as follows:

The Reverend Fathers

F. Gouesse	Thos. Flynn	N. Gillespie
R. Shortis	Ed. Kilroy	L. Letourneau
Ch. Schilling	A. Brisard	P. Gillen
M. Rooney	J. Curley	A. Mayer
R. Wallace	J. Force	

Eight of these are still here, engaged in the exercise of the holy ministry, except one whom God is visiting at present with a terrible malady and whom we have been waiting upon day and night for a month. He has lost his mind. Three others have left the society for family reasons, one died here, a victim of his zeal for the mission. Of the fourteen, no one, so far as we know, has been suspended, and twelve have been, ever since their ordination, esteemed and honored and doing good.

But it is time to come at last to the famous list of the resources of the house. Here it is, year by year, from the beginning. It includes absolutely everything that was received as stipends for masses, fees for marriages, for baptisms, in pew rent, collections, offerings, etc.

In 1843	for one missioner	$ 112.08
1844	for two missioners	213.59
1845	three	121.37
1846	three	142.13
1847	four	286.54
1848	six	1,034.18
1849	five	650.89
1850	four	609.48
1851	five	989.93
1852	five	744.50
1853	six	908.24
1854	five	726.17
1855	four	901.00
1856	four	735.70
1857	four	569.82

This would give an average of $143 per year for each priest, that is to say, a sum on which no bishop in the United States would ask his missioners to live. And yet this is all that went into the treasury of Notre Dame and that was brought in by this long and hard labor of fifteen years. That is to say, the combined efforts of five and six missioners in their best years did not gather what a single priest can reap in twenty places in this country without ever going outside of his parish.

This, we think, is answer enough to the second accusation. The third accusation is a double one. The College and the Sisters have taken up too much of our time, it is said.

If by this is meant that besides the institute of the Brothers, for which we had been principally wanted, we also did what was not asked of us, namely, put up a college and established Sisters, we grant it; but we cannot see that in this we were wrong, not even when we take the good of the Brothers into consideration; for we have already proven that they gained by the establishment of the other two branches, which took an equal interest in them as in their own members, and which have, in fact, procured for them their best vocations.

The question here is certainly not one of strict justice, since it is well known that we came to the United States at our own cost, and that the diocese never made us any other advance than a piece of land already offered to two communities. Therefore, since we were working at our own risk, a certain latitude should be allowed us for our activity, and this Bp. De la Hailandiere himself accorded us. The charter of the University bears his seal, and the Sisters likewise received his approbation and even presents from him.

We are aware that some bishops in the United States are not in favor of colleges; but everybody also knows that the majority show by their acts that they are of a different opinion. If, today, a bishop who knows us but imperfectly questions the utility of our college, we have reason to rejoice, since the same bishop, nine years ago, expressed his regret that it was not burned down instead of the workshops, which had just been reduced to ashes by a fire. We are no less thankful to the good Lord who has built this College, as stands written on the front, *Dominus aedificavit domum*, and no less convinced that it is for us a means of doing good, and especially of smoothing the way for our successors. And if there is no reason to boast, neither is there cause to despair of a house which is growing year by year, and which this very year has about 150 boarders and enjoys the confidence of the public.

Even were it true that Sisters can be easily found everywhere, it would not follow that ours are superfluous nor that our sacrifices to establish them were a mistake. We are, on the contrary, happy to see them established and doing good in their sphere of action. We could not regret our sacrifices of time and money unless they had interfered with the success of the Brothers or with anything of more importance. Now this did not occur, and if at this day, after fifteen years of painful labors, there is anything to console us, it is to see that Providence has given us the means to keep the three Societies which had been confided to us under obedience marching side by side. And if the crisis which torments the country leaves us on our feet, we will see in this a new proof that, even when all human aid is lacking, the arm of the Almighty protects us, and more lovingly than ever we will say: *In te Domine speravi; non confundar in aeternum.*

The institute of the Sisters of Holy Cross is not known. It is quite recent; have but the patience for a little and you will see, at least we hope so, that it is not a work of supererogation, but quite to the contrary, a work raised up precisely to meet some of the most pressing wants of existing society, strongly organized by the immediate direction of Rome, at present occupying all the attention of the venerable founder of Holy Cross, until he shall have exactly seized and reproduced in their Constitution and their relations with the other two societies, the views and desires of the tribunal which is to approve them. For our part, and we think ourselves well informed, we believe in their future and we bless God beforehand, even amidst the embarrassments which they cause us.

The fourth accusation, "that Fr. Sorin had kept the money collected for the asylum at Vincennes," needs no other answer than the exhibition of the receipt for this same money, written entirely in the very hand of the good bishop, who must have forgotten. Here it is in full:

"Vincennes, 22 March 1858
Bro. Lawrence, Steward
Dear Brother:
The money for the orphans arrived here yesterday by express. Accept my sincere thanks and believe me always,
Your very devoted
†Maurice, Bp. of Vincennes."

The letter in question also mentions another complaint, namely that Fr. Sorin had his subjects ordained by visiting bishops, and that at one of those ordinations he left the bishop of the diocese two months without informing him.

Having no remembrance of this delay of two months, Fr. Sorin can only humble himself for it and say, that it could only happen through forgetfulness on his part. If, however, the good bishop did not bestow holy orders on all that were ordained at Notre Dame, it is because he authorized this proceeding, as appears by a permission signed by himself on November 14, 1849, and worded thus:

"We humbly beg of the Bishop of Vincennes the following permissions:

"1. To have our own subjects ordained by another bishop during his absence from the diocese, or when it would be difficult to send them to Vincennes;

"2. To invite any bishop that may honor us with a visit to officiate pontifically, and even to administer confirmation and receive a profession.

"Signed: Maurice, Bp. of Vincennes."

Moreover, having received from the same worthy bishop the faculties of vicar general for all his mission, and amongst others, that of giving jurisdiction to every priest ordained at Notre Dame for the society, it does not appear that there was matter for a serious reprimand as for a grave fault.

In terminating this review of the first fifteen years of Notre Dame du Lac, let it be permitted us to add here that in this country the community has hardly found real and permanent sympathy except from the illustrious Archbishop Purcell. It was doubtless the will of heaven that one part of its trials should consist in this painful disappointment; but the more it felt the lack of this direct encouragement from those from whom it felt that it had the right to expect it, so much the more appreciative did it feel for the kindness and protection of the glorious archbishop, which was a sufficient compensation for all the rest.

These pages will remain for our successors, and it would
not be just for them to be left in ignorance of the apprecia-
tions of their predecessors in regard to the men and things
that concerned them. Probably everyone, according to his
own views and the designs of God, has served, although in
different ways, in strengthening and developing the Work.

On all without exception we invoke blessings from
above, and we earnestly beseech the Divine Majesty to
grant us time and means to prove to all that in sacrificing
our existence to the foundation of a work which we thought
worthy of the sacrifice, we had no other view but the good
of the Church, without any personal considerations, since
each one of those that is working for it today may be far
away tomorrow. In the thought and words of the most
eloquent prelate that has visited the institution, we had to
consent to bury ourselves in its foundations. If the edifice
stands, we will never regret the price and the sweat that it
has cost us.

CHAPTER 18

1859

The year 1858 had ended peaceably. The existence of the house was hardly any more secure than at the same time the previous year, but the confidence of each of the members had increased by a year of daily and providential assistance. The amount of the debts had been lessened, but that of the assets had taken the same direction. The balance of accounts showed that, in spite of the economy that was practiced in everything, the institution was hardly self-supporting. Yet all extraordinary outlays had been avoided, and even things which in ordinary times would be considered necessities were dispensed with, and in many points the community was destitute, even in the matter of clothing. *State of the house at the end of 1858*

The College did not appear to suffer from the hard times, the number of pupils remaining about the same as the preceding year, and the payments being made with about the same regularity. The novitiates were in better condition, and there was better order than ever in them. *The College* *Community*

The state of the foundations had somewhat changed. Milwaukee was suspended for an indefinite period, in accord with Bp. Henni, for want of a suitable place. Hamilton had just closed in the last days of 1858. Br. Dominic, who had kept a German school there for two years and a half, had fallen sick, and the physician declared that a change of occupation was necessary for his recovery; whereupon the good Brother decided it was best for him to make an *Foundations* end of everything in one stroke. Without asking the advice of anyone, he left his post and his vocation. In vain did his superiors and his brothers try to bring him to more religious sentiments; he persisted in his infidelity, and the matter was referred to the superior general.

On the other hand, two new schools were opened, in Fort Wayne and in Toledo, where the community had already been established since 1844 and 1854. Columbus had added an English school to its German foundation. The state of the foundations was at least equal in prosperity to 1857-58.

Poor harvest

The beginning of this winter was not severe. This was a blessing for many, and especially for Notre Dame du Lac. The harvest had been a failure in almost all crops. Wheat was not two-thirds of what it is in an ordinary year; Indian corn still less, and potatoes did worse. Fruits had been a complete failure. This deficit (nearly two thousand dollars) added considerably to the embarrassment of the administration. At the beginning of December wheat gave out, and from twelve to fifteen bushels a day were needed, at a dollar and a quarter a bushel.

Repayment of $10,000 demanded

To add to the difficulties, a certain gentleman, who in 1856 had lent the community for two years the sum of ten thousand dollars at ten percent, indicated that he wanted his money. Where was such an amount to be found in the depth of winter? The administration began to look for money on all sides; but the more it looked, the more did the conviction impress itself on the seekers that there was no money in the country.

Extraordinary prayers

Extraordinary prayers were prescribed. Everybody tried to interest heaven in the affairs of Notre Dame, and awaited with confidence the result of this long crisis.

Solemnities

To divert the somber thoughts of the future, indulged in by certain timorous people who had too much of the prudence of the world, more attention than ever was devoted to religious solemnities. Christmas, New Year's Day, and the Epiphany were celebrated at Notre Dame with all the magnificence possible. On the latter festival there was a grand representation of the mystery of the day. More than

fifteen hundred candles reminded the spectators of the star
and of the coming of the Gentiles to the uncreated Light.

Yet, three days afterwards there was an uprising, or   *Mutiny*
rather a mutiny, of about forty young men of the College,
such as had never before been witnessed at Notre Dame.
And had not the spirit of religion, which had its weight
with the greater number, been brought to bear, nothing
more would have been required to ruin the prospects of
the whole scholastic year. And all this came from a want
of tact and from an overzealousness in the punishment
of certain faults whose gravity had not been sufficiently
explained and which it is hard to make non-Catholic students understand. We speak of particular friendships. Two
boarders were dismissed on the spot, and the departure
of several others was resolved upon, although deferred for
prudential reasons.

This year, the Christmas vacation which some of the
pupils were accustomed to take disturbed the order of
classes and the discipline more than usual, and it was
resolved not to permit this in the future.

February

The statistics and the budget were delayed on account   *Statistics and*
of the sickness, which lasted more than a month and a half,   *budget*
of Br. Vincent, who had charge of this great and important
work. Regular statistics had been sent for a number of
years to the Mother House, but a budget had never been
asked for. The work was finished and signed in Chapter on
3 February. The amount of expenses calculated for 1859
could not be reduced, notwithstanding the general desire
of all the members to pay off the debt of the establishment;
it was necessary to petition His Reverence to authorize an
expense of $64,000.

This matter of the budget was long but very useful,   *The result*
because it gave the administration new light. All possible economy had been practiced everywhere, but details
were not so well known. When signing this budget, every
member felt that he had acquired a certainty which he did

not before possess. Each felt more thoroughly the need of renewed attention, of new devotedness, of new efforts to draw down the blessings from on high.

Mortgage of $10,000 to pay

The amount of the floating debt was slightly diminished since the visit of His Reverence in September 1857, but it was still very high. For the present, there were hardly means to meet the daily expenses. And yet it was necessary by the nineteenth of this month to find ten thousand dollars, that is, fifty thousand francs, or to lose twenty-five thousand dollars. Great indeed was the embarrassment. An attempt was made in various directions to borrow this sum, but without result. Still, there was at the bottom of each one's soul a conviction that the same providential hand which had to often drawn the Lake out of its difficulties would not fail it in this critical case.

The very day on which the budget was signed and a crushing debt was again verified, a letter was received from Paris announcing a subsidy of ten thousand instead of seven thousand francs from the Propagation of the Faith. Next day, a gentleman brought two little boys to the College and placed in Fr. Sorin's hands a mortgage of two thousand dollars as security for the payment of the education of his children, not being able to pay immediately in cash. Now under the circumstances, this mortgage was almost equal to its face value in gold for the establishment. It was at least a beginning of hope that Divine Providence would again save the house in this new crisis.

Besides, it was the opening of a new session, and nearly two thousand dollars were due. The number of pupils remained the same. Not only was the existence of the establishment the object of the special attention of Divine Providence, but also that of each member of the institution.

Fr. Sorin runs the risk of being poisoned

The day immediately following the signature of the documents just mentioned, Fr. Sorin barely escaped being carried off at a time and in a way that would be least expected. The Brother infirmarian, who had been accustomed for some time to bring him a dose of bitters before dinner, made a mistake one morning and presented him with a large dose of the preparation known as Pain-Killer.

He would unfailingly have soon been a corpse if he had taken the dose.

Contrary to his usual practice, he asked the good Brother what the dose was and examined it before even raising it to his lips. The dear little Brother in vain urged him to take it. The glass remained on the table until he had reported in the infirmary the refusal of the Fr. Superior; and having thereupon examined his flasks and discovered his mistake, the dear good Brother returned breathless, and cried out when he saw the glass on the table, "Oh! How glad I am that you did not take those bitters!" The Blessed Virgin has doubtless watched over that life which may still be useful to her work of the Lake. It was an additional proof of the uncertainty of life and of the necessity for a religious as well as for any other Christian to be always prepared.

The first quarter of this year was an almost unbroken *Trials* series of trials of all kinds: their number and gravity for a long time prevented the author of them from being suspected.

The demon had asked for power to sift the Congregation in France, in Bengal, and doubtless also in the United States. Fr. Sorin did not hesitate to say at several Chapters that if he saw the demon with his own eyes, he would not believe more firmly in his presence and his efforts to destroy the work.

The effects of those temptations were first visible in what was most lax in the Congregation, the enemy got his first subjects cheaply. But he did not stop there. He stirred up trouble, distrust, and the spirit of party and of nationality amongst the Brothers. The temptation was evidently gaining ground.

Prudence fled from those that should have remedied the evil; a blindness heretofore unknown seemed, at least for a time, to have fallen upon even those that had never before compromised themselves. Falsehood fell from lips that had never before been suspected; multiplied and ruinous negligences were of daily occurrence even amongst members of the Chapter. All suffered, even where you would have sought in vain a reasonable cause. The College table was sometimes neglected in a manner that was the height of folly. The acting steward declared that there was nothing to be had at a time when the market was glutted, and the cook had nothing to put on the table when the storeroom was full.

The same vertiginous spirit seemed to blind the members of Notre Dame even beyond the ocean.[1] The Brother who was then managing the affairs of the Province at the Mother House lost five thousand francs in the printing of a series of books in English which had to remain in the customhouse at New York. And all that he had purchased in France he left behind him in such a strange way that a boy of twelve would have seen in such conduct an attack of madness. It was a new loss of two thousand francs, not to speak of seven or eight hundred francs that were stolen from him in New York; from him, a former sailor accustomed to travelling by sea and land.[2]

Rev. Fr. Kilroy
withdraws

One of the Fathers of the society who ought to have been most devoted to it, seeing that he had made all his studies in it, was this same year the instrument of whom God allowed the enemy to make use in order to add to its trials.[3] Not only did he leave the society, but he tried to

1. "et tolle hinc. E.S." is written in the margin next to this sentence.

2. The following prayer is written in pencil in the margin at the side of this paragraph: "O Mary, you are the Mother and at the same time the perfect model of mercy. You who have never broken the branch in half or extinguished the smoldering wick, hear my filial supplications and grant them by giving to the author of this chronicle the tenderness of mercy. Give him also a great love of justice and a strict fairness in his ways, you whom we like to call the mirror of justice. Deign to hear me, a poor plaintiff, and be kind to me, O Virgin Mother of God, O Mary."

3. Edmund Kilroy was born Nov. 24, 1830, in Ireland and entered the Congregation of Holy Cross at Notre Dame on Nov. 8, 1848. He professed vows on Aug. 15, 1853, and was ordained in either 1853 or 1854. He withdrew from the community in February 1859. He then held several pastorates in the diocese of Fort Wayne, accepted a commission as chaplain in the Union Army in 1861, and attended Oxford University from 1863 to 1867, whence he went to Canada. M.g. and Alerding, *Fort Wayne*, 127.

justify his withdrawal, like all those that look back with regret to the onions of Egypt, by speaking badly even of those who twelve or thirteen years before had [brought life] by the fruit of their sweat and fatigues; and as a natural consequence of an unsettled and strange character, speaking in turns of the same society, well or ill according to the whim of the moment; without real malice, but without any fixed principle of justice or of truth.

In the opinion of the community he did no injury to the house by leaving it, but was rather doing it a service. But the world was not likely to understand the peace that he was leaving to his associates when he took himself away from amongst them. He had even a certain influence on the mind of another Father, who was at the time superior of an important house in Chicago; and if he did not directly shake his vocation, he at least contributed much to make it unsteady, and thus to ruin totally that foundation, which had cost much, and which appeared to be full of promise for the Congregation. This matter will be spoken of in due time and in detail.

The same year was marked by the withdrawal of a greater number of Brothers than usual. A certain professed Brother, Ambrose,[4] who had been an annoyance to the society for nearly ten years by his spirit of conviviality, levity and murmuring, took matters in his own hands and went his way whence he had come, with the promise of the Provincial to have his withdrawal accepted. Another professed member named Arsene,[5] whose brain had been weakening by degrees for more than a year and who began

4. Br. Ambrose (John Daxacher) was born Oct. 25, 1818, at Marienthal in the Tyrol in the archdiocese of Salzburg, Austria. He entered the Congregation of Holy Cross at Notre Dame on Feb. 2, 1851, and professed vows Aug. 7, 1854. He was serving in New Orleans when he withdrew from the community in September 1859. M.g.

5. Br. Arsene (Patrick Murray) was born in August 1826 in Ireland. A painter and mason, he entered the Congregation of Holy Cross at Notre Dame on June 22, 1852, and professed vows on Aug. 15, 1855. He withdrew from the community in September 1858, re-entered it at the end of the year, and was dismissed in 1859. M.g.

to excite apprehension by his Cassandrian predictions and his threats of fire and ashes, one fine morning declared positively that the Pope had called him to Rome and that he was going, adding, however strange his language might appear at the time, that he had no doubt of his future election to the See of St. Peter.

Seven other Brother novices disappeared successively, either of their own accord and with the consent of the superiors, or because it was not thought advisable to keep them. None of them was regretted as a loss, and at the annual retreat in the month of August the Congregation had an appearance of health, life and zeal such as it had never had before. The society of the Fathers was represented by eleven professed and four novices; that of the Brothers by 107 members professed, novices and postulants; in all, 122.

Archbishop of Baltimore at Notre Dame

On the fifth day of the retreat the seven bells of Notre Dame rang out at full swing during the particular examination. The archbishop of Baltimore had come to visit Notre Dame and to spend twenty-four hours amid this young family, some members of which he had had for several years in his archdiocese (at Washington), and a new colony of whom were preparing to start for the city of Baltimore.[6]

His visit could not have been more opportune. He came from Chicago, whose bishop at the time was very unfavorably disposed and whom he had greatly surprised by telling him that he was coming to Notre Dame. The difficulties of Notre Dame with Bp. Duggan[7] were submitted

6. Francis Patrick Kenrick was archbishop of Baltimore in 1859. Born Dec. 3, 1796, in Dublin, Ireland, he had been educated in Rome and ordained a priest in 1821. That same year he emigrated to America and served in the diocese of Bardstown, Kentucky. He was ordained a bishop in 1830 and served as coadjutor bishop of Philadelphia, becoming bishop of that see in 1842 and archbishop of Baltimore in 1851. Code, 152–153.

7. James Duggan became administrator of the diocese of Chicago in 1858 and bishop of Chicago on Jan. 21, 1859. Born in Maynooth, Ireland, on May 22, 1825, he had been educated in Ireland and in the United States. Ordained a priest for the diocese of St. Louis in 1847, he had been ordained coadjutor bishop of St. Louis on May 3, 1857. Code, 77.

to him, and he did not hesitate to give his opinion and his counsels in favor of the Congregation. The venerable archbishop seemed to be well pleased and even edified by what he saw, repeating that he had not suspected that the Congregation had such an establishment in the West, and that the hand of God was manifest in this work.

The scholastic year 1858-59 had terminated with success; and in spite of the financial crisis which still prevailed in the West, the receipts fell only a little short of those of the two previous years. One hundred and eighty-seven entries had been recorded, and there was an average attendance of 125 pupils for the year. This was a gain of some pupils over 1858; but what was perhaps equally consoling was the excellent spirit that prevailed in the College at the end of the year and which presaged well for the reopening in the month of September following.

About the middle of the year the pupils had organized *Military company* a military company, the members of which, thirty-seven in number, adopted a very graceful uniform. This company, even till the very last day, bore itself most honorably and added much to all the celebrations at the end of the year.

The novitiate of the Brothers had never yet been filled *New novitiate* with such a large number of postulants; at the annual retreat there were twenty-one. The house was crowded. The old novitiate had been torn down and a new one was going up on a somewhat larger scale. Five thousand francs had been allowed for this new building, which was put up by the workmen of the Congregation, i.e. the Brothers.

The wheat this year, without being a very large crop, *Good harvest* was better than last year. There were 2,500 bushels, or about half of what would be consumed in a year. This was a great help, because the year just ended had cost more than twenty thousand francs for this article alone, wheat having gone up to $1.50, that is to say, 7.50 francs a bushel, where it remained for the last six months. There were also grounds to expect some fruits, wine and Indian corn, perhaps even sugar, or at least molasses.

This year the Provincial Chapter adopted the resolution to purchase at wholesale, for six months, sugar, coffee,

*Wholesale pur-
chases; no
contact with
strangers*

tea, leather, butter, etc. It was also decided to send away the
hired men and to have the work done by Brothers, except
that it was necessary to keep a hired carpenter until such
time as a Brother would be able to direct that work himself.
This was a means of lessening expenses and of preserving
the community spirit from contact with strangers.

The Father Salvatorists were successively recalled from
their missions and gave up their pastoral charges to devote
themselves with the Brothers to the work of education: still,
they might accept parishes where there was a possibility of
establishing schools of the Brothers and Sisters, but only
when two Fathers could find employment.

But it is time to speak of Chicago, since the entire year
was preoccupied with this establishment. It is quite a story.

The Congregation Leaves Chicago
Homo sic, Deus aliter cogitat et disponit

Preliminaries

To understand fully this withdrawal, it is almost indispensable to go back to what has been said already or,
rather, to briefly retrace the history of the foundation in
Chicago during the three years of its existence.

*History of this
foundation*

In the year 1851, Bp. Van de Velde, then the bishop
of Chicago, the protector and devoted friend of the Congregation of Holy Cross in the United States, had invited
the society to make a foundation in his diocese, and as an
inducement he purchased a magnificent piece of ground
near the city of Chicago, which he offered to the Brothers;
the following year he offered Fr. Sorin his St. Mary's University, on the sole condition of doing there all the good
he could. The lack of subjects caused the execution of the
project to be delayed.

Like his illustrious predecessor, Bp. O'Regan[8] visited
Notre Dame and appeared soon to have become its warm

8. Anthony O'Regan was born July 27, 1809, in Lavallegro,
County Mayo, Ireland, and was educated at St. Patrick's Seminary
in Maynooth. Ordained a priest for the archdiocese of Tuam, Ireland,
in 1834, he emigrated to the United States in 1849 and served as
rector of St. Louis Seminary in Carondelet, Missouri, until 1854,

friend. He often expressed the hope of seeing members of Holy Cross doing in Chicago the good that he witnessed in Indiana. Finally, on May 26, 1856, he made a formal proposition to have his desires in this matter carried into effect. He proposed to sell St. Mary's University to the Congregation for sixty thousand dollars, payable in twelve annual installments of five thousand dollars each, without interest. All things having been maturely weighed by both parties, it was agreed to put the fundamental points of the contract in writing, and the document was drawn up and signed in duplicate by both parties. Here is the literal translation of this document.

Bishop O'Regan, wishing to introduce the Congregation of Holy Cross into his diocese, has had an understanding with said Congregation in the following terms, after mature deliberation and serious examination of all things.

1. His Lordship desires that the Congregation of Holy *The Chicago* Cross shall as soon as possible open a day school in the *house* buildings known in Chicago by the name of St. Mary's University, and afterwards, as soon as possible, parish schools in four or five parishes of the city, under the direction of the Brothers of St. Joseph. It is also his desire to see an Industrial school annexed to the day school, on the same ground as the University and under the direction of the same Brothers.

2. His Lordship also desires that the Sisters of Holy Cross open on the same grounds, *servatis servandis*, a day school for young German girls, and an industrial school for young people with a parish school for St. Joseph's congregation, and other German schools whenever they shall be requested.

3. His Lordship gives the Congregation charge of St. Joseph's parish as soon as a German Father of the Society shall be ready to assume charge of it.

---

when he was named third bishop of Chicago. His administration of the diocese met with opposition from the clergy, and in 1857 he left for Rome, where he resigned his see, effective May 3, 1858. See Code, 231; *The Catholic Encyclopedia* (1907–1914), 3:654.

4. Moreover, it is the intention of His Lordship to protect this new community by all means in his power in his episcopal city and throughout his diocese, whose most precious interests are evidently bound up with the success and the development of this Congregation.

5. The Congregation of Holy Cross enters fully into the views and intentions expressed above, and pledges itself to fulfill them as soon and as completely as possible.

6. To carry out this contract, His Lordship sells the said Congregation the property known as "St Mary's University" for the sum of sixty thousand dollars, payable in twelve annual installments of five thousand dollars each, without interest; as surety for the payment of this sum, the Provincial of the Society in the United States signs twelve separate notes and gives a mortgage on all the property thus acquired by the Society, one half of which is transferred unconditionally and the other half expressly for a special object, namely education.

It is understood and agreed between the two contracting parties that if any portion of said property shall be ever sold by the Congregation of Holy Cross, a sum shall be refunded to the ordinary at a pro rata of fifteen thousand dollars on the first part or portion, today valued at forty-five thousand dollars.

This 28th day of May, 1856

(Signed) † Anthony O'Regan
Bp. of Chicago
E. Sorin, Prov.

This decision once terminated, Bp. O'Regan promised to have drawn up without delay the papers necessary for the consummation of this transaction, and in particular to call together the legal officers of the university to obtain their consent in writing to this transaction. All formalities were soon complied with, and Fr. Sorin was invited to Chicago for the signature and the exchange of deeds.

Chicago continued

Meanwhile, a distinguished lawyer came to Notre Dame, Mr. H. Ewing of St. Louis, son of the ex-Secretary

of State of the United States,[9] and a very devoted friend of
the Society. The affair in question was immediately placed
in his hands. Not only did he examine it seriously, but
he went in person to Chicago as the representative and
attorney of the Congregation to see that all things be done
in a legal manner.

Having had several long interviews with the Bishop
of Chicago and his lawyers, Mr. Ewing returned to Notre
Dame two days afterwards, declaring that he could not
advise Fr. Sorin to proceed farther in this purchase, that the
bishop could not legally give such a title as he thought he
could offer, and that by signing this contract the Society of
Holy Cross would expose itself to serious difficulties, adding
that he had tried, but in vain, to convince the bishop of
this. Naturally, this advice was followed and the contract
laid aside.

However, Bp. O'Regan was by no means satisfied with
this result, and he returned to his first idea, namely, to
lease the college to the Congregation for a certain number
of years. He said that after all it mattered little to him what
the mode or the regime was under which the Congregation
entered the diocese, provided that it entered and that it was
there to do all the good that he expected of it; that in any
case, whether it purchased or leased the property, he would
do for it what he had promised.

The new proposition of leasing the college was seriously
examined at Notre Dame. Bp. O'Regan became impatient
at the delay and wrote several times to hasten the conclusion of the affair. The following is a copy of one of his
letters:

Episcopal Residence, Chicago
July 26, 1856

To the Very Rev. Fr. Sorin.

Very Reverend and dear Sir, I very much regret that   *Chicago*
you place me in the necessity of reminding you once more   *continued*
to bring to an end all the arrangements regarding the

9. Hugh Ewing was the son of Thomas Ewing and the brother
of Philemon Ewing. See chapter 14, note 5.

college in this city. It is expedient that everything be finished without more delay; for every delay, I assure you, gives me much embarrassment and has already caused me a considerable loss.

It is surely unnecessary for me to remind you that this transaction should be brought to a close, otherwise the pecuniary loss for our college would become a most serious matter. Be good enough therefore to come immediately and settle this business properly.

Wishing you all kinds of prosperity,

I am, Very Reverend and dear Sir,

Very faithfully yours,

†Anthony, Bishop of Chicago.

The Chapter of Notre Dame, however, remained some time longer undecided. The bishop could not suffer this and came himself on 3 August with all the documents prepared and ready to be signed, as might have been expected. The bishop repeated the encouragements and the promises that he had formerly made, and finally, on 4 August, the contract was signed at Notre Dame for fifty years at an annual rental of $2,150. The bishop demanded that this sum, for this time only, should be paid him in full in advance because of the urgent needs of the moment, saying that nothing more would have to be paid on the rent for eighteen months. Thus far, everything passed off agreeably.

Chicago continued

It was soon discovered that the Congregation had bound itself to more than it had reckoned on. Instead of fifty dollars which it was said would be sufficient for repairs, it was absolutely necessary to contract at once for seven hundred dollars for a single item; moreover, the bishop required the Congregation to take the old furniture of the college, which made an additional sum of five hundred dollars, including a piano.

By the contract the Congregation had bound itself only to maintain in the apartments or on the grounds of the college, not a regular university, but a respectable day school. Properly speaking, this is all it was the first year, and the bishop found no fault with it; nor during the fifteen months that he remained in Chicago after the opening of the schools did Bp. O'Regan make any complaint either of the college or of the schools of the Brothers or the Sisters. Quite the contrary, he spoke of the Society only to praise it and he wrote of it in the same strain until his departure for Europe.

More than once, by word of mouth and by writing, Fr. Sorin reminded him of his promise to build new school houses, but he always answered that he was obliged to defer this expense, however pressing he himself considered it. Yet such was the deplorable condition of those poor hovels in which the schools of the Brothers and the Sisters were taught that it was out of the question to expect any but the children of destitute families, especially when the free schools of the city were provided with magnificent buildings in which nothing was wanting.

Moreover, the Brothers and the Sisters, as well as their children, had to suffer from the negligence or the poverty of the carriers who often left them in midwinter without wood or coal, etc.

When, at the beginning of September 1857, the Very Rev. Fr. Moreau, founder of the Order, made his visit to the establishment of Chicago, the only schoolhouse that he had time to inspect, that of the Cathedral itself, appeared to him so unfit that he forbade the Brothers who taught there at the time to continue school until the building had been thoroughly repaired; he at once notified the bishop whilst thanking him for a favor which it may be well to mention here.

The Very Rev. Fr. Moreau, having gone with Fr. Sorin to present his respects to the bishop of Chicago, the latter was eulogizing the Rev. Fr. Sorin, whereupon the Very Rev. Founder remarked that he did not consider Fr. Sorin deserving of much praise in the contract he had made with His Lordship, and that unless some help were given him, he did not see how the establishment could pay the annual rental of $2,150. The bishop answered immediately that he was well aware that the schools had brought in but little, and to make up for the deficiency, he would order a collection to be taken up for that purpose in all the churches of the city, and that this collection would continue every year on the same Sunday, and would bring in, he was sure, a thousand dollars. A circular to this effect was addressed to the pastors, but the collection was made in only one church, and brought in sixty-six dollars instead of a thousand. It was no more spoken of by either party.

Chicago continued

Soon afterwards the bishop set out for Europe; the monetary crisis was on, the monthly payments of the scholars became still more insignificant, and the debts of the community were on the increase. Meanwhile, His Lordship's agent demanded the payment of the rent six months in advance, contrary to the promise of the bishop. Fr. Sorin considered himself justified under such circumstances in refusing it for the time being.

Some time afterwards Bp. Duggan, administrator of the diocese, also demanding the same payment and for the same reasons, received a similar answer. Everything was explained to him in a subsequent interview, and the conclusion to which he came was that things should be left *in statu quo* until the regular nomination of a bishop for Chicago; and this was agreed to without hesitation.

But hardly had Bp. Duggan received his bulls[10] for the diocese when a rumor was spread that he was going to take back the college. Fr. Sorin wrote to him to ascertain the facts, and in answer received, on Good Friday, the following letter, which needs no commentary:

Chicago, April 18, 1859

Very Reverend and dear Sir,

Chicago continued

It was my intention before receiving your letter to write to you immediately after the Easter holidays; but your letter of inquiry makes me do so sooner than I had intended. I write therefore to inform you that you should recall your community and have the college and the premises vacated by the beginning of vacation, which, I expect, will be in the early part of summer.

10. Papal documents appointing him bishop of Chicago.

Since I have been here I have always desired to see this property restored to the diocese, and as you have not fulfilled the contract, you leave me no alternative but to rescind it. I do not think that the gain received by the diocese from the presence of the community compensates for the property that it holds. We know nothing of the youth of this city and we have no place to instruct them; they are compelled to seek elsewhere what they could easily find at home.

Without further useless discussion of what is unalterably decreed in my mind, I request that you take your measures, because I am myself beginning to take mine.

I remain, Very Rev. dear Sir,

Sincerely yours in X.,

†James, Bp. of Chicago

It would be useless to tell of the surprise and the pain caused at Notre Dame by this first letter. To dismiss more than thirty members without any other pretext than that of the violation of a contract in regard to which he himself had said that the affair should be left *in statu quo* until the regular nomination of a bishop, was something hardly credible.

The following week, a Chicago lawyer was consulted on the question of the contract, which he declared to be perfectly valid. The Rev. Fr. Sorin then went to see the bishop, who agreed as to the validity of the contract and who admitted that it was the option of the Congregation to retain the college on the condition of paying the rent in the precise terms of the contract or of giving it up as it was.

Fr. Sorin begged the bishop to bear in mind that the Congregation could not thus, either in honor or in justice or according to its Constitutions abandon the establishment, and concluded by respectfully declaring that it was obliged to retain it. The question seemed to be settled, and for about two months nothing more was said of it.

Chicago continued

About the middle of June, the rumor became current once more that the bishop was going to take back the college. The Rev. Fr. Sorin once more went to Chicago, visited the bishop, and learned from his own lips that he was really determined to carry out his first idea, and that he was allowing no other choice, saying that Bp. O'Regan had no right thus to alienate this property and he said several other things more or less surprising and painful to listen to.

The Rev. Fr. Sorin then proposed that in the case of retiring from the college, select schools should be established in different parts of the city for the Brothers and the Sisters. The bishop answered that he would think about it, whereupon Fr. Sorin replied that he was not prepared to decide anything, that in a few days he expected to see his own bishop, the bishop of Fort Wayne, and the archbishop of the province,[11] whose advice he would ask.

Archbishop Purcell advised that the archbishop of St. Louis be written to and asked whether he would be pleased to lend his attention to the difficulty and settle it. The Rev. Fr. Sorin did write, but the archbishop answered, with all the delicacy that is characteristic of him, that he would rather be excused from interfering.

On 12 July, the Rev. Fr. Sorin went again to Chicago to see His Lordship; but as he had nothing new to lay before him and his last two interviews had been extremely mortifying, he thought it as well to address the bishop the following lines:

Chicago continued

St. Mary's University, July 13, 1859

My Lord,

After having prayed, reflected, and consulted, we respectfully beg to inform you that we have come to the same conclusion as at first, namely, to keep our contract, and whilst we are determined to do our best to correspond to your views, we think ourselves secure in the expectation

11. While the diocese of Chicago was in the ecclesiastical province of St. Louis, headed by Archbishop Peter Richard Kenrick, the diocese of Fort Wayne was in the province of Cincinnati, headed by Archbishop John Baptist Purcell. An appeal would be complicated, since two archbishops were involved. See Shea, 4:181–182, 219–220.

that you will appreciate our efforts and will grant us your protection.

Very respectfully,

Your obedient & devoted Servt in Xt.

E. Sorin, S.S.C.[12]

The next day, the fourteenth, the bishop answered by letter as follows:

Very Rev. and dear Sir,

In answer to your note in which you inform me of your final resolution, I now write to let you know mine. It is simply this: that you vacate the college and the premises by the first of next August, and that the community, men and women, leave the city by that day. I will take the property such as it is, with its improvements whatever they may be, and will be satisfied not to demand the payment of arrears for the past two years. You will have the kindness to take notice of the terms and of the day mentioned, for I have already taken my measures for that day. To prevent all useless discussion for the future, I will simply add that my decision is final and decisive.

I remain, Very Rev. and dear Sir,

Sincerely yours in J.C.

† James, Bp. of Chicago

On the same day, the Rev. Fr. Sorin acknowledged the receipt of the message in the following terms:

My Lord,

Your esteemed letter in answer to my last astonishes me. If I were the only one interested, I would not have waited for a second similar injunction; but I am charged with the interests of other people who trust to me to protect them. To carry out your orders without offering a word in

12. S.S.C. stands for *Salvatorist a Sancta Cruce*, a designation used by priests of the Congregation of Holy Cross in this period.

their favor would be simply betraying their confidence. If we differed still more from your manner of judging of our difficulties, it seems to us that we have still a right to our convictions, especially when everything seems to depend on a legal and common document which should afford an answer and a decision. Your order to vacate the college can be founded only on the fact of the nullity of our lease. Without doubt, your lawyers have told you that it was in effect annulled; but ours tell us just the contrary, including even the lawyer that drew it up for Bp. O'Regan. Up to the present therefore I see no legal decision in virtue of which we should give up our possession.

Chicago continued

Permit me to remark here that the document of which I speak gives us legal rights; if ours are extinguished, I beg as a favor that the declaration may not be looked upon by anyone as an arbitrary proceeding on your part, but rather as the decision of a legal and competent judge.

I think that without the least noise or scandal this affair can be easily examined, and if we must withdraw, we desire at least to be able to do so without the slightest resentment against Your Lordship.

> Very respectfully,
> Your Obedt. Servt.,
> E. Sorin

His Lordship made no reply. On the nineteenth, the Rev. Fr. Sorin visited him, but could not obtain an interview on business. The bishop positively refused to treat otherwise than in writing, and ended by saying that it was altogether useless to return to a subject definitively settled in his mind. In vain did the Rev. Fr. Sorin try to induce him to read some lines of the treatise of Bouix, which reserve exclusively to Rome the right of judging the question; he would not read, but added that the next day he would take legal measures to obtain an eviction, in force as of 1 August.

Chicago continued

On the twentieth the Rev. Fr. Sorin addressed him the following letter:

My Lord,

In submitting to you the attached copy, I humbly beg to present you here some of the remarks that I wished to make yesterday evening.

1. If up to the present I have refused my consent to our withdrawal from Chicago, it is because I thought it contrary to Canon Law, to our constitutions, and to the laws of the country.

2. We have never denied our obligation to pay the rent, and when our request for the performance of certain promises was rejected, we positively declared that we would pay the rent according to the terms of the contract, including the past as well as the future.

3. If the Congregation or any of its members had not done their duty, I ought to have been informed of it before receiving orders to leave the city. The former was one of my duties, the latter was beyond my powers.

4. We were urged by Bp. O'Regan to come to Chicago. I cannot see that we failed through our fault in anything that we had undertaken to do, except in the payment of the rent, which we thought ourselves justified in delaying for a time.

5. If an impartial judge would make a comparison between the state in which we found all things three years ago and that in which we leave them, we should not fear the result.

6. We made no profit, but rather find a deficit of more than a thousand dollars, not to speak of about thirty members for nearly three years, because of the hard times and the non-payment of schooling. It is easy to ascertain the condition of the school-houses where our teachers were obliged to teach from the beginning, and also the circumstances of the parents whose children they were to receive, and then the blame will not fall on them, but instead of being blamed they will be pitied. The Rev. Mr. Dunn who has always had the largest number of Brothers and the most numerously attended school, told me some weeks ago that he was pleased with the Brothers, and that he never had any fault to find with them.

7. The great reason that seems to make our withdrawal a necessity is your regret, ever on the increase, that Bp. O'Regan had thus disposed of the college, etc.; but to what extent this regret constitutes a right to take it back is a point that does not easily ally itself to the fundamental ideas of contracts.

8. The frequently repeated declaration of Your Lordship that you are not bound by any promise of your predecessor, and that if you could find in the writing of the lease any legal subterfuge to evade it, you would unhesitatingly avail yourself of it, is something that I cannot understand.

9. You seem to have no fear of the scandal that would result from legal proceedings in this matter. I assure you that I could not be so insensitive thereto, although it seems to me that I should have no reason to fear. Because I assure you that I have full faith in the goodness of our cause, if it ever could be brought into our courts. When I proposed a legal arbitration, I gave a sufficient proof of this.

But sooner than go before court in a suit with a bishop, I would prefer even a greater loss and a more humiliating disgrace to the assurance of gaining a case of such a ruinous nature. You must have foreseen from the first that this would be our final determination. That is say, when you seriously threaten to resort to legal means to evict the community, you take a high-handed way of settling every difficulty to your own satisfaction. As to your doubts as to whether our Congregation is approved, however painful it was to me yesterday to hear you express them, I humbly beg you to permit me to say that I think it is.

If I have written one word to cause you the least pain, I beg you to forgive it; it never was my intention to pain you in any manner whatsoever. But you cannot be surprised to find me personally sensitive to such a termination of three years of hard work recognized in such a pitiful manner. Fortunately, I cherish the hope that I have not lost all merit before God.

To be frank to the very last, whilst I reverence your great virtues and your sacred character, I remain painfully convinced that you have not done us justice as we expected it of you.

I still hope that you will deign to consider this matter anew, and that you will see things in a very different light. If we can no longer continue our labors here, we can at least retire with your blessing and your wishes for our success.

Very respectfully,
Your humble Servt. in X
E. Sorin, S.S.C.

The following is a copy of the Latin text of Bouix accompanying the above letter.

Semel autem legitime constituto in aliqua diocesi conventu, jam non poterit Episcopus conventum hunc supprimere seu congregationem jure ibi conventualiter existendi spoliare. Nam Sedes Apostolica, Institutum hujusmodi approbando, hoc ipso jus ei confert, per varias mundi partes sese propagandi, et solummodo [explenda] remanet conditio de jure communi requisita, ut pro qualibet nova fondatione interveniat ordinarii consensus. Unde expleta hac conditione, id est, semel obtento episcopi loci consensu, jus conventualitatis in illa dioecesi congregationi acquiritur, vi pontificiae approbationis. Jam ergo nequibit Episcopus ille, aut ullus hujus successor conventum supprimere. Sed si forte suppressio necessaria videbitur, ad Sedem Apostolicam recurrendum erit.[13]

Bouix, Book 2

13. Rev. Marie-Dominique Bouix (1808–1870) was a well-known French canonist. *The Catholic Encyclopedia* (1907–1914), 2:711–712. The following is a translation of the Latin text: "A religious house once legitimately established in a diocese, the bishop can no longer suppress this house or deprive a (religious) congregation of the right to maintain a house. The Apostolic See, in approving an institute of this sort, confers upon it thereby the right to extend itself into various parts of the world, the only requisite condition remaining to be fulfilled being that the consent of the ordinary be had for any new foundation. When this condition has been fulfilled, that is, once the consent of the ordinary of the place has been obtained, the right of domicile in that diocese has been acquired by a congregation by virtue of papal approval. Thereafter, neither the bishop nor any of his successors can suppress the religious house. If, however, suppression seems urgently necessary, recourse will be had to the Apostolic See."

Immediately after this, the Rev. Fr. Sorin prepared to recall all the members of the two communities: two priests, ten Brothers, and nineteen Sisters. There remained only ten days more to move, dispose of all the furniture, pay the debts, and collect what was due, not to speak of a store of Catholic books which the Sisters had opened in their Industrial House at the request of Bp. O'Regan, and which left them now with a capital of four thousand dollars on their hands, with which they did not know what to do.

Chicago
continued

It was adding great embarrassments and considerable losses to the disgrace of such a retreat, which the fear of scandal hindered them from even explaining to anyone. But without the protection of the law, which was to be invoked against them, there was no way of holding out longer. It seemed better to them to sacrifice everything to the fear of a scandalous suit, leaving it to the superior general to judge whether it would be expedient to follow up the matter, or to let it be gradually forgotten.

The writer of this memoir does not wish to act in any way contrary to the profound respect due to the bishop of Chicago. He thinks that he sees things just as he has set them down. He believes himself to be quite sure that the default in the payment of the rent was merely the occasion for the bishop to carry out a preconceived plan, namely that of resuming possession of the college as soon as possible; this desire having only increased after the removal of the cathedral, which is now separated from the college by only a single street. But he seems to have consulted his own views only with reference to a temporary advantage for the diocese, without regard to the rights there acquired by the Congregation.

This opinion (which is nothing more than an opinion, however) is supported by the positive and repeated declarations of His Lordship that "if he found a subterfuge in the contract, he would unhesitatingly use it," and that "Bishop O'Regan had no right to make this contract and that therefore it was null."

Hence it would follow, if this way of acting was lawful: 1. That little faith could be placed in the word and the promises even of a bishop, and that every agreement should be put in writing, since his successor would not be obliged to recognize it, even when on this word or on these promises a whole community should have relied and acted.

2. That contracts, no matter how well worded and how conformable to law, would be of no effect and would not protect the interests of a community making a contract with a bishop, except insofar as it would please the latter to maintain them, or unless there was question of something that does not fall under public opinion, such as the cultivation of a field, etc. For it would be rash for a young community to try to manage a college successfully under the very eyes of the bishop, and contrary to his will; and if the moral influence of such opposition did not at once discourage a Society, the serious threat of a suit, even if there was no cause, would assuredly prevent all resistance to a bishop, since to make such opposition would be to take a stand amongst the enemies of the Church or amongst those who have lost their self-respect.

3. In the present case, the desire of the bishop to re-enter into possession of the college required the withdrawal of the whole community, since if any member of it remained in the city, he would be considered merely as an agent of the Society for Notre Dame, to the detriment of the college in Chicago.

It is useless to answer what must have been brought forward to justify the charge that the members of Holy Cross were incapable. They have always been sufficient for the class of students that frequented their pitiful schoolhouses. Who could reasonably demand that the Congregation sacrifice its best subjects where there was no encouragement and no prospect of success? During the first year, Bishop O'Regan, whilst showing himself the protector of the Society, made only promises; the second year was when the see was vacant, and the Congregation did not receive the least help; the third year was still worse, since from the beginning Bishop Duggan himself declared his intention to resume possession, and the more surely to succeed in this, he refrained from bestowing the least attention on the

*Chicago
continued*

*Chicago
continued*

Congregation, although it was giving a Christian education almost gratuitously to more than a thousand children in his episcopal city.

Matters stood thus when the time came for the annual retreat; Fr. Sorin used this occasion as a pretext to cover the departure of the members of this establishment.

In the middle of the second retreat, during the particular examen, the bells of Notre Dame were suddenly heard, as for the arrival of a bishop. It was the archbishop of Baltimore, the primate of the United States. He had heard of the difficulties of the Congregation with Bishop Duggan, and, as he himself said, those difficulties made him wish to see the house. He remained for twenty-four hours, showed himself most gracious to everybody, listened to the whole story of Chicago, suggested what was to be done, and all but gave the assurance that everything would be arranged.

Fr. Sorin wrote to the bishop of Chicago, almost at the dictation of the archbishop, renewing his offers of service. The letter remained unanswered, which left the impression that all was at an end. A memorial of twenty pages had been addressed by Fr. Sorin to the archbishop of Baltimore on the occasion of his going to Chicago, and the archbishop, after reading it, gave it to Bp. Duggan. The archbishop, when leaving Notre Dame, had told Fr. Sorin to claim the return of this memorial if matters were not arranged, and to send it to St. Louis[14] to the metropolitan.

In conformity with this advice, the Rev. Father P. Dillon[15] was charged to proceed to St. Louis with the memorial, but when he presented himself to the bishop of Chicago to reclaim the memorial, all was changed, and His Lordship now only desired to have an understanding with the Rev. Fr. Sorin and to retain the Society that it might continue to do there all the good possible.

14. The metropolitan, i.e., the archbishop of St. Louis, was Peter Richard Kenrick, the brother of the archbishop of Baltimore.

15. Patrick Dillon was born Jan. 1, 1832, at Ballymacwarck, County Galway, Ireland, and entered the Congregation of Holy Cross at Notre Dame on Aug. 15, 1856. M.g.

The following week, Fr. Sorin went to Chicago with *To Chicago*
his bishop and found the bishop of Chicago most favorably
disposed. All things were settled without the least difficulty
on either side, and the Congregation found itself more
firmly established than ever in a city where a few days
before it saw no possibility of remaining. *Haec mutatio
dexterae Excelsi* was the thought and the conviction of
Fr. Sorin and of his counselors. It was a genuine triumph
for all the friends of the Society in Chicago.

However, new expenses had to be incurred at once *New expenses;*
to establish the two Societies permanently on the same *repairs*
grounds in a becoming and religious manner. Ten thousand
francs were employed for this purpose in the course of the
succeeding five months. In compensation the two schools
took on a new development beyond what they ever had, *Success*
and by the end of December the college had one hundred
and twenty pupils and the Sisters nearly one hundred in
their department.

The affair of the superior, who was suspected of being *Providence on*
the prime cause of all the trouble, settled itself without any *the withdrawal of*
of the vexations, which the superior had delighted in mak- *Fr. Force*
ing them fear and rather to the advantage of the Society.[16]
He had believed himself very beloved by the parishioners
of St. Joseph's; he had the humiliation of hearing and of
having repeated just the contrary; he imagined that the
parish would be glad to retain him and would even prefer
him as a secular priest. Providence allowed that the bishop
should speak in time and that their desire to have the
Rev. Mr. Mayer,[17] whose superior talents they had learned
to value during about two years, should be encouraged.

16. Bernard Joseph Force (or Voors) was born Mar. 17, 1828,
at Verthe in Germany. He entered the Congregation of Holy Cross
at Notre Dame on Nov. 8, 1848. He had been ordained a priest
when he withdrew in 1859. M.g.

17. Aloysius Mayer was born Oct. 4, 1819, in Fitten Kofen,
Bavaria, and entered the Congregation of Holy Cross at Notre Dame
on Sept. 1, 1857. Formerly a Redemptorist Brother, he appears to
have been a priest when he joined Holy Cross. He withdrew in
1858. M.g.

Return of Rev.
Mr. Mayer
Mr. Mayer, who had always regretted (leaving) Chicago, lent a willing ear to the proposition for his return. It was a way for him to be received back into the Society, and in some months, peace reigned, and all was moving smoothly in the college and in the magnificent St. Joseph's parish, which counted four thousand souls.

Peace and
harmony
God grant that in return for all the anxieties caused by this establishment in 1859, peace and harmony may so reign that Heaven will send down blessings proportioned to the needs and the hopes of the Congregation. Its future has not been dimmed nor its importance lessened in the State of Illinois, especially since a new foundation has been authorized and established in the diocese of Alton.[18]

The State of Illinois more than any other (state) is going to become a great center of Catholicity as well as of the Union itself. Twenty-five years ago, Chicago formed as it were the limit of the United States in the West; today civilization has advanced so far that Chicago finds itself in the very center.

New mutiny
Towards the middle of December there was a new manifestation of insubordination amongst the pupils, in which the same number (forty) were involved. Much prudence was required to restore order. Six were sent off and as many others withdrew as a consequence; but the right spirit was not so speedily restored, and until the end of the year the relations between professors and students were strained. Ordinarily, such impulsive acts leave an unpleasantness in the mind, which is no longer disposed as it was before.

This time the cause seemed to lie with the Prefect of Discipline, who was not sufficiently feared and who allowed too much liberty.

18. The diocese of Alton, Ill., was erected in 1853 as the diocese of Quincy. The title was changed to Alton in 1857 and to Springfield in 1923. Code, 419. It included the southern half of Illinois. Shea, 4:625.

Notre Dame faculty, ca.1866

Rev. Neal Gillespie, C.S.C.,
president of St. Mary of the Lake,
Chicago; editor of *Ave Maria*

Brother Francis DeSales
(Andrew Sweeney), C.S.C., with
Professor Joseph Lyons, class of
1862, first historian of the
University; Lyons Hall is named
after him.

Rev. Joseph Carrier, C.S.C.

Rev. James Dillon, C.S.C.

Rev. Paul Gillen, C.S.C.

Rev. Peter Cooney, C.S.C.

Rev. William Corby, C.S.C.

Rev. Patrick Dillon, C.S.C., second president of the University of Notre Dame, 1865–66

Hon. Schuyler Colfax, Indiana Congressman, 1855–1869; Speaker of the House of Representatives, 1863–1869; Vice-President of the United States, 1869–1873

ATLANTA CAMPAIGN.

ARMY OF THE CUMBERLAND.

HOLY COMMUNION.

SISTERS IN FIELD HOSPITAL.

35TH OF INDIANA VOL.

1ST IRISH VETERAN REG'T.

1861. EASTER SUNDAY 1864. 1865.

Divine Service by Rev. P. P. COONEY C.S.C. Chaplain Gen. of Ind. Troops in the field.

Sacred Heart Church and Main Building, ca. 1866

Bishops of the Province of Cincinnati, 1868. Left to right: George Carrell of Covington, John H. Luers of Fort Wayne, Sylvester Rosecrans of Columbus, John B. Purcell of Cincinnnati, Peter P. Lefevere of Detroit, Louis Rappe of Cleveland, and Maurice de Saint-Palais of Vincennes.

Hon. Timothy E. Howard, historian of Notre Dame and St. Joseph County, Indiana

Rev. John M. Toohey, C.S.C. translator of Sorin's Chronicles.

Bishop James Duggan of Chicago

Rev. E. Sorin, ca. 1873

CHAPTER 19
1860

The year 1860, which was destined to have the first General Chapter of the Congregation of Holy Cross, was looked to by all the members of the Society as a year that would mark an epoch in the annals. For the Province of Indiana it opened with brilliant colors and full of consolations, hopes and encouragements. *Favorable state of things*

An extraordinarily mild winter, which prevented the greater part of the sufferings that otherwise seemed to be inevitable in a country exhausted by the consequences of a financial crisis which had raged for three years; an appearance that boded well for the success of the seeds entrusted to the earth the previous autumn; the College better equipped than ever; the novitiates filled; more numerous and more advantageous applications than in the past for new establishments; the schools already founded giving general satisfaction; the amount of the floating debt finally diminishing gradually and the dangers that had formerly threatened the existence of the Society lessening; public confidence growing strong; and the spirit of the community improving in proportion as the number and accommodations permitted more regular and freer movements in the general course. God made his presence felt and peace reigned in the provincial house and its dependencies.

It was to be regretted that the new Constitutions in English could not be placed in the hands of the religious, *Rules in English held up*

who had impatiently waited for them so long; but seeing the grave inconvenience of a miserable translation
and poor print, and the probability that numerous changes
would be made by the General Chapter, it was decided
that those new books should be kept locked up until the
Chapter had decided. This was a real sacrifice, but it seemed
out of the question even to try to escape it. However,
the Rules and the Directory were read and explained in
each house.

One of the first measures that the Chapter of Notre
Dame thought it advisable to adopt for the general welfare,
spiritual and temporal, was to regularize the existence of the
Sisters necessary for the work of the house. The Chapter of
St. Mary's was called upon for its opinion and cooperation,
and by common consent it was agreed that the decree of
His Reverence in regard to the cloister of the Sisters should
at last be carried out to the letter, and that the number of
persons required for all the work of the house should be
filled up as soon as the Brothers had vacated the building
occupied by them, and that a suitable washhouse would be
built. All was to be ready at the latest by Easter.

Then it would be no longer necessary to send anything to St. Mary's, as had been done for some years but
not without inconveniences. The Sisters, being numerous
enough, would form a regular community, with all the
privileges of cloistered religious, and would be protected
by their enclosure against the dangers which the growth of
the institution was gradually making greater.

This change would have been deferred until the general retreat, but it was thought desirable to have at
least some months' experience, so that the advantages and
disadvantages of it might be placed before the General
Chapter, enabling this same chapter to determine in a permanent manner all the relations of the two Societies with
each other.

A priest sent
to preach in
the cities on
the religious life
and education

Towards the beginning of this same year the administration thought it advisable to make an effort to fill the
new novitiate of the Brothers which was nearly completed,
and which appeared to justify new sacrifices to procure

for it some promising subjects. The Rev. Fr. J. Dillon,[1] then vice president of the College, was chosen to go and preach this new crusade against the inroads of infidelity and of Protestantism, and to seek young men of faith and devotedness to enroll under the banner of the cross.

At the same time, he received the obedience of the Visitor, and he proceeded first to call on the bishop of Alton, who had just opened a Brothers' school, and who seemed to be very desirous of obtaining subjects for several other localities. After some months of this new effort, there remained no doubt that it was worth continuing and that from it the Congregation could not fail to draw some precious advantages. In America people must make themselves known, must show themselves to the world if they expect anything from their efforts.

Some months afterwards, the same considerations prompted the appointment of an agent in the West to canvass for pupils, sell scholarships, and collect the debts of the College and of St. Mary's Academy. The choice that was then made of a non-Catholic gentleman may appear strange; but when it is carefully examined, it is easy to see that such a man, well known in a big city like Chicago, will succeed better than a Catholic in breaking down a host of prejudices against Catholic institutions, especially if he is a man who has the confidence of the public and he can say that he himself has placed his children in those institutions, and that his son has been at Notre Dame for three years where he is happy and is making progress. It is an experiment, which seems to justify the expenditure of more than thirty-five hundred francs for six months.

An agent is hired in Chicago for 7,500 fr. a year

The financial crisis continued to rage and became more severe; money seemed to be growing scarcer, and serious fears were entertained as to the future of a College which, as everybody knows, needed an easy circulation of money

University gains in number

1. James Dillon was born Nov. 18, 1833, in County Galway, Ireland, and entered the Congregation of Holy Cross at Notre Dame in 1853. His brother, Patrick, however, was vice president at Notre Dame in 1860. M.g. See chapter 18, note 15.

to sustain itself and to supply itself with students. Such were the conjectures of men, founded on a state of things easy to grasp and analyze. And yet from this state of the country, God drew entirely different results. The number of boarders increased by one-fifth, and payments were better, comparatively, than in previous years. There were as many as one hundred and seventy-eight students at one time in Notre Dame, and St. Mary's Academy followed in the same forward march.

Finances

As to the finances of the institution, there was not a great change in the treasury. The amount of the debt was going down very little; it was fortunate that it did not rise at a time when people had to live on their actual resources and meet enormous interests without being able to sell anything.

Foundations

The establishments of the Province were gradually becoming more regular, and were growing more and more productive for the Provincial House. Baltimore, Philadelphia, Cincinnati, Toledo, Columbus and Zanesville, were beginning to have the look of regular foundations with good prospects for the future.

Chicago

Chicago was still under the painful yoke of pecuniary difficulties; its debts had even increased considerably, and yet its actual state gave more satisfaction and more promise for the future. The college had as many as one hundred and twenty-five day scholars, and the parish schools were in better condition than ever as regards numbers; but they were the same pitiful shanties as ever.

The select school of the Sisters had also grown satisfactorily, containing seventy-five young ladies, that is to say, more by half than any other school of the same kind in the city. The two parish schools which the Sisters taught, at the cathedral and at St. Joseph's church, were flourishing and in good repute.

St. Joseph's parish itself, after having threatened to give trouble, did not break the peace and was established on a more solid footing, the bishop having formally transferred it over to the Congregation of Holy Cross for fifty years, in the same manner as he had given St. Michael's to the Redemptorist Fathers.

Considering the improved condition of the two Societies which were at this time decently and canonically established on the premises leased from the bishop; considering the dispositions of the bishop which seemed to be excellent; considering finally the standing on which the schools and the parish had been placed, the future of the Congregation in this city was more encouraging than it had been for two or three years. Unfortunately, the resources of the West were exhausted; the lack of money had become really embarrassing and Chicago is the center of the West, which it represents in times of want as well as of plenty.

Hardly were the Easter holidays over when St. Joseph's congregation in Chicago began once more to be restless. This time the people were dissatisfied with Fr. Exel.[2] He was recalled and Mr. Mayer left alone. Some months afterwards, Mr. Mayer himself having left the Society and having been named pastor of another German parish in the city, the trustees went in a fury to the bishop, declaring that they no longer wanted to have anything to do with the Congregation of Holy Cross, since they could get no one but Fr. Exel. The bishop quieted them and told them to remain in peace until 1 September following. Another aged German priest, Mr. Hartland, was given them, and peace was restored for awhile.

At this same time a second fair was held in the city for the Holy Cross foundation in Chicago. It was a brilliant affair, the grandest that had ever been seen in the city, and without doubt it made an impression most favorable for the institution. It lasted four days and cleared five thousand francs.

Fair — $1,000

The end of the scholastic year showed a deficit of three thousand dollars for the college and of four thousand for the Sisters, that is to say, a debt of seven thousand dollars. It is true that two thousand dollars was spent for

Finances

2. Charles-Antoine Exel was born May 18, 1826, at Strasbourg (Bas Rhin), France, and entered the Congregation of Holy Cross at Ste-Croix on Sept. 27, 1858. He left France for Notre Dame in January 1860, and he withdrew from the community in America, July 1, 1863. M.g.

repairs and a thousand for rent, paid in advance, and the following year would have the benefit of saving this expense of two thousand and three thousand in rent, in all, five thousand dollars. It was therefore resolved to continue the experiment of this college for another year and to abide by the result.

State of Notre Dame and its dependencies, July 1, 1860

At this epoch, when the first General Chapter of the Congregation of Holy Cross was about to open at the Mother House, the foundation of Notre Dame du Lac was very close to the nineteenth year of its existence. The following lines give a faithful statement of its present condition.

Notre Dame has been known for some years past as one of the leading Catholic institutions of the West. It possesses a little domain of seven hundred acres of land on the banks of the St. Joseph river, two miles from South Bend, the county seat of St. Joseph county. This property contains two little lakes or bodies of spring water, on the banks of which, to the east, the University of Notre Dame is built. It has today the appearance of a most agreeable and most romantic little village.

The principal buildings are the university and its church, the novitiates of the Salvatorists and of the Josephites, the workshops, the farm-house, etc.; then, to the rear of the College, the infirmary, the kitchen, and the Sisters' house, all constructed of brick except the workshops, and all comparatively new.

The number of entries this year was 224. Each year shows an advance on its predecessor, not only in the increased number of pupils, but in the more elevated tone of the studies. Thus the classical course was one-third larger this year than in 1858–59. The University as such enjoys at present a reputation more flattering and more encouraging than ever. But it still has pressing needs; for instance, classrooms and an observatory. It can accommodate and probably will have two hundred boarders this year.

The University and the Salvatorists

The University of Notre Dame is, properly speaking, the establishment of the Salvatorists in the United States. Of itself alone, it would be sufficient to secure their future.

If the debts weighing on the institution should be some day paid off, it cannot be denied that Notre Dame du Lac will be for the Congregation of Holy Cross a foundation worthy of being preserved. With its resources in land, it could support itself without the least dependence on public patronage. Its little domain and its lime and brick kilns afford it a surer source of existence than the number of its pupils.

What has for a long time checked its forward march is its floating debt, the interest on which absorbs all its profits. Were not this the case, it could now afford to hire the best professors of the country at good salaries. When it can add ten thousand dollars to its actual budget for professors, it will soon find them.

The religious character of the institution draws to it a class of young men amongst whom the Society of Salvatorists will as a matter of course draw some recruits every year for its novitiate. It is thus that two-thirds of those that compose it today have entered, and it has never been in better condition. There are at present a dozen novices who are all choice and promising young men. *Salvatorists' Novitiate*

In front of St. Aloysius's novitiate and close to it is that of the Brothers, recently built on the site of its predecessor, but half again as large. It has at present some fifty novices and postulants. It is the only house at Notre Dame where the Brothers are represented by themselves, and not very suitably overall. The St. Joseph's novitiate is built on a charming little island which forms a considerable elevation between the two lakes. It is the most beautiful spot of the whole property, and in a short time, when the plan shall have been fully carried out, it will be quite delightful. *Josephites' Novitiate*

There also the Josephites, like the Salvatorists, will have in time a foundation to be envied, an existence less precarious, perhaps, than anywhere else. East of their novitiate and on the opposite side of St. Mary's Lake, is the house of the working Brothers, and around this house are grouped their barn, stables, cattle-sheds, etc., all on a scale proportioned to the extent of their domain and of their *Farm house*

Workshops number. Farther on, on the public road, are their work-shops, and the house for their apprentices of whom there are forty, divided as follows: five with the tailor, eight with the shoemaker, five with the carpenter, two with the blacksmith, and the other twenty on the farm, at the lime kilns, and at the brickyard. Without going out of their own premises, the Brothers can here advantageously employ any number of workmen.

The value of Notre Dame in dollars and cents can hardly be set down; but if it were necessary to make a rough estimate, it could hardly be less than seventy-five thousand dollars.

Dependencies

Foundations The Congregation having of its own accord given up all its missions except those of Lowell and of South Bend,[3] which are at the very doors of Notre Dame, and which are attended to by the Rev. Fr. Exel and the Rev. Fr. CarRoll,[4] the consequence is that all of its efforts are directed to only one object, education. In Chicago, eighty-six miles west of Notre Dame, it has a university and four parish *St. Mary of the Lake, Chicago* schools where fifteen members are at work. The University of St. Mary of the Lake was delivered over to it by special contract in 1857, at an annual rental of two thousand dollars. This contract, entered into when times were better, was not one of the most advantageous, since thus far it has brought in nothing, and the time of fifteen religious has been absorbed in it without compensation, leaving con-trariwise a deficit of two thousand dollars. But indirectly, by the influx from the West that it has caused to Notre

3. These two missions were St. Alexis's, which was later called St. Joseph's, established in 1853 in Lowell, on the east bank of the St. Joseph River, opposite South Bend, and St. Patrick's, established in 1859 in the town of South Bend. See chapter 14:10; Howard, 419–420.

4. Thomas Carroll was born Aug. 17, 1836, at Andaghe, Ire-land, and entered the Congregation of Holy Cross at Notre Dame on June 30, 1857. He withdrew from the community in 1863, but in 1895 he donated the Lourdes Grotto at Notre Dame. M.g.

Dame, it was not a loss, and just now there is reason to hope that it may turn to the advantage of the Society. Last year there were 125 day scholars.

The four parish schools count eight hundred children and give entire satisfaction to everybody this year. St. Patrick's especially is doing wonders. The teaching Brothers are each paid two hundred dollars. They have just rented a house for themselves for five years at two hundred dollars a year near St. Patrick's with the view of having it serve as a residence for all the teaching Brothers in Chicago. Besides, the Congregation has a large German parish connected with the University. It counts from three to four thousand souls, and affords a means of doing good and of supporting the University.

Cincinnati

Next in point of importance comes Cincinnati. St. John's German school counts 575 children, under the tutelage of five Brothers. It brings in a thousand dollars or two hundred per capita. It has a great reputation on account of being the first Catholic school of the city, and it has given rise in a number of priests to the desire of obtaining Brothers of St. Joseph. Br. Boniface,[5] who has been its director for two years, deserves great praise for his devotedness and his success.

St. John's

Philadelphia

Two parish schools were founded here, one at St. Paul's four years ago, and the other at St. Augustine's last year. Each of them employs three Brothers for two hundred and fifty to three hundred children. By special contract the latter assumes the payment of $1,000 annually, the former

St. Paul's

5. Br. Boniface (Franz Rudolph Mühler) was born Jan. 4, 1826 or 1828, at Neiheim, Westphalia, Germany. He came to America in 1851, and entered the Congregation of Holy Cross at Notre Dame on July 7, 1853. He professed vows on Apr. 8, 1855, at St. John's Church, Cincinnati. M.g.

is paid through the scholars, which gives more annoyance than profits.

Baltimore

St. Patrick's

The Brothers have two houses in this city: one a parish school at St. Patrick's and the other an orphan asylum[6] two miles from the city. The school has hardly more than one hundred and fifty children, and the asylum thirty-five. Their salary is fixed at $150, with board and lodging. This new foundation, which is not yet one year in existence, is doing very well under the direction of Br. Edward,[7] one of the best members of the Society. The pressing demands for Brothers that come from this city are the best proof of this.

Toledo, Diocese of Cleveland, Ohio

Two schools

This is also a double foundation. Three Brothers live together in one house, and have an English school for the Irish congregation and a German school for the German parish. The former has about 150 children, the latter eighty. Their salary is eight hundred dollars. This is a good institution which may be developed to advantage.

Columbus, the Capital of Ohio, Archdiocese of Cincinnati

Two schools

Here also the Congregation had a double school, but for want of numbers the German school had to be given

6. Established in June 1815, St. Patrick's was Maryland's first public as well as its first parochial school. The parish is the second oldest in Baltimore, and by the late 1850s was populated by Irish immigrants. In the summer of 1859, four Holy Cross Sisters and three Brothers were assigned to St. Patrick's, and in September they began to teach in the parish schools, one for boys and one for girls. The orphans were on a farm near Darby Park. See M. Campion Kuhn, "The Sisters Go East—And Stay," 15–19.

7. Br. Edward (John Fitzpatrick) was born Mar. 1, 1836, in Liverpool, England, entered the Congregation of Holy Cross at Notre Dame on Sept. 26, 1852, and professed vows on Aug. 15, 1855. M.g.

up for a time. During the past year the Irish school is the only one that the Brothers have. It has 160 children under two teachers, whose salary is $150 with board and lodging. This is a valuable foundation which should be well cared for and which has a promising future.

Zanesville, Ohio
Archdiocese of Cincinnati

An Irish congregation, St. Thomas's, is under the charge of the Rev. Dominican Fathers. Two Brothers are employed here at the same salary as in Columbus, and they are giving full satisfaction. They teach 150 students. Here also the future is promising. *St. Thomas*

Fort Wayne

It is now several years since the Brothers have resumed charge of this school, which is very satisfactory and gives no trouble. There is only one Brother, but two will be needed at the next reopening, as well as at Madison, Indiana. *Cathedral*

Madison, Indiana
Diocese of Vincennes

The Brothers have been re-established for a year, to the great joy of the pastor and his flock. There are one hundred and twenty children; the usual salary, $150.

Alton, Illinois
Diocese of Alton

Two Brothers have here a fine school of 160 children. The Brothers have been living with the Bishop for nearly two years, and they seem to come up to the expectations of everybody; the usual salary. *Cathedral*

Sorinsville

This is the latest foundation of Brothers, one mile from the University, in the midst of some twenty Irish families who have settled between the town and the College, and *Little school* for whom a schoolhouse was built last year and a teacher provided, who goes every morning to take charge of some thirty to thirty-five children. They almost pay for wood and candles.

Recapitulation	
Foundations	11
Schools	17
Teachers	37
Salaries	$8,000

Of this amount, one-fourth might be considered as clear profit, did not Chicago turn over its surplus to the support of the college. The balance goes in rent, clothing, and in some cases for board.

CHAPTER 20

1861

In ending the Chronicles of the Congregation of Holy *Chicago*
Cross in Chicago towards the end of July 1859, Fr. Sorin
was far from expecting to find it so soon in the like difficulties, made quite painful by a series of acts which must
show, according to the evidence, "a gross injustice," as will
presently be seen. The author of these pages only repeats
here the expression of the bishop of Chicago; any impartial
judge can easily determine on which side is the injustice.

But before beginning, he wishes to remind the reader
not to lose sight of the fact that it is with a bishop that
the Congregation is in dispute, and that any justification of
the Congregation implies a grievance or a reproach against
His Lordship or his counselors. He would also remark that
all the proceedings of the bishop for the last two years are
such as to leave no doubt in regard to his wish and his
plan to take possession of the college as soon as it would
be possible for him to do so, without any regard to the
engagements of his predecessor, which he never recognized
in this matter. Now he knew better than anybody that
in a city like Chicago it would be rash for a religious
congregation to attempt to hold a college or a school of any
kind without the good will of the bishop; but that it would
be folly to hope to succeed against his will. In vain would
talent and devotedness combine; they would fall against
the opposition of the Ordinary.

Deception

When, therefore, in the month of August 1859, Bp. Duggan appeared to have returned of his own accord to such dispositions as Fr. Sorin could desire, and when he promised the establishments of Chicago the protection that was necessary for them, the Congregation believed in his word and had not the least doubt but that he would be a benefactor, and would more than repay them for the considerable damage that his opposition had caused since his coming to the episcopal see.

As has been said, the Congregation by its contract was only bound to keep a respectable day school, without any collegiate course whatsoever. The better to show his desire of pleasing the bishop, Fr. Sorin then promised to neglect nothing to keep up classes of Greek and Latin, French and German, mathematics and vocal and instrumental music, etc., and this he continued to do, employing men of ability at considerable cost.

On the advice of the archbishop of Baltimore, the Congregation had promised to settle the arrears of rent for the three past years, as soon as any profits came in, which did not seem to be an unlikely or remote probability, owing to the confidence inspired by the declared and efficacious protection of the bishop. On his part, the bishop had promised that he would give in writing to the Congregation the St. Joseph's German church, on the same conditions which he had ceded St. Michael's to the Redemptorist Fathers. And when later some members of this congregation tried to make trouble and to have it taken from the Fathers of Holy Cross, His Lordship repeated his declaration that there was no danger, and that he would rather close the church than yield to their insolent demands.

New expenses for the Congregation

Almost at the time of the reconciliation just mentioned, the bishop made known his pressing need of money, and his wish to get three thousand dollars before the month of May, promising that if it were advanced to him, he would make no further demand till the month of May of the next year. With considerable difficulty, the Congregation managed to pay him that sum by the specified time.

Up to this time no doubt had arisen as to his real dispositions, and in its full confidence in him the Congregation had made improvements costing more than twenty-five hundred dollars, and put up such buildings as would set the Sisters on a regular footing, so that by the following spring the Congregation had expended thirty thousand francs in buildings and repairs on the grounds. It is true that the Sisters had obtained from their benefactors nearly half the amount; the rest was paid from the funds of the Congregation.

Thus far, all things seemed to be progressing in peace and harmony. The bishop was pleased, as he himself wrote to the superior general in France when mentioning the services rendered him by the Congregation. However, this good will, real or apparent, was soon to pass away without any possibility of assigning a cause for the change. A pretext was sought in the change of the superior of the college, but before there was even talk of naming a successor for him the bishop had already changed. The Father himself could not be mistaken in that.

Changes in the bishop's disposition

At the solemn distribution of premiums in the college, the bishop, who was in town and whom everybody expected, did not make his appearance. If the cause of his return to his earlier coolness was not easy to discover, the object was less enigmatic; the bishop again wanted to resume possession, and to bring this about he had only to attack the Congregation on the one point the facility and efficacy of which he had discovered.

Meanwhile, the mean spirited persons who have been referred to in the matter of the German church, returned to the attack, and by means of representations that would not have been even listened to by a well disposed bishop, they persuaded him to take St. Joseph's church suddenly from the Congregation and to transfer it to a secular priest, whom they afterwards drove away; and this contrary to all justice as well as to the repeated assurances of the bishop. Thus, after four years of devotedness and of services such as had never before been bestowed on this parish,

Difficulties with the Germans

the Congregation was deprived of the principal support which it found there to meet its engagements. This was not merely withholding his protection, but it was ratifying a loss which he well knew would be fatal to the Congregation in Chicago. This church had been given from the first as the only assured source of revenue from which to pay the annual rent of the college.

This act, which needed no commentary, received one that left no doubt. Some weeks afterwards, the Fr. Superior went to the bishop to ask for some compensation for the loss of the church, for instance, the charge of a little Irish congregation which he had already been attending at the request of the vicar general. The latter could hardly attend to it, seeing that he was pastor of the cathedral and of a large parish of five or six thousand souls. This simple request was simply rejected.

Offer of a French priest for Chicago refused

Shortly afterwards, when the newspapers of the city announced that the Canadians of Chicago were going to build themselves a Protestant church, the same Father presented himself to His Lordship and offered him the services of a French priest of the Congregation. The bishop knew that those poor Canadians, as well as a certain number of Belgians, had been without a pastor for five years, and that their abandonment had become a serious matter. He seemed to be pleased with the offer and requested the Father to go to Notre Dame du Lac and arrange the matter, but on his return next day everything was changed. The Father was refused, although he asked the bishop for absolutely nothing more than permission to work in the city for the salvation of some thousands of his countrymen who were daily leaving and apostatizing for want of a priest who understood their language and would take an interest in them.

The dispositions of the vicar general were hardly less discouraging. It had been agreed with the bishop that the teaching members whom the priests should employ would be paid two hundred dollars each. The Brothers engaged in teaching at the cathedral were thus entitled to four hundred dollars, and the Sisters to the same amount. When the end of the scholastic year came, he positively refused to pay the Sisters any salary. Under other circumstances, this injustice might have been let pass unnoticed, but the Sisters had to pay for their board and lodging; and without wishing to cause any trouble to the vicar general for the payment of the four hundred dollars in question, they were obliged to tell him that they could not continue the school without a salary. *Inde ira.*

Would it be believed? He preferred to employ a married lady at $450 a year rather than to leave his little girls under the care of two Sisters against whom he had no other complaint. As to the salary of the two Brothers, and of the other three whom he employed at St. Patrick's, he paid in notes on time, some of which were protested, and others have not been paid to this day.

New offenses at the School of the Holy Family

The Brothers' school at the cathedral was also given up, seeing that no Brother had the courage to continue it in the state of total abandonment in which it was left. The three other Brothers at St. Patrick's and the one at the former cathedral remained at their posts, but till the present day they have not received the least part of their salary. Last Christmas, with the consent of the pastor, they got up an exhibition at St. Patrick's for their own benefit. It brought in two hundred dollars, which His Reverence took for himself without leaving them a cent. And this is the gentlemen who tells all that will listen to him that the Congregation does not pay its rent and, consequently, should retire.

There is certainly reason to be surprised that the Congregation held out so long against such opposition; but if we consider the expenses it had gone to and the considerable debts it had made to establish itself respectably in Chicago, relying on the promises of two bishops on which it tried to hope, *spes contra spem*, we shall perhaps better understand how, even to the last, it tried not to see what was only too plain, namely, that the bishop would hold to his first declaration, that he was not bound by his predecessor's act, and that he would take back the college without any regard to what losses the Congregation might thereby suffer.

The injustice of the bishop

To gain his end he did not hesitate to adopt measures that he himself would have unhesitatingly condemned in others. Nothing was easier for him than to place the Congregation in a position to pay the rent, supposing he ought to have exacted such a sum, which many called a "permission to do good in his diocese." The schoolhouses were left in a shocking state of neglect. The efforts of the most devoted members were thwarted; each superior lost courage when, year after year, he saw not only the precarious condition of the establishment, but the unmistakable proofs of bad will on the part of the ecclesiastical authorities, whose object was perseveringly followed up, to drive the community out by small annoyances.

This state of things was communicated to Fr. Sorin when he was still in Rome. He was on the point of making it known, but preferred to allow some time yet, to see the evil with his own eyes and to see once more what remedy could be applied before laying the matter before the tribunal that could by right do the community justice. Moreover, the rent was paid up to the month of May, and till then there was nothing to fear.

On his return at the end of April, civil war had broken out; everything was changed in the United States; commerce was entirely paralyzed, and in money transactions everybody understood that patience towards a debtor had become a necessity. In such a state of things no one would think that a bishop would avail himself of the physical inability of a Congregation which was sacrificing itself under *His orders* his very eyes, to declare to it that since it was not paying, it must leave the city, otherwise he would take legal measures to have an eviction in form. Let us quote his very words.

Fr. Sorin presented himself to offer his respects to His Lordship, but finding the bishop absent, he deputed the superior of Notre Dame du Lac,[1] who was acquainted with the bishop, to learn from his own lips what credit was to

1. Since Fr. Sorin himself was the superior of Notre Dame du Lac, the chronicler probably meant to say here "the superior of St. Mary of the Lake," the college in Chicago.

be given to the rumor that was abroad that he intended to take back the college. The bishop confirmed the rumor, adding that he expected all the members to be gone before the first of August. The Father Superior, being very much surprised at such an arbitrary command, wished to know the cause; but none was assigned except that of the poet: *Sic volo, sic jubeo, sit pro ratione voluntas.*

For an hour and a half the same Father set before the bishop all the complaints that the Congregation thought itself justified in bringing against the manner in which it was treated since its coming to Chicago. He listened to all, admitted most of the charges, and ended by saying that he had the greatest esteem for the Fathers of the Congregation and that he was ready to give them proof of this at all times and throughout his whole diocese; but as for the college, his decision was irrevocably made. Some days later the same Father was sent back to the bishop with the following letter from the provincial.

> Notre Dame du Lac, June 8, 1861
> to Bp. Duggan, D.D., Chicago

My Lord,

I request that if you in reality want us to leave the premises which we occupy in Chicago, you will have the kindness to give us in writing your orders to this effect, so that we may have some document to justify us, if necessary, in this step.

> Very respectfully,
> E. Sorin.

The following is the answer:

> Chicago, June 11, 1861

Very Reverend and dear Sir,

In answer to your letter I have only to repeat to you what I have often said before: that since the contract between you and Bishop O'Regan has been violated by you in almost every point, I have only to take back the property of the Church which you are occupying. The college has not been properly kept; the schools in the parishes have been neglected; and the rent which you agreed to pay has not been paid. For these reasons and others, I require that you no longer retain the property of the Church; and remitting you the several thousands of dollars now due, I simply demand possession of our own property. If I must resort to legal measures to attain this object, let all the scandal and all the consequences fall back on you. For three years I have borne much for the sake of peace; but I am now resolved not to be any longer trifled with. Your positive refusal to comply with any of the obligations of your contract forces me to adopt the course against my inclination. I give you three days to answer, after which I will consider myself at liberty and will employ the only means left me to redress this grave injustice.

Respectfully,
†James, Bp. of Chicago

On the twelfth, Fr. Sorin, to whose eyes and conscience this letter did not contain a truthful phrase, answered as follows.

My Lord,

In answer to your esteemed favor of yesterday permit me to tell you that I yield to your orders and to the fear of scandal, however different from yours may be our manner of appreciating our labors in your city these three years. You say that we have not fulfilled our obligations; we believe on the contrary that still less have you complied with yours. But since we must go, we will do it religiously, I hope, in peace and humility and with your blessing.

Very respectfully your humble servant, etc.
E. Sorin, C.S.C.

Evacuation of the college

Three days afterwards, the college and the two Brothers' schools, the Sisters' day school and their German parish school were closed, without the utterance of the least complaint as to the bishop's conduct. But it seems that the more each member of the Congregation was on his guard, so much the more free did public sentiment feel to express itself in their regard. The sensation was too profound not to become annoying to the bishop. Two days later, he wrote to the Father Superior to tell him that, instead of six weeks, he could allow him only one in which to vacate the premises, and that if all the members were not gone in eight days, he would have recourse to the law.

Thus it was ever the law, scandals, and the threat that if the Congregation gave him the least trouble, he would forbid all his clergy to send even one child to Notre Dame, and he would not even give permission to any of the Fathers of Holy Cross to say mass in his diocese.

From all this it follows that, however firmly the Congregation may be convinced of the injustice that is done it, it can appeal neither to Rome to protect and safeguard its rights, nor to any other authority, without causing a fearful scandal in the Church. *Domine adjutor meus et liberator meus.* This was the last trait to show in a clear light the spirit of persecution of which the Congregation was the object in Chicago.

The college had a number of old accounts to collect and debts amounting to three thousand dollars to pay. The Sisters had on hand a sum total of five thousand dollars to pay to various booksellers and dealers in church goods, one-half of which they still had in their store and of which they could now make no use. This store had been opened at the request of the bishop for the convenience of the clergy and of the people, and now it is peremptorily closed, as were the classes, to the great loss of the good Sisters. God alone knows how great is their embarrassment just now.

Financial losses of the Congregation

Moreover, they also leave on the portion of the grounds which they occupied buildings and improvements to the value of five thousand dollars, one-half of which they paid out of their own funds, and the rest they collected, whilst at the same time they were not receiving one cent of the salary to which they were entitled. Seeing that in the terms of the contract, which was to last fifty years, the improvements belong to the bishop, those five thousand dollars of improvements and the $5,500 paid the bishop in cash for five years use of the property more than compensate him and cause him not a fraction of loss in the operation;

whereas the Congregation has given gratis for five years the services of thirty members, who are now withdrawing under duress, with a debt of eight thousand dollars which they must liquidate, and all this as the result of a deception the mere suspicion of which would have seemed to them a crime.

Moreover, they are not even permitted today to make known their grievances. On the contrary, they must go their way in silence, as if incapable or unworthy of the confidence of the bishop, who would have neither arbitration nor reference to the Sacred Congregation of the Propaganda, but who was always ready to appeal to the secular arm to force them to obey, because he knew very well that they would all sooner lose eveything than cause scandal in a diocese that has had more than enough of scandals. Happily, in withdrawing they had the consolation of having given no scandal before God.

The strange attitude of the bishop of Chicago

But they cannot understand how a bishop, dealing with a religious congregation approved by the Holy See, refuses it the privilege of carrying to Rome its difficulties with the ecclesiastical authority, but will call only on the secular arm whilst he is reminded in every tone that it belongs to Rome to settle the question and not to the secular tribunals.

Nothing would have induced Fr. Sorin thus to drop the matter before Rome had decided; but when only three days, that is to say, some hours, were left him in which to forward his answer to Chicago, before the bishop would begin a suit whose disastrous consequences no one could foresee, he did not hesitate to yield to the moral violence to which he was subjected, leaving it to God to do him justice, and seeking in the treasure house of hope a compensation for the injustice of this world.

Br. Amédée

The difficulties of Chicago are followed by those of Brother Amédée[2] of St-Laurent near Montreal. This

2. Br. Amédée (Jacques-Pierre Dayres) was born Jan. 24, 1824, at Agen in the diocese of Lot et Garonne, France. He entered the Congregation of Holy Cross at Notre Dame on Oct. 15, 1853, and

Brother had left Notre Dame in the month of July 1860, to enter the Province of Canada, with the written permission of the Very Reverend Father General, but contrary to the formal prohibition of Fr. Sorin, whom he thus placed in the greatest embarrassment, quitting his obedience of book-keeper just at a time when he was alone in the office, and when his departure left it closed without anyone to take charge of it. He had sent his trunk to the railroad station without having it examined according to custom, and he himself set off in the middle of the night, without handing in any accounts or leaving any statement or memorandum of what he was taking with him.

His history

He was a man of a fickle, somber, mysterious character, whose ways were secret and erratic, having the zeal of a Pharisee in regard to others, but with a way of his own of understanding poverty and obedience as applied to himself. He was eager for news and confidences or meddling gossip; he knew well how to make all those who came in contact with him unhappy, and to sow discord around him. In a word, he had the talent to make himself detested and almost insupportable to all in the house.

When the Very Reverend Father came to make his visit in 1857, he could not see clearly through his books: the three years that followed left the same veil over his operations. Mystery was his element. When Fr. Sorin went to St-Laurent in the following October, the Brother handed him, unsolicited and without a word of expla-nation, a check for four hundred francs. On his return from France in April 1861, he met this same Brother in Philadelphia, where he passed several days with the Broth-ers of Notre Dame, to all appearances courteous and cheerful.

---

professed vows on Feb. 2, 1856. He served as provincial treasurer from Aug. 30, 1857, until he left for Canada. He had visited France from September 1858 until March 1859. After leaving the U.S. for Canada, he returned to France and there withdrew from the community on July 8, 1866. M.g.

Difficulties with
Br. Charles
Borromeo begin

Towards the end of May, Brother Charles Borromeo,[3] whom Fr. Sorin had brought from France the preceding autumn at an expense of twelve hundred francs, asked permission to go to Canada. As he was urgent in the matter, Fr. Sorin told him to write to St-Laurent that he would be permitted to go, if he were still wanted there, provided Canada first reimbursed the Provincial of Indiana for the money advanced for him, but that on no other condition would Fr. Sorin consent to the change.

The letter was sent accordingly, but without any regard to it, Br. Amédée sent Brother Charles Borromeo a check on New York for an amount sufficient to pay his travelling expenses from Notre Dame to St-Laurent. Fr. Sorin opened the letter, as he does for all the correspondence of members of the community, and returned the letter and the check to Brother Amédée.

Insolence of
Br. Amédée

The Brother then begins a pitiable series of threatening, insulting, pedantic and arrogant letters. He repeats over and over again that he holds the fate of Notre Dame in his hands, and that it depends solely on him to sink the institution. He has three ways of doing this, one of which consists in certificates that he can put in circulation and thus ruin it; the other two more dreadful and more infallible, etc., etc.

Papers fraud-
ulently taken
from Notre
Dame du Lac
by Br. Amédée

What could those certificates be that were in the hands of a professed Brother who had been for four years the secretary-treasurer of the house, and to whom the house owed absolutely nothing at his departure?

At the very start, Fr. Sorin, more disgusted than angry at such language, sent copies of the first letters of Brother Amédée to the Mother House in France as well as to his immediate superior at St-Laurent; for the Brother had had

3. Br. Charles Borromeo (Jules-Charles Petitpierre) was born Apr. 25, 1825, at Neuchâtel, Switzerland. He entered the Congregation of Holy Cross at Ste-Croix and began the novitiate on Mar. 19, 1859, as Br. Victorin. His name had been changed to Charles Borromeo by the time he left for America on Sept. 16, 1860. He withdrew from the community briefly, Aug. 8, 1864 to Oct. 12, 1864, and then left finally on Mar. 15, 1866. M.g.

the impudence to give it out that he wrote under Fr. Rézé's eyes and that the Mother House sustained him; he appeared to have no doubt of the truth of his assertion.

Be this as it may, neither the Reverend Fr. Rézé, nor the Very Reverend Fr. Superior General seemed to have approved of his conduct. The former answered evasively, *Evasive manner* attempting to prove that he had tried all possible means *of Fr. Rézé* to quiet this Brother, but without success, adding that the danger seemed to him imminent, and advising great prudence and even concessions. It began to appear that he would be well enough pleased to get Brother Charles Borromeo for nothing, although the question admitted of no doubt that he should first reimburse the advances for his voyage from France to America. He even promised that if *He states his* this satisfaction were granted to Br. Amédée, there would *conditions and* be an end of the whole matter, saying that Brother Amédée *violates them* himself had assured him that he would be content with this, and that on the arrival of Br. Charles Borromeo at St-Laurent he would at once send a receipt in full to Notre Dame, with all the notes and certificates that he held in his possession against the house of the Lake. The Rev. Fr. Rézé himself went security for the keeping of this promise.

Fr. Sorin, who, on the word and the writings of his actual superior, believed Brother Amédée to be capable of ruining the institute, and who had no ulterior purpose other than, if necessary, to bring the matter to the knowledge of Rome, preferred, for the sake of peace, to sacrifice the twelve hundred francs, and, what cost him far more, the feeling of honor and justice which he was obliged to lay aside before an injustice and provocation that went beyond all bounds.

But what can a victim do who is attacked on the high road by an assassin who holds the knife to his throat? He sent the Brother, therefore, not expecting very strongly that a man capable of writing such threats and of convincing his superior that he would put them in execution, would keep even promises attested by this same superior.

And in fact, instead of doing as he had engaged to do, Br. Amédée on the following week sent Fr. Sorin a letter similar to the others, stating that he had just received from Sainte-Croix the letters in which he had denounced him to His Reverence, and that consequently he would not now keep his promise unless he received from Fr. Sorin a new cloak of French cloth, a complete new outfit of clothing, etc., etc.; and then he repeated his insulting declaration that the fate of the Lake was in his hands.

The action of His Reverence

Meanwhile, the answer of His Reverence had also reached Notre Dame du Lac. It seemed to Fr. Sorin to be favorable to him, settling in his favor the question of the twelve hundred francs, and offering to expel Br. Amédée from the Congregation if he demanded it. Moreover, it stated that St-Laurent was informed of this decision. It might be expected that the result of this intervention of the Mother House would manifest itself, but it did not. Fr. Sorin, finding that the letters of Sainte-Croix, like his own, had no effect, demanded reimbursement, but in vain.

It would be hard to find anywhere else a series of letters from the pen of a religious more disgusting than these. And yet, strange as it may appear, his immediate superior, who could not pretend ignorance of the facts, did not hesitate to write to Fr. Sorin that in this matter, Br. Amédée had shown more delicacy than might be thought. Let us devote some lines to an analysis of the whole affair.

Abridged story of the difficult Br. Amédée

In the month of July 1860, Brother Amédée, secretary and treasurer of Notre Dame, leaves his post by stealth, telling no one what money or other valuables he takes. In the month of October following, he hands Fr. Sorin four hundred francs without saying why or whence the money comes. In April 1861, the same Brother meets Fr. Sorin in Philadelphia and shows himself to be animated by the best dispositions. On his return from Europe in May, Fr. Sorin finds that this same Br. Amédée is at work to bring Br. Charles Borromeo to Canada. The year before, Br. Charles had been promised to St-Laurent by France, but His Reverence afterwards gave him to Fr. Sorin.

At the entreaties of Br. Charles, Fr. Sorin permits him to inform St-Laurent that he may go there, provided the

twelve hundred francs in travel expenses which he cost
Notre Dame du Lac shall first be refunded to Fr. Sorin.
Br. Amédée answers for St-Laurent by sending only the
amount necessary to pay the journey from Notre Dame to
St-Laurent. The check is returned to him by Fr. Sorin,
whereat Br. Amédée is displeased!!! He insolently writes
that he has five means to destroy Notre Dame, that he
holds the honor of his superior in his hands, and that his
superior, under whose eyes he is writing, thinks as he does.

A copy of this letter is sent to the superior referred
to, who answers evasively. A second copy is forwarded to
the Mother House, which is greatly alarmed by it. The
Brother repeats his threats and insults without seeming to
fear the least blame either from St-Laurent or Sainte-Croix.
Finally, he promises that if Br. Charles Borromeo is sent
to him, he will cease and will deliver up all his means
of destruction. The Brother is sent to him, but he lays
down new conditions. He requires a general declaration
from Fr. Sorin that Canada owes him nothing, and he
promises that if this receipt is forwarded to him he will
return all his documents. The receipt is sent, but the same
infidelity! He now demands a cloak, clothes, etc. Fr. Sorin
refuses to make any further sacrifices even for the sake
of peace.

It is doubtless painful to have to record things of such *Declaration of*
an irreligious nature in the annals of a community; but *intention*
if those annals are to be considered as a truthful history,
they must either speak the truth or be silent, unless it
be understood that they show only the fair side. But that
would not be doing justice to the institute, nor even to the
action of Providence; because unless we see the obstacles
and the difficulties of all kinds that have been met, it will
not be possible to appreciate the triumph of grace. Moreover, those miseries contain lessons and warnings which
will at least not be useless for our successors.

Although the personal dispositions of Br. Amédée were
alone the ostensible object of the complaints of Notre
Dame du Lac from the month of May to the end of this

year, it nevertheless appears probable that they would have had no importance if his superiors had been better disposed towards Notre Dame.

St-Laurent has for a number of years shown feelings of a kind of envy, sometimes poorly disguised, which have never allowed the administration of Notre Dame to be on terms of cordiality in matters that would be for their common good. Br. Amédée, who without a doubt is a firebrand of discord and does not know what it is to live in peace with everyone, profited from this defect to turn to the annoyance of the province that he had deserted, all the projects for the expansion of the province of St-Laurent, which he

wished at any cost to see take the first place, if only to justify the preference that he had shown for it. Hence, the pompous announcements of foundations requested for and made in the United States. To believe him, Canada was going to overrun everything and Notre Dame would soon be only a secondary concern. That the administration of St-Laurent lent a ready ear to the suggestions of the Brother in question can hardly be doubted.

At just what point the Mother House itself had let itself be taken in by the trickery of this dangerous Brother does not appear so clearly. But one thing is certain, that he considered himself perfectly assured of the support of Sainte-Croix, even in this last dispute. In addition, there is within reach a secret agreement between Sainte-Croix and St-Laurent to deceive Notre Dame, as witness the

opening of New York, not only without the knowledge of Notre Dame, but with a formal denial of the fact after it had been resolved upon.[4] Nevertheless, the Very Rev. Fr. General had himself declared, on his visit at the end of September 1857, that the house of New York would not be re-established without the consent of Notre Dame du Lac.

4. After Fr. Sorin had closed the Sisters' house in New York City in 1856, the house had been reopened in 1860 by the Marianite Sisters of Holy Cross, by then a separate and autonomous congregation. See chapter 15. See also Catta, *Moreau*, 2:470–478; and Catta, *Mother Mary*, 202–208.

This kind of underhand dealing towards the first foundation of the Congregation in a foreign land surely proves that there is resourcefulness at Sainte-Croix; but that the voice of honor and of peace is always consulted, is far from being as well established.

The administration of Notre Dame is quite willing to see herein one more effect of perfidious insinuations and intrigues of Br. Amédée, but it is none the less convinced that this establishment at New York, under the circumstances in which it was made, is an apple of discord very unwisely cast by the general administration, and that no honorable nor religious principle ever justified it. It is a shameful piece of underhand work deliberately and unnecessarily perpetrated on the administration of the Lake, which in 1856 was sanctioned and directed by Sainte-Croix in its act of closing New York.

The two facts that we have just related will perhaps seem to be marked with some bitterness. But if one knew the memories still fresh in the mind of the narrator, they paint very imperfectly the anguish caused by the former and the vexations of the second. Fr. Sorin had returned from Europe with increased devotedness to the Mother House; but to his unspeakable regret, the conduct of Sainte-Croix towards him in those two events singularly disenchanted him. Hence the coolness with which he listened to the demands of Ste-Croix, which asked for favors whilst multiplying injuries.

On 15 April, the Very Rev. Fr. Superior General paid two notes for Fr. Sorin amounting to fifteen thousand francs as a loan in return for a similar favor for a like amount in 1855. This sum was to be refunded in three installments of five thousand francs a year on the future allocations of the Propagation of the Faith. This loan and this promise of repayment were a proof as well as a result of the reciprocal sentiments of the Mother House and of her eldest daughter.

Soon after having signed those notes, the Mother House was subjected to the agony (which no one understands better than Fr. Sorin) caused by the catastrophe of

Marie-Julien.[5] Even before the first payment on the fifteen thousand was made by Sainte-Croix, Fr. Sorin was asked to hasten his payment, and at the beginning of April he sent a thousand francs to the treasury of Sainte-Croix, and had made arrangements to hasten the other payments. It was his intention to settle the whole account this year, in order to help the Congregation, whose existence was threatened. Here Fr. Sorin thought he had some claim to be believed on his word, after having paid out thirty thousand francs in 1855 to save the Congregation.

He would have been only too happy to prove anew, in a similar manner, his personal affection for the Very Reverend Father General, whose critical position he understood; and even if prudence had condemned him, filial love would have prevailed and Sainte-Croix would have received even more than it advanced. Unfortunately, the two incidents just spoken of caused bitterness of heart, and when the heart was no longer with Sainte-Croix, it was all the worse for the latter.

Besides, the condition of the two houses was far more precarious than could have been anticipated before this matter of the fifteen thousand francs came up. Sainte-Croix was far more embarrassed than could have been supposed. The Lake was in the midst of the horrors of a war which no one would have believed. Sainte-Croix wanted to have its funds come in sooner than was agreed upon. Notre

5. Br. Marie-Julien (Joseph-Eugene Bayen) was born Aug. 14, 1813, at Notre Dame de L'Epine (Marne), France. He entered the Congregation of Holy Cross at Ste-Croix on June 3, 1843, and professed vows Aug. 23, 1846. He served for many years as the general steward of the congregation at the motherhouse and was elected one of the six general assistants of the congregation by the General Chapter of 1857. M.g. Assigned to the community's college in Paris, Les Ternes, he became involved with unscrupulous promoters and, without authorization, he made the congregation liable in 1860 for large sums of money. When this came to light in January 1861, Br. Marie-Julien was dispensed from his vows and expelled from the congregation, but the congregation had to pay the debts that he had incurred in its name. Catta, *Moreau*, 2:395–446.

Dame was hardly able, on account of the war, to meet its engagements. Seventeen times Sainte-Croix insisted on payment before the time, and just as often Fr. Sorin was obliged to defer. He had promised to make his repayments from the grants of the Propagation of the Faith, and he had to wait to learn what allowance would be made him and until the usual checks were received.

Father Sorin was urged to obtain a draft on the treasurer, contrary to the confidential instructions which he had received from this officer, and which he had made known at Sainte-Croix before leaving France. And because Fr. Sorin did not yield to the appeals of Sainte-Croix, for the simple reason that he could not, cruel reproaches were heaped upon him, orders were issued and reiterated in virtue of holy obedience, even when the execution of those orders was out of the question. Sainte-Croix refused the sanction of professions requested by the Lake, and all the imaginable means were employed to compel Fr. Sorin to do the impossible. Things were even carried so far that the budget was retained, and at the end of 1861, it had not been returned from Le Mans.

Let us sum up once more. Br. Amédée, the Sisters in New York, the affair of the fifteen thousand francs, these were for this year the three chief sources of vexation such as Notre Dame had not previously known.

Portiuncula, or Our Lady of the Angels

On his return from Europe in the month of May, Fr. Sorin found the new chapel of the Brothers' novitiate almost finished. It had been begun the previous fall on the plan of the very chapel of St. Francis of Assisi, forty feet by twenty. Fr. Sorin had obtained for the new sanctuary all the indulgences of the Portiuncula[6] in perpetuity. It was blessed by the bishop of Fort Wayne on 29 May, and the altar was

Facsimile of the Portiuncula of Italy

privileges

6. Portiuncula: a small chapel near Assisi which was the birthplace of the Franciscan order in the thirteenth century. See Donald Attwater, *A Catholic Dictionary* (New York: Macmillan, 1962), 390.

made privileged[7] by him for every day of the year. Soon afterwards, Fr. Sorin asked of Rome permission to have this chapel declared a regular pilgrimage, and on date of [no date given] the Pope granted this petition. These two favors were received by the Congregation at Notre Dame du Lac with the liveliest gratitude.

Tombs of Fr. Sorin and Br. Vincent

Here Fr. Sorin had dug for Br. Vincent, his first companion, and for himself a burial vault where they are both to rest in the expectation of a blessed resurrection. The vault is under the floor in the center of the nave. In this spot is to be erected a little monument in the shape of a priedieu to receive the right hand of the Very Reverend Fr. Moreau, the founder of Holy Cross. The hand will be suspended as if giving a blessing. All this was explained in writing to the Very Reverend Father himself in 1861, and his answer approved the design, which is not altogether devoid of sense, as can be seen on a little reflection. There it is that people will come to pray and meditate. The right hand of the venerable founder and the body of the pious patriarch of the Brothers of St. Joseph will be two of the most precious relics possessed by the Congregation. It is already the resort of all those that are anxious to pray and to obtain some favor.

The professor of painting in the College has set above the altar a Virgin of Foligno which is not without merit. Preparations are being made to begin the beautifying of the grounds next spring, which will greatly enhance the external charms of the chapel.

Ecclesiastical House of Retirement

Missionaries' Home encouraged by His Holiness, the bishops of America and the clergy

On 25 September, the first stone was blessed by Bp. Luers, of Fort Wayne, surrounded by all the clergy of the diocese, who had just ended their ecclesiastical retreat, preached by the Rev. Fr. Smarius[8] at Notre Dame. This

7. Privileged altar: one at which a plenary indulgence may be gained for a soul in purgatory by the celebration and application of a mass. Ibid., 18.

8. Probably Rev. C. F. Smarius, who was active in the diocese

undertaking had received the encouragement of the Holy Father as far back as 1852, but it had to be deferred for want of funds, etc.

On his return to Rome in the month of January, Fr. Sorin was questioned on the progress of the work. The Holy Father himself was pleased to start the list of subscribers and sent two thousand francs to Fr. Sorin, who was thus placed under the obligation of beginning as soon as possible. Other offerings for this purpose came in and were added to that of the Pope so that before leaving Europe, Fr. Sorin had received five thousand francs for the Missionaries' Home. The document in which the Holy Father was pleased to recommend the work was subscribed to by fourteen bishops before the end of the year, and a number of priests hastened to show their sympathy for the work.

A plan was prepared *ad hoc*, and the estimated cost was $20,000 – 136 feet in length, 66 feet wide, three stories high, with forty-eight private rooms, besides the common rooms. The location at the head of St. Joseph's lake is both charming and convenient. The foundations being once blessed, the work was continued during the autumn by the workmen of St. Joseph's Novitiate, who took the bid in the amount of [no sum given] dollars. *Dimensions of the home*

The undertaking was announced in the Catholic papers of the country, and other donations were added to those of Europe. A society of priests was organized on the plan of that already established in several dioceses of France and Germany, but on more advantageous conditions, since from every priest who wished to come and end his days there, an annual subscription was required in proportion to his age when he became a subscriber.

The undertaking has received the highest praise, and is destined to render eminent service to the American Church, as the Rev. Dr. Keogh recently said in *The Pittsburgh Catholic*. Its object is to gather aged missioners together and to provide a place of retirement to those that desire it, when they need it and are suitably disposed. It *Encouragements and advantages*

of Fort Wayne in the 1860s. See Alerding, *Fort Wayne*, 205.

places the bishops of North America under a certain obligation and makes interested friends of all the subscribers, who look upon Notre Dame du Lac as their future home.

War between the North and the South

Contrary to all the anticipations of thinking men, war broke out at the beginning of spring by the attack on Fort Sumter near Charleston, and before the end of the year more than a million men had taken up arms, each in defense of his rights. For more than fifteen years the South had been complaining of the North, and every year the Union seemed to be threatened in the Congress. People were accustomed to those threats, which had come to be but little regarded.

The South was in earnest, had taken action, and had prepared. The first cannon fired in South Carolina took the people of the North entirely by surprise. In some months two hundred thousand soldiers were in the field, and by the end of autumn about six hundred thousand had abandoned everything to defend their country.

Of this number, one third were Catholics. Notre Dame du Lac at once thought of providing those Catholic soldiers with the helps of their holy religion. Fr. Paul Gillen was the first sent to Washington, the headquarters of the grand army, towards the end of June. He did much good there. In succession, three other Fathers were likewise deputed and accepted by the Government as chaplains, namely, Fathers J. Dillon, P. Cooney and W. Corby.[9]

The Sisters were also called by the Government to take care of the wounded. In autumn, twenty-two Sisters

9. Paul Gillen was born in Ireland on Nov. 24, 1810, and joined the Congregation of Holy Cross at Notre Dame, where he received the habit on Dec. 1, 1856, and professed vows on July 2, 1857. On James Dillon, see chapter 19, note 1. Peter Cooney was born in Roscommon, Ireland, on June 20, 1822, and entered the Congregation of Holy Cross at Notre Dame, probably in 1858, and was ordained a priest on July 1, 1859. William Corby was born in Detroit on Oct. 2, 1833, and entered the Congregation of Holy Cross at Notre Dame on Apr. 8, 1854. He was ordained a priest on Dec. 25, 1860. M.g.

of Holy Cross took charge of several military hospitals at Cairo, Paducah, and Mound City.[10] In this latter hospital there were about one thousand beds.

It would be hard to speak too highly of the good done by those Sisters wherever they went. Before the end of this year they baptized forty dying soldiers, after having instructed and prepared them all.

Never had circumstances been more favorable to the progress of the Catholic religion. In the presence of death man reflects. The devotedness of the missionary and of the good Sisters cannot escape his attention, especially when, in spite of himself, he contrasts it with the coldness and the helplessness of Protestantism.

The University

The hard times this year, which caused half the colleges of the country to close, has thus far had no such effect on this institution. The number of boarders has even exceeded that of last year, owing to its distance from the theater of the war.

Hard times

These same hard times have had several other advantageous results for Notre Dame.

1. It has suggested the plan of making the bills of each director of a school payable in three, six and nine months by each according to the presumed revenues of each establishment, an excellent means of obtaining without trouble a considerable sum total and of compelling each director to practice economy, so that he may be able to pay his bills when they fall due.

Advantages

2. In order to save on professors, the novices of the two novitiates have followed the courses of the University, which are more thorough than ever, and in which they make more progress without causing any trouble. This plan should not be abandoned.

10. Cairo, Illinois, is at the confluence of the Mississippi and the Ohio Rivers. Paducah, Kentucky, is on the southern shore of the Ohio River, about forty-five miles upstream from Cairo. Mound City, Illinois, is eight miles upstream from Cairo, on the Ohio River. See Brosnahan, 233–236.

3. Finally, these same hard times have compelled everyone to look more carefully to a stricter economy, and if there has been suffering in one sense, there has been gain in another; the morale of the institute has been the gainer, and that is the main point.

St. Joseph's Novitiate

Novitiates: numerous, regular, edifying

This year has been like a year of rebirth for the Brothers' Novitiate. Hardly had the building been finished on the plan of the former house much enlarged, when it was filled with novices and postulants. Soon what had been considered sufficient for a number of years was found to be too small, and it was deemed necessary to think of adding the two towers which had been left for the future. Fifty-five novices and postulants spent the year there as models of regularity and in the observance of the rules set down for the novitiate. The classes were followed at the College and there was greater regularity in the exercises, the number there present representing the community better than ever. The spirit of piety became established, peace reigned without interruption, and it could be said of the house all year long that it was truly a regular and edifying community.

CHAPTER 21

1862

The year 1862 must for several reasons be a memorable one in the annals of the Congregation of Holy Cross in the United States. The continuation of the civil war, the sending of new chaplains and of a still larger number of Sisters to the army; their successes, their dangers, their trials, the deaths taking place in their ranks; the repercussion of the miseries of the Mother House; the suspense for more than six months in expectation of the Visitor General, who instead of improving the condition of things with the lapse of time, only increased the trouble; the lack of financial resources to meet the continual needs of the institution; the prosperity of the College and of the Academy despite the hard times; the success of the Brothers' schools; the desertion of some among the Brothers; the necessary enlargement of their novitiate, as well as of the house of the apprentices; the sudden erection of a new hall for exhibitions and recreation; the completion of the new St. Mary's Academy; the continuation of the work on the house for aged ecclesiastics; some urgent requests for new foundations at Alton and Springfield, Lafayette and Washington City; these are the principal chapters that deserve attention if they could be developed without danger of offending anyone.

Without a doubt the most charming side of the Society of Holy Cross in the United States this year was that of the war. There were at one time five Fathers and more than forty Sisters in the Armies of the Potomac and of the Tennessee, and in the hospitals of Paducah, Louisville, Cairo, Mound City, Washington City, and Memphis; and whilst the Reverend Chaplains followed their regiments or their brigades amidst the bullets and all the dangers of the war, the Sisters (were) in the middle of the hospitals, some of which occasionally contained as many as fifteen or sixteen hundred wounded or sick soldiers at a time, and the most consoling conversions multiplied around them, the number of baptisms in the hospitals becoming greater every day.

During the course of this year the Sisters of Holy Cross baptized with their own hands more than seven hundred soldiers, after having duly prepared them and made them desirous of belonging to the Religion of their good nurses. Nothing could be more edifying than the conversion and the last moments of those brave soldiers, who blessed Heaven while dying for having granted them the grace to find true life at the very gates of death.

Two of those devoted Sisters fell victims of their zeal in the same hospital, Mound City, as well as one of the Fathers, sent temporarily to help the many wounded men crowded together in this vast building. The two Sisters were Fidelis and Elise,[1] and the chaplain was the Rev. Fr. Bourget,[2] who had just come the year before from the Mother House in France. All three were excellent religious. They were greatly lamented by those for whom they had sacrificed their lives, as well as by their fellow religious at Notre Dame and at St. Mary's.

1. Sr. Fidelis (Bridget Lawlor) was born in 1831 in Queen's County, Ireland, received the habit at St. Mary's, Notre Dame, on Aug. 6, 1857, and professed vows, Aug. 15, 1859. She died on Apr. 18, 1862. Sr. Elise (Unity O'Brien) was born in 1838 in County Donegal, Ireland, and received the habit at St. Mary's, Dec. 8, 1860. She died on July 9, 1862. ASHC.

2. Julien-Prosper Bourget was born June 16, 1831, at Crehan (Côtes-du-Nord), France. He entered the Congregation of Holy Cross at Ste-Croix on Apr. 22, 1858, and professed vows on Aug. 15, 1859. He left for America with Fr. Sorin on Sept. 16, 1860. He died at Mound City on June 12, 1862. M.g.

Those sacrifices were undoubtedly a gain for each of these dear victims; they gave the Congregation of Holy Cross, in the eyes of the public, a consecration that it had not before received and which must surround it with a happy prestige in the midst of the New World.

Whilst it was thus gaining a more enviable reputation in the outside world, the demon, jealous as always of all that is good, and especially of the salvation of souls, made ready to attack the Congregation at the very center of its life and its prosperity, and he very nearly succeeded in utterly destroying it. Never perhaps were men more united in a common devotedness to the same work, and never did the spirit of darkness succeed better in setting them at cross purposes as to the means of reaching the end which they all had in view.

The Mother House appeared to her elder daughter to misconstrue entirely her real sentiments, and vice-versa; soon, on the one side and on the other, everything was interpreted in the worst sense, until religious, who still loved and esteemed one another, began to spy on one another like veritable enemies. There is no doubt that all this trouble was the devil's work.

A Visitor was sent from France. Instead of the favorable results that everybody looked for from this visit, through some mystery not to be explained unless by the wiles of the evil spirit, none of those hopes was realized, and a series of troubles that had not even been suspected began one after the other to arise, in a manner as surprising as it was distressing. Neither party had foreseen the lamentable consequences of the first disagreements, which were in themselves slight and of little importance. But when a man is once aroused to what he considers his duty, there is no knowing how far he will go. At the end of the year the Visitor was in New Orleans, without having arranged anything satisfactorily in the Province of Indiana.[3]

3. The visitor was Rev. Charles Moreau, the nephew of the superior general, Rev. Basil Moreau, and his assistant in the general administration of the Congregation of Holy Cross. Fr. Charles arrived in the United States at New York on Dec. 31, 1861, and returned

Amidst the internal vexations and agonies caused by this misunderstanding, Heaven kept up (our) courage by precious blessings. The College and the Academy were in a prosperous and most encouraging state. The war had ruined several institutions on the lines between the hostile armies; thus far, the north of Indiana had lost nothing by this scourge of the nation, but on the contrary had, in a way, gained by the misfortune of others. The same reflection applies to public institutions.

Unfortunately, confidence, which is the soul of commerce, no longer existed. Whoever happened to be in debt when the war began, could not escape being embarrassed to meet his liabilities. Notre Dame had to suffer from this, especially since provisions and all other articles were going up in price, and paper money was daily less trusted by merchants.

However, with the protection of its heavenly patroness, it maintained its credit and position, and this critical year, which might have entirely ruined it, left it more solidly established than ever in public confidence.

This same year the increasing number of boarders made it more necessary than ever to have a recreation hall for the Junior Department. There were now seventy juniors, who in winter and in bad weather had to take their recreation in the study hall. Mrs. Phelan generously offered $1,000 for this purpose. With this amount not only was a recreation hall built, but a hall in the upper story for the distribution of premiums, thus saving the institution an annual expenditure of from eighty to one hundred dollars for the erection of a theater and a suitable place.

The work on the house of ecclesiastical retreat was continued, in proportion to the resources. The Rev. Father Dillon spent some weeks in the city of Pittsburgh,

---

to France in September 1863. During the intervening twenty-one months he visited all the houses of Sisters, Brothers, and Priests of Holy Cross in the U.S. and Canada. See Catta, *Moreau*, 2:480–504; Catta, *Mother Mary*, 219–242; Leandre-M. Frechet, *Les Archives Générales: Chronologie des évenements qui ont marqué la vie de Sainte-Croix* (Rome: Curia Generalizia de Sainte-Croix, 1968).

where he collected nearly eleven hundred dollars for this project.

The first trial of steam heating was made this summer at the new St. Mary's Academy, and it gave all the satisfaction that could be desired.

CHAPTER 22

1863

The unfortunate war, which has been desolating the country for the last two years, was destined to be prolonged with all its horrors throughout this whole year, the principal events of which bearing on the Congregation of Holy Cross in this Province we are going to relate.

The four missionaries continued their dangerous work with the same courage and the same results. The Rev. Fr. Carrier[1] joined his confreres at the beginning of spring. He was chaplain of the Catholic soldiers in the army which had the signal honor of taking Vicksburg, but he was recalled the following summer and returned about the beginning of October.

The Rev. Fr. James Dillon, whose health had been failing for some time, was obliged to seek to recover it in a foreign climate and in repose, and he left for Europe in the month of August.

Sisters were sent in larger numbers to the hospitals, and baptisms multiplied more than ever amongst their wounded and sick. Before the end of the year the number of those whom they had thus prepared and regenerated ran up to

1. Joseph Carrier was born on Dec. 20, 1829, at La Moutade (Puy-de-Dôme), France, entered the Congregation of Holy Cross at Ste-Croix on July 24, 1851, and professed vows on Aug. 15, 1852. M.g.

eighteen hundred, not to speak of all those that went home edified and devoted for life to the Sisters of Holy Cross.

The visitation was resumed in May,[2] but with hardly any serious result. After spending some ten days at Notre Dame du Lac, the visitor departed and was heard of no more, leaving it to the General Chapter, which was to be held in the month of August, to pronounce on the difficulties of which this visit had been the unexpected and probably also the involuntary occasion.

The Chapter did meet at the appointed time and the question was examined at some length. The results are known, and this is not the place to make any comments on the subject, on which the highest tribunal of the Congregation has pronounced its judgment. However, Rome has kept silence at least all this year on the difficulties of the Congregation, and at the end of December there was nothing authentic or official from this supreme tribunal.[3]

This year the number of entries was greater than ever. The pupils came the first days in such numbers that soon every spot was occupied, and beds had to be placed wherever they could be crowded in.

Then, laborers became so scarce that it was hard to find men to cut wood in the country. The Council of Notre Dame suddenly found itself face to face with the almost impossible task of obtaining the amount of wood necessary for the winter, which had already set in. After the most serious deliberation, it was resolved to introduce steam heating as an escape out of the difficulty, as had been

2. Charles Moreau was at Notre Dame du Lac from July 11 or 12 until Aug. 25, 1862. Cf. Catta, *Moreau*, 2:484. The dates and events of a second visit, here referred to, are uncertain. See chapter 21, note 3; see also Frechet.

3. The General Chapter of 1863 erected two canonical provinces, one for France and one for North America. The North American Province was not officially established until 1865. See minutes of the general chapters, sessions of Aug. 14, 18, and 19, 1863, GA; Catta, *Moreau*, 2:612–658.

done at St. Mary's. There was not a day to spare: it was November. The work was urged forward with all possible haste, and by Christmas the College was heated delightfully and economically, as it had not been before.

The steam heating at St. Mary's a year earlier had much to do with the great reputation of the new Academy. The Council hoped that something of the kind would happen for the College, nor was it disappointed.

The advantages of this new system were not known until it was in full operation. Soon afterwards, steam was introduced into the kitchen and the wash-house. It was everywhere considered a blessing, saving on an average twenty to twenty-five dollars a day. The administration took this occasion to raise the board by twenty dollars, and no one found fault.

Towards the end of the year, His Reverence having ordered Fr. Sorin to protect the Brothers against conscription, the latter sent the original to Bp. Wood of Philadelphia, who exonerated him from all blame, although he expressed his regrets that such were the unhappy consequences of the fratricidal war between the North and the South.[4]

The four Brothers in Philadelphia once being withdrawn, it was impossible to continue the three schools, seeing that only novices would be left, who by themselves would be incapable (of managing the schools). Fr. Sorin gave no orders in this matter, but was content to send the Brother Director an exact translation of the letter of His Reverence.

Meanwhile, the Rev. Fr. Carrier, who had obtained

4. The Conscription Act of 1863 provided for a draft by lottery of eligible men in July 1863 and in March, July, and December 1864. The chronicler cites the fear that the Brothers working in Philadelphia would be exposed to the military draft as the reason for withdrawing them from the schools in which they were teaching there. Kuhn, "Philadelphia," 111–113, suggests that Sorin wanted an excuse to close the congregation's houses in Philadelphia, lest that city be designated as the seat of administration for the North American Province, as had been recommended by the General Chapter of 1863.

excellent recommendations from General Grant to the President for the exemption of the members of the Congregation, proceeded to Washington, and obtained, in effect, the verbal promise of the Secretary of War that our Brothers residing at Notre Dame, in consideration of their workshops, would be exempt if the lot fell on them. Therefore, instead of proceeding to Canada, as His Reverence advised, not knowing of the exemption, the Brothers, who were just as safe at Notre Dame, resolved of their own accord to return thither.

The Rev. Fr. Stanton of St. Augustine's found the greatest difficulties, real or imaginary, in replacing those Brothers, and protested against their recall. He unjustly laid the blame on Fr. Sorin, who was only carrying out the orders of his superiors.

One thing that contributed not a little to tranquilize the members of the Council during those two years of trouble, was that they all along expected the visit of the Superior General himself, of whom they had not the slightest fear, if only they had a chance to show him how much the dispositions of the Province were misjudged. They never doubted that his presence would have restored perfect harmony in a few days.

In the month of August of this year, the Brothers' school at St. Paul's, Philadelphia, was closed during Fr. Sorin's voyage to France, the pastor refusing obstinately to give or promise a fixed salary such as the Brothers receive in all their other establishments. Experience had proved that the good Brothers did not make their expenses there.

CHAPTER 23
1864

This year was to be marked by several events: sudden increase of the College which was to count 360 boarders present, so that Notre Dame became one of the most numerously attended boarding schools in America; the decrees of the Holy See reuniting the three Provinces of Indiana, Canada, and Louisiana, and fixing the seat and the novitiate of the American Province at Notre Dame du Lac, thus giving hopes that peace, harmony, and union, equally desired by all, would soon be firmly established. On this occasion, His Reverence was invited jointly by Bp. Luers and Fr. Sorin to come and preside over the future chapter and to regular all matters, and also to persuade the Reverend Mother General of the Sisters to fix her general administration at St. Mary's, near Notre Dame du Lac.

Whilst Providence was more evidently than ever bestowing blessings on the Congregation of Holy Cross in America, the demon was striving as usual to destroy it.

Elections in the States are generally an occasion of some commotion. This year, amidst the horrors of war, they could not but be the object of general interest, seeing that on them depended the continuation or the termination of those same horrors. The Council of Notre Dame felt how necessary was prudence in such delicate and dangerous circumstances. It took the matter into consideration and adopted a resolution which was calculated to have the best results. Unfortunately, it was badly carried out, or rather was not carried out at all, the member to whom it had been entrusted foolishly relying on a third party who did not understand the consequences and took no steps in the matter. The result was that the house was very seriously compromised in the eyes of the country.

Mr. Colfax, the Speaker of the House of Representatives in Washington and an old friend of Fr. Sorin, as a matter of course counted on the votes of Notre Dame. Now, as most of the Irish in this country imagine, rightly or wrongly, that the Republican Party is hostile to them, three-fourths of them voted against him. He and his friends were indignant at this. The following month, the exemption which Fr. Carrier had obtained for five members on whom the draft had fallen, was revoked, the post office threatened, and all those privileges were going to be suppressed in a moment.

In this crisis, Fr. Sorin did his best to direct all minds and all hearts to the glorious Patroness of the Lake. This time, as so often before, she showed that her arm was not shortened and her maternal heart had not grown cold. Every member promised to say one thousand Hail Marys. Fr. Carrier was once more sent to Washington, where, after a week of long and earnest work, he succeeded in having the recall of the exemption revoked.

Fortunately for the community, Mrs. Sherman, the wife of the famous general of that name, a fervent Catholic and a friend of the institution, had some months before taken up her residence in South Bend for the sole purpose of having her young family educated at Notre Dame and at St. Mary's. She took a lively interest in the case of the five conscripts, and wrote immediately to President Lincoln and Secretary of War Stanton. Heaven permitted that those letters were received in Washington on the very day when the general telegraphed to the government the fall of Savannah. It seems evident that the Blessed Virgin this time employed the excellent general to secure this favor.

The unexpected success of the College had given rise since the end of summer to the desire of increasing or repairing the building. A regular petition to this effect was addressed by the Council of Notre Dame to the Mother House, and then by the advice of Sainte-Croix to Rome, asking for authorization to devote ten thousand Roman gold crowns to the enlargement of the university buildings. In the same document, the Cardinal Prefect of the Propaganda was asked to permit the weekly publication of a magazine in English especially devoted to the honor of the Most Blessed Virgin, in the style of the *Rosier de Marie* and of several religious publications lately established in Italy. The answer of the Cardinal was most gracious, and the two petitions were granted.

In times of war, and especially of national or civil war, all the passions of the poor human heart are to be dreaded. More than once, the institution of Notre Dame du Lac would have had to tremble for its existence, were it not that it never doubted of the protection of its patron. Whenever the revolutionary storm became more violent, Notre Dame being the central point of a considerable radius, naturally became the object of an attention that was rather hostile than favorable. Never had it been more indispensable to make use of the greatest prudence, to keep up to the ideas of the times, and especially to focus the eyes of Providence on the institution. Its position, although brilliant, was none the less insecure. A false step, a mistaken measure, would compromise everything, destroy everything.

The more the number of students increased in the College, so much the more serious did the danger become; because there was far from being anything like unity of views amongst them in political matters: the two camps were, on the contrary, clearly divided, and were it not that the Blessed Virgin protected all, there would have been quarrels and even the shedding of blood elsewhere besides in Virginia and on the other battlefields.

But it is a testimony which it is consoling to record, that those young men who at Notre Dame du Lac represented the various shades of the politics of their families and of their States, lived in harmony even whilst their fathers and their brothers were slashing one another some hundreds of miles away.

Happily, at the very beginning of the war, Divine Providence had inspired the sending of chaplains and of Sisters to the armies of the North. Their devotedness was as a buckler to protect those that remained at home. The death of several of those noble victims at their post of duty and of honor increased the good will of the country.

The community had no reason to regret its advances. The devotedness of its members was appreciated by the government, the generals, and the officers, whose public eulogiums testified loudly to the country in what estimation their services were held. Out of a hundred others, here is the public testimony borne recently by the commanding general of a brigade in his official report after the battle of Nashville:

"As to the Rev. Fr. Cooney, chaplain of the 35th regiment of Indiana Volunteers, he cannot be too highly praised. I am happy to be able to point him out as one of the model chaplains of the army: gentle, pious, and brave as a lion. He marched without fear in the midst of his heroic regiment, in the shadow of death, affording the wounded and the dying the aids of his holy religion, encouraging each soldier by his example and his words, without distinction of faith or of religious opinions."

Such a testimony from the pen of a man who before the war was at the head of the Know Nothing movement against Catholics is above suspicion. At that terrible and bloody day of Nashville, 16 December, there were two Protestant ministers also present: the official report does not even mention them.

When this same Father, worn out by fatigue and almost a wreck, some weeks afterwards, preaching at mass, announced to his regiment that his superior recalled him, and it was evident that his state of weariness did not permit him any longer to continue a ministry which was too burdensome for him, these veterans, as he himself relates, who during nearly four years had fearlessly met all the imaginable dangers of war, began to weep like children. On that very day a petition was drawn up and signed by all the officers of the regiment and by the general in command of the division, who with his own hand declared that the recall of Fr. Cooney "would be a calamity." This document is a real masterpiece of the noblest sentiments of the human heart. The superior of Notre Dame could not resist; Fr. Cooney could nowhere else be more highly esteemed, more loved, in a better position to do good.

A similar scene was enacted twice in regard to Fr. Paul Gillen in the Army of the Potomac; it was found equally impossible to recall him, although the state of his health seemed imperatively to demand it.

When Fr. Corby returned to Notre Dame after three year's service with the Army of the Potomac, it required a positive order to tear him away from amidst the dangers that he had over and over again confronted without showing the least symptoms of fear. He had literally been present at all the battles of the Peninsula (Campaign) under McClellan and Meade, and afterwards under Grant. He also, and more frequently than any other, had marched amongst bullets and balls, and under the same aegis as his confreres had never received the slightest wound. All of them had unbounded confidence in the protection of the Blessed Virgin; they placed their trust in her, and were neither confounded nor forgotten.

The Rev. Fr. J. Dillon, director of the missionary chaplains, was the first to be put out of action. At the end of two years his lungs became affected. Against the advice of the best army physicians he remained in the army much longer than he should have done. Finally he went to Europe, but returned after twelve months in about the same state of health. The doctors that had observed the course of his malady were of the opinion that a trip to California would be beneficial to him, and in the month of October he started for San Francisco. His first letters seemed to indicate a change for the better in the health of the pious missioner;

but it will take a year to pronounce on the improvement in his health.

The sudden increase in the number of pupils in the College this year is due in the first place to the Patroness of the institution, who was more importuned by prayers, more honored, more loved than ever. The secondary causes are chiefly the following:

1. The harmony and devotedness of the professors, both members of the Congregation and hired. A little more attention to their general comfort, a higher salary for those that were not members of the community, a well established assurance in their minds that the administration esteems them and desires their happiness: in a word, there has been in the faculty everywhere this year, more than any other, contentment and devotedness to the success of the College.

2. Everyone loving his duty and performing it *con amore*, the progress of the students was the more marked; parents understood this as soon as did their children.

3. The table kept pace with the times, nothing was lacking, nor were any complaints made. The good Sisters who devoted themselves to providing, three times a day, not merely for three hundred and sixty pupils, but for nearly six hundred persons, deserve all praise, for it was no easy task to please such a family with the imperfect means at their disposition. But that devotedness which is the fundamental characteristic of those good daughters of Holy Cross makes up for many things.

For twenty years those dear Sisters have devoted themselves to the service of Notre Dame du Lac, and the success with which it is crowned at the present day is in no small measure due to them. During the first twelve years, when they formed an integral part of the community, their fidelity in all their trying labors was simply beyond praise. Since the separation, separate accounts are kept at St. Mary's, as is but right; but the devotedness of the forty Sisters at Notre Dame du Lac has remained the same, equal to all the requirements of the institute which they love as in the first days.

They were born here in the paternal house, and the mutual desire is that the sentiments of their early child-hood never undergo the slightest change. What is done contentedly and lovingly is generally well done. It is not only in the kitchen, but in all the important employments wherein they are engaged that they need to be sustained, by this interior content. Their devotedness is a blessing to the whole institution.

The most important of the improvements at Notre Dame du Lac this year was the rebuilding of the infirmary, which from a little old cabin was changed by Christmas into a respectable building, one hundred feet long, forty-five wide and three stories high.

This building, like the College, is heated by steam. For the present the second story is entirely taken for classes, and a part of the ground floor by the professors. The re-mainder, that is to say, what is strictly speaking about half of what is actually necessary, for the infirmary.

CHAPTER 24

1865

In the annals of Notre Dame du Lac this year forms an epoch in more than one way, but chiefly by the holding of an extraordinary Provincial Chapter by order of the Holy See and presided over by an Apostolic Delegate, and also by the rebuilding of the College or, rather, by its being built anew.

Thus far the Chronicles of the Congregation in the United States have only been able to be written with such reserve that one is compelled to acknowledge that they do not state the half of what the impartiality of history would demand. It is hard for a son that has the least regard for the honor of his father to reveal weaknesses which he would infinitely sooner keep forever secret.

But if, however, one must transmit to successors a true account whence instruction can be drawn and the Providence of God towards his work can be admired, it would be unjust, we think, always to present accounts not only incomplete, but directly false and unjust.

The writer of these memoirs does not wish to judge of the intentions of anybody; God alone has reserved it to himself to pronounce herein. But it would be making truth to lie to seek in all circumstances to screen from blame those whom he heard blamed in the most positive manner by His Holiness himself. For instance, it was to him and to the Procurator General that the Holy Father said one day when speaking of the Very Reverend Fr. Moreau:

"An admirable head for himself, but abominable in the guidance of others." His Eminence the Cardinal Prefect of the Propaganda was often heard by the same Fathers to speak in the same sense of the Superior General and of his nephew.

If the Very Reverend Father Moreau and his nephew have been so long spared in these pages, it is not because they were thought blameless in regard to the embarrassments in which the administration of the Province was involved, but in order to avoid any reflection disadvantageous to them. We now resume more freely the history of 1864 in a few pages.

Fusion of three provinces into one

The General Chapter of 1863 had decreed the fusion of the Provinces of Indiana, Canada and Louisiana into one, whose seat was to be fixed later on. This measure was simply an act of resentment of the Very Rev. Fr. General and of his nephew, who sought merely to lower Notre Dame du Lac. It was pitiful to hear them talk of its insolence, etc.; according to them and some others, this poor mission of Notre Dame hardly deserved to live, and its suppression or its ruin would not cause a single tear.

This fusion caused by the resentment of the Superior General and his nephew

Painful though the admission may be, there appears to exist no doubt that His Reverence and his nephew were constantly seeking means to be revenged on Notre Dame. The fusion just mentioned had no other cause; this was no secret to any of the members, not only of the Chapter, but of the Congregation. The intention was to fix the seat of the new Province in New York. The Superior General himself said to the writer of these pages that he was thinking of placing his nephew in New York as Assistant General in charge of all the American foundations; but as the General Chapter was so near, he preferred to leave all to its decision.

Superior General's warning

The suppression of the provinces having been resolved upon, nothing was easier than to have it passed by a chapter in which the Superior General had taken care to assure himself of a majority of votes, which left Indiana neither

The Superior General caught in his own net

chance nor hope of success. The pretended impartiality of His Reverence was from the beginning to the end of this assembly nothing but a thinly disguised mockery. Probably the matter did not escape the discrimination of the Sacred Propaganda,[1] which, instead of leaving to the Superior General the decision of the question of residence, decided it itself and located it at Notre Dame. The bishop of Fort Wayne was named Apostolic Delegate and charged to call together a chapter in which the election of a Provincial of America would take place, and the revision of the Constitution on Provincials.

Triumph of Notre Dame just when it was to be deeply humiliated

The chapter met at Notre Dame in the third week of Easter, and Fr. Sorin was elected to the new charge by an absolute majority. The chapter seemed to have established peace and harmony, and during some months it might have been believed that concord would finally succeed the interminable miseries of the past. If His Reverence had accepted with a good heart the result of those measures which his bad will had called forth, there is no proof that the consequences would not have been happy. But everything had turned against him, and Notre Dame, which he wished to humiliate and reduce, had gained a victory which it had not even desired. The defeat was too humiliating to be accepted by him. That was not the spirit of the Superior General nor of the nephew.

Fr. Sorin elected Provincial of America

Ste-Croix cannot accept such a defeat

It is hardly necessary to state that the decrees of a chapter so unfavorable to the higher authorities were of no effect. Even before putting them to the test, the union of the novitiates into one, which had been decreed, was pronounced to be an impossibility, as also the administration of so vast a province by one man. The Rev. Fr. Charles (Moreau) in New York would have been equal to the task; but the idea of entrusting to Fr. Sorin of Notre Dame

Provisions of the chapter remain without effect

1. After the Congregation of Holy Cross received papal approval in 1857, its affairs were supervised at the Vatican by the Sacred Congregation for the Propagation of the Faith. (Propaganda Fide).

the government of Canada, Louisiana, and New Brunswick was a . . . .[2]

The great event of the year 1865 was the call of the Superior General to Rome with the positive intention of keeping him there. It was only after the third summons that he finally obeyed. The Reverend Fathers Drouelle and Champeau were summoned at the same time. This does not belong to our annals of America, and yet it is not out of place in them, since it is at this epoch that all is about to change for the Congregation, and in particular for Notre Dame. The resignation of His Reverence was accepted at once, although the fact did not become public till the following year.[3]

His Reverence summoned to Rome

His resignation accepted

This same year His Reverence had sent the Rev. Fr. Charles (Moreau) to Rome. He was a declared enemy who would do everything to justify his acts in America. Besides his own cause, he represented in Rome that of his uncle and of the whole general administration. He lodged with the Procurator General, whom his Reverence had designated as one on whom he might rely without fear. However, Fr. Charles ruined himself forever at Rome.

2. Toohey, the translator, wrote in the margin at this point: "See p. 351 of the original. The words are here cut off, and I cannot pretend to supply them, though the sense is evident." The bottom line of p. 351 appears to have been cut off when the page was bound.

3. Pope Pius IX accepted Basil Moreau's resignation as superior general of the Congregation of Holy Cross on June 10, 1866. Invited by Cardinal Barnabo, the Prefect of Propaganda Fide, to come to Rome for consultation by a letter of Nov. 17, 1865, Moreau left Le Mans for Rome on Jan. 29, 1866, and returned to Le Mans on June 10, 1866. See Catta, *Moreau*, 2:659, 669, 689, 695.

CHAPTER 25

1866

The Superior General had only obeyed under duress the order of the Cardinal Prefect to proceed to Rome. After some months, seeing clearly that instead of gaining anything, he was gradually losing in the estimation of all those that had at first taken some interest in him, he left the city as if by stealth. This irritated not only His Holiness, but also all the Cardinals. From this time forth the Rev. Fr. Moreau had no friends at Rome. His resignation, once accepted, was promulgated, and the Rev. Fr. Chappé named Vicar General Apostolic provisionally until the chapter.[1]

The Superior General flees Rome

His resignation proclaimed and a Vicar General named by Rome

This time His Reverence could not accuse anybody of influencing Rome against him. He had been himself the author of his own downfall. He had been seen, heard, followed, examined. No one had remained to answer him. It is said that he formally demanded the expulsion of the Reverend Fathers Drouelle, Champeau and Sorin, with whom he declared it was impossible for him to govern the Congregation. He also wished to sell Santa Brigitta,[2]

Himself the author of his downfall

---

1. On Pierre Chappé, see chapter 12, note 5. Fr. Moreau's resignation as superior general was announced to the community at Ste-Croix on June 21, 1866, along with the pope's appointment of Chappé as the provisional head of the congregation until the general chapter could meet and elect a new superior general. The general chapter met at Ste-Croix, Aug. 25–29, 1866. See Catta, *Moreau*, 2:698–699, 712ff.

2. Santa Brigitta (St. Bridget's) was a monastery in the historic

without even informing the Propaganda beforehand, and he actually did sell it quietly. He wished to leave Rome, which he no longer loved. The 31 May of this year will remain memorable in the minds of the inhabitants.

General Chapter   The year 1866 must form an epoch in the annals of the Congregation of Holy Cross. The resignation of the Superior General having been accepted by the Pope, a Vicar General was at the same time named by the Cardinal Prefect of the Proganda, with all the powers of the Superior General, until the regular election of a new General by the next chapter. Fr. Chappé, first Assistant, was chosen to administer the affairs of the Congregation and to convoke the General Chapter which met at the usual time at Sainte-Croix. It was presided over by the bishop of Le Mans as Apostolic Delegate; all the members summoned were present with the exception of the Rev. Fr. Charles Moreau, who on a whim thought that he ought to deprive the chapter of his lights and his cooperation. Bp. Fillion[3] in this delicate circumstance showed more consideration than the lack of politeness of the dear Father deserved; but he went right on without paying any further attention to this act of singularity.

                      The acts of the chapter having been made known to
Bp. Dufal elected   the Congregation, it will be sufficient for us to remark
General   here summarily that Bp. Dufal, (titular) bishop of Delcon (and vicar apostolic of) Eastern Bengal, was elected general, and was afterwards confirmed by the Holy See.[4]

---

center of Rome acquired by the congregation in 1855 and used as its headquarters in the Papal States as well as a house of studies for seminarians. See Catta, *Moreau*, 2:152.

3. Charles-Jean Fillion, a priest of the diocese of Le Mans, had been appointed bishop of Le Mans in 1862, upon the death of Bp. Nanquette. See Catta, *Moreau*, 2:508.

4. Pierre Dufal was born Nov. 8, 1822, in St-Gervais d'Auvergne (Puy-de-Dôme), France, entered the Congregation of Holy Cross at Ste-Croix, Sept. 29, 1848, and withdrew the following year. He re-entered on Jan. 5, 1852, professed vows Aug. 15, 1852, and was ordained a priest on Sept. 29, 1853. After service in the congregation's houses in Rome and Le Mans, he was sent to Bengal, India, in 1858, appointed vicar apostolic of Eastern Bengal in 1860, and ordained a bishop, May 15, 1861. M.g. Although he had been

The Congregation was divided into four provinces: France, the United States, Canada and Bengal.[5] To relieve the pressing necessities of the Mother House which was loaded down with debts, America subscribed a sum total of seventy thousand francs.

Unfortunately, the provisional government was (*sic*) until almost everybody was beginning to lose patience and hope. The whole Congregation had necessarily to suffer, although the Mother House, where the ex-Superior General resided, naturally suffered much more from this state of things than any of the other houses.[6]

Finally, on 12 September of the following year, official news was received at Sainte-Croix that (the Superior General, Dufal) had arrived at Marseilles, and everybody began to breathe more easily.

Immediately after the General Chapter, Fr. Sorin proceeded to Rome with the Rev. Fr. Procurator General as deputies of the chapter to lay its acts before the Holy See. He remained there three weeks, and obtained from the Holy Father the approbation (*propria manu* in five lines) of the Ave Maria and the blessing of the crown of Our Lady of the Sacred Heart.

On his return to the States at the beginning of October, he proceeded to Baltimore to assist at the National Council

---

in India since 1858 and had not been present at the general chapter of 1866, Dufal was elected to succeed Moreau as superior general. See Catta, *Moreau*, 2:718–719.

5. France had been canonically erected as a province of the congregation by the General Chapter of 1863. See chapter 22, note 3. The Chapter of 1863 had decreed that all the houses in North America should constitute one province, but Canada and Louisiana had appealed to the General Chapter of 1866 for autonomy and the Chapter canonically erected Canada as a separate province and Louisiana as a vicariate depending on the general administration. Bengal was not erected as a province. See minutes of the General Chapters, sessions of Aug. 27–28, 1866, pp. 273–279, GA.

6. Dufal, the superior general-elect, at first asked that the election not be confirmed and then pled his unworthiness. Consequently, he did not arrive at Ste-Croix to take up his duties and responsibilities as superior general until Sept. 25, 1867, more than a year after his election. Catta, *Moreau*, 1:726–728, 752.

to which he had been invited by Archbishop Spalding, and this delayed his return to Notre Dame till the twenty-first of the same month.

The scholastic year was already well under way, nearly 350 boarders had entered, and everything promised a most successful year. However, as soon as he learned of the reduction of fifty dollars that it had been deemed expedient to make in the former cost of board, he felt that the profits would not correspond to the number, and he expressed his fears to the administration. But it was for the time a misfortune that could not be helped. The books showed a loss, a real deficit of ten thousand dollars at the end of the session. After such an experience, he insisted on having the former charges restored, which was done at the return of the pupils in September 1867.

Deficit of
$10,000

This year 1866-67 was necessarily affected by the inaction resulting from a state of expectancy: expectation that the decrees of the chapter would be approved by Rome; expectation of the new (Superior) General; expectation of the Rules as revised by order of the General Chapter but which could not be distributed before the arrival of the new general. But if in the Province of the United States there was not much initiative, there were at least patience and peace.

Year of expectation

The novitiate of the priests needed repairs; it was discontinued this year. When all had been brought to a state, not only passable, but even more satisfactory and comfortable than it had ever been, the Rev. Fr. James Dillon, elected master of the Salvatorist novices by the Provincial Chapter, took possession towards the end of August with six excellent novices, all chosen from amongst the pupils of the University. The novices no longer have anything to do with the College.

Novitiate of
the Salvatorists

The Rev. Fr. Letourneau[7] having been named chaplain at St. Mary's and pastor of the Assumption at New Lowell, the Rev. Fr. Carrier was appointed his successor in

St. Joseph's
Novitiate likewise
separated from
the College

7. Louis-Job Letourneau was born Oct. 3, 1828, in Detroit, Michigan, entered the Congregation of Holy Cross at Notre Dame,

St. Joseph's novitiate. He undertook all the teaching of the novices, who thus ceased connection with the College. The two novitiates were thus for the first time on a regular footing according to the letter of the Constitutions. Hence, they inspire new hopes.

Another step in the same direction was taken this year by the decree of the Provincial Chapter to finish the Missionaries' House at the expense of the Congregation to make it the residence (besides some priests that might wish to come and make retreats there) of novices who, finishing their novitiate before the age required for profession, would there continue their studies until they made their perpetual vows. The work is going forward and will be completed by Christmas. On the north tower will be placed the telescope presented to the institution by His Majesty Napoleon.[8]

Scholastics' House

Observatory

Since the return of Fr. Sorin, the community has gained in its religious life by its more complete separation from the College. It has passed the year in this happy separation, occupying all by itself the two lower stories of the infirmary. At the last reopening of school, it exchanged the first story with the Minims[9] without suffering much in its isolation.

The missions have equally been making progress. Cincinnati has made the acquisition of a suitable house for the sum of eight thousand dollars, which the establishment will pay by degrees. Besides, St. Philomena's school has been taken again, so that fourteen teaching Brothers reside there

Missions: Cincinnati

---

probably in 1853 or 1854, and was ordained a priest Sept. 20, 1857. Having completed his novitiate and his theological studies in Rome, he accompanied Fr. Basil Moreau on the latter's journey to North America in 1857. M.g.

8. Napoleon III had been Emperor of the French since 1852. Seeing the University of Notre Dame as an outpost of French culture and influence, he presented a telescope, over seven feet long with a six inch aperture, to Rev. Joseph Carrier, a professor of science at Notre Dame, when the latter was in France during 1866. See Hope, 156.

9. The Minims were boys between the ages of six and thirteen who were students in the primary division at Notre Dame. See Hope, 221.

this year, each at the head of a large class of from 100 to 150 scholars.[10]

Fort Wayne

Fort Wayne is likewise to have a pied-à-terre of its own for the Congregation. The four Brothers who conduct this school are doing well and are very happy.

Lafayette

Four other Brothers are established by an ancient authorization in Lafayette, where by mutual agreement they are to build on their own ground, at the charge of the pastor, a house costing $25,000 on condition that they relinquish their salary for five years.

Alton, Springfield

The two schools of Alton and Springfield employ, the former four Brothers, the latter only two. They are also promising houses.

St. Patrick's

The new foundation of St. Patrick's is still in swaddling clothes, but will, perhaps, emerge from them some day. The Rev. Fr. Cooney is superior.

New Dublin

Brother Raymond is still at New Dublin, where he rules all things, if not according to his own best judgment, at least with great liberty.

Baltimore

Baltimore, not having signified by one side or the other, any intention to continue, remains closed, seeing that no signs of reopening were manifested.

Holy Cross

Holy Cross is a recent foundation of four Brothers on Mr. Murphy's land. The Rev. Fr. Paul Gillen is the superior, and he has just built a house there for his little colony. It is a mission that will probably be blessed by Heaven, and will be consoling and fruitful.[11]

10. St. Philomena's parish had been founded in 1846 for German-speaking Catholics. The school stood on East Third St. and had been opened in 1865. Archives of the Archdiocese of Cincinnati, parish files, "St. Philomena, Pearl St., Cincinnati." The fourteen teaching Brothers apparently refers to the total number of Brothers teaching in the parish schools of Cincinnati.

11. The foundation was near Luzerne (later Keystone) in Benton County in east central Iowa. Paul Gillen, born in Ireland on Nov. 24, 1810, had entered the Congregation of Holy Cross at Notre Dame on Dec. 1, 1856, and had professed vows July 1, 1857. Ordained a priest, he had served as a chaplain with the Army of the Potomac during the Civil War. The community records specifically mention three Brothers as having been involved in the opening of

The Rev. Fr. Letourneau, superior of the Brothers at St. Mary's, takes his meals with them and assures to all for the future the satisfaction and the advantages of community life.

The Brothers at St. Mary's

The Congregation has made a valuable acquisition this year in the purchase of 1,320 acres from Mr. Irwin, five or six hundred of which are a deposit of turf. About one thousand tons have already been taken out and will replace twelve hundred cords of wood. Our neighbors are astonished beyond measure to see that Catholics from beyond the sea have come to discover such a treasure for them. They could not be convinced until they saw the fire that this black earth made in our boilers.[12]

Discovery of turf

The event of the year is the great bell, which everybody wants to see and to hear. It is the largest bell in the United States, and unquestionably the most perfect and most sonorous. It can be heard for fifteen or seventeen miles.

Great bell

The material improvements this year at Notre Dame were the painting of the exterior of the College, and the painting of the interior in the color of oak, which wonderfully adds to the beauty of the two. Then the erection of two lodges on the principal avenue, at the point of intersection of the road going towards St. Mary's, with a view to prolong thither the gardens that begin under the

Two lodges: new post office and new porter's house

---

this foundation. Br. Matthew (John Carroll) was born about 1822 at Killashiula, County Tipperary, Ireland, and entered the congregation at Notre Dame, Nov. 19, 1850. Br. Cesaire (Peter McMahan) was born in November 1829 at Rossley, County Fermanagh, Ireland, and entered the congregation at Notre Dame, Apr. 25, 1854. Br. Aloysius Gonzaga (Edward Barnes) was born Oct. 18, 1843 or 1844, at Annistaig, County Kilkenny, Ireland, and entered the congregation at Notre Dame, July 19, 1860. He died at Keystone, Iowa, July 25, 1869, and is buried there. M.g. See also Franklin Cullen, "Holy Cross in Iowa: Five Apostolates, 1844–1977," unpublished ms., 3–5, IPA.

12. This property, which became known at St. Joseph's Farm, was in Harris Township, St. Joseph County, Indiana, eight miles northeast of Notre Dame. See Carl Tiedt, *The Peat Bog, St. Joseph's Farm* (South Bend, Ind., 1987).

windows of the College. The two lodges are joined by a rail fence which closes the road, that to the east being used as a post office and the other as a porter's lodge and the little store of (religious) objects kept by Br. Francis.

Color of the future

The number and the spirit of the pupils of the College seem to be improving upon preceding years. If nothing happens to darken the horizon, the future appears consoling and full of promise. God grant that His kingdom be sought first and always and by each and everyone, and that we may thus deserve the continuance of the blessings without which we can do nothing.

CHAPTER 26

Additions or Reminiscences (1880)[1]

While reading over again the foregoing pages, nearly forty years since they were commenced, I was not only interested in this faithful record of so many proofs of Divine Providence's visible and constant attention and tender solicitude, but I sincerely regretted they were so poorly related, and even some, at least, totally overlooked. But who could say all Divine Providence has done, since 1841, for the children of the Holy Cross in this New World? Every day from the first to the last should have its chapter, and each one, as the work went on, developing itself and increasing the number of its devoted laborers, should multiply its pages, in order to show the real and true cause of the growth of such a small and insignificant seed into a tree, the shade of which already protects so many innocent souls and pure hearts.

Indeed, if there is a man upon earth who can account for the steady progress and unceasing development of the work of the Holy Cross in America, it should be the one who came first to commence it and who to this hour ever

1. This last section, written in English in what appears to be Sorin's own hand, has been reproduced as it is in the original manuscript except for the following. Toohey's reordering into one or more paragraphs of passages more than a page in length has been retained. Numbers and other abbreviations, e.g., U.S., have been written out. Otherwise, Sorin's spelling and punctuation, or lack thereof, have been kept.

remained its principal Director. But he, more than anyone else, feels absolutely convinced that whatever the devotedness of his associates and co-workers may have been, it would have amounted to and resulted into (sic) a complete failure, if God had not blessed their puny exertions in the undeniable manner He did, making of us as many living witnesses to the truth of His apostle's solemn declaration; that the weakness of God is stronger than men; that the foolish things of the world God hath chosen that He may confound the wise; that He hath chosen the weak things to confound the strong; and the base things and the things that are contemptible hath God chosen, and the things that are not, that He might bring to nought the things that are, that no flesh should glory in His sight. 1 Cor. ch. 1:27-29. This precious and most consoling text is familiar to all missionaries. I learned it by heart, or rather took it to my heart long since, and God alone knows how well it has served me.

Hence I repeat without a particle of shame, but with a readiness equalled only by an absolute conviction, that if there is anything praiseworthy in the rapid growth of the mustard seed brought over from the old world and planted by us in this new one, it is to the abundant dew, the incessant and every-increasing blessing from above, it is due. *Non nobis Domine, non nobis, sed nomini tuo da gloriam.*

Our share in what the world may perhaps admire, what is it? Simply and honestly, to have checked and opposed the workings of divine grace, instead of cooperating faithfully with it. Ah! If we had all and every one of us duly responded to the advances of the Divine Master, what glorious results would now rejoice the guardian angels of this New World! But alas! the more forcibly we feel obliged to confess our infidelities, the more evidently we prove that what little good has been done must be wholly credited to the protection of Heaven.

One thing, perhaps, will appear evident more than any other, viz: that the Blessed Virgin has taken this mission of the Holy Cross in America under her special protection, from its very incipiency throughout. To me the evidences of the fact, if I can use the only expression I know to convey my conviction, are such, so numerous and palpable, that, when I think of them, Notre Dame and what has sprung from it stands beyond doubt the work of our glorious and Immaculate Virgin Mother.

5th of August. Our Lady of the Snows

Long before we left France for this New World, I remember very distinctly that there was in my mind a predominant thought and in my heart a special, an abiding desire, which I might call a hidden passion, viz: to devote my time somewhere, to consecrate my life to preach what I knew of the Blessed Virgin. My first sermon, written at home in 1837 when I was only subdeacon, was on Our Blessed Mother, from the sacred text: *Qui elucidant me, vitam aeternam habebunt.* I read it all to my dear Parents before I preached it, and they seemed to feel more than pleased with my first oratorical essay. From this first debut until I left all, I preached often, my first love increasing year after year.

But on the day of our departure, when I opened my new Breviary for vespers, (until then the Roman liturgy was totally unknown to me, having never used but that of our Diocese) I was struck to see that we were starting on a beautiful festival day of the Blessed Virgin, Our Lady of the Snows. The impression I received from the happy coincidence was not to be soon obliterated. I had absolutely nothing to do with the choice of the day. How often have I not thanked her since, for choosing it Herself, as a proof that she wished us to leave for our new Mission under her maternal protection! To look up to Her as to our guiding Star! Mr. Leo Dupont was with us in the coach from Mans to Havre.

He had volunteered to accompany us to the sea and to arrange everything for our embarkation. We were intimate friends. He served us admirably for three days; without him we might have found it impossible to take the sea. He was the last to shake hands with us several hours after the boat had left the shore. One may imagine his joy and his comments when he learned the name of the festival on which we were leaving our friends at Mans. A few weeks before we had made together one of the three hundred and sixty-five pilgrimages which he published some years later in his beautiful *Année à Marie*, in two vol.

I knew his admirable love of the Mother of God; he thanked Her as only Saints know how to thank Heaven for deeply felt favors. I said my office in the coach, Vespers and Matines (sic): I never felt happier; it seemed the B. Virgin claimed not only my thoughts and affections but my whole life; She wanted all I could give. Oh! how glad I would have been to give her something worth offering and receiving! My only consolation then was to make no reserve. But insignificant as was my poor return She seemed to accept it.

Since this first mark of maternal tenderness, who could enumerate the daily proofs She has given us of her undying love? To whom were (sic) I indebted a little later on for celebrating my first mass in Indiana on Rosary Sunday?[2] And for reaching Vincennes our long journey's end in time to say my 2d mass and preach before our venerated Bishop on the Solemnity of Her Divine Maternity? I should have been stone blind not to recognize on the above 3 occasions the loving hand of a Mother even if she had entirely withdrawn her sensible protection all the time intervening. But of the 2 months and 6 days that our journey lasted, I could not point out to a single one on which she forgot us & left us in want. If time permits, I will relate some more were it only to show to our dear Religious of the Holy Cross in America how good the Mother of God has been to them from the beginning; how much they owe her & what boundless return of gratitude & love She has a right to expect from each of them.

2. Here, above the line, appears a cross. On the facing page (blank back of p. 366) is a similar cross followed by the words, "in Logansport, invited by the V. G. A. Martin since Bp. of Natch." See above, chapter 1, note 13.

The above three first delicious *Etapes* in a little more than two months were too significant to be passed unnoticed by young missionaries whose souls were wholly absorbed in one same thought viz: to make known in the New World the Holy Mother of God, to whom they had consecrated their best love. For Her they had left all; for Her they actually lived; for Her they passionately wished to spend themselves and be spent to the end of their life. If She blessed their labors, they had not even a doubt their Mission would prove a success. Without Her they could not account to any man for the first elements of Christianism; (they could) not even explain to Heathen the Apostles' Creed itself; like the happy Shepherds of Bethlehem they themselves had been wont to find Mary and Joseph and the Infant; in the same order they intended preaching the Gospel to the Indian and to the Citizen of the New World; in their deep convictions, Mary was the key to open to all the mysteries of the Gospel. How could the Son be preached without speaking of his Mother? And how could she be made known, without being admired and praised and loved?

1843

Towards the end of the extraordinary winter of 1842-43, on the 15th of March, a remarkable event happened in the mission of St. Mary's of the Lakes, which alone was more than enough to console our New Missionaries, of (sic) the little trials unavoidably imposed upon them by the rigor of the season and its unprecedented duration; (the snow covering the ground for full five months, with the exception of two days) two serious causes of the sufferings of the country at large, but particularly for our newcomers, whose arrival at South Bend had been preceded by a heavy fall of snow, ten days before, and who found in their long wished for new quarters no preparation whatever but an old log cabin, completely abandoned since three years, without any furniture except a bed and three chairs.

For three days they went to town in the evening, and
returned early in the morning to fit up the venerable old
Mission House. They went to their task with a will; and the
fourth night, they all slept deliciously in their new lodging,
more precious in fact to each one of them, than any palace
in the New World could have been. By degrees, all their
real wants were successively supplied: not a complaint nor
a murmur, nor even a regret was heard in the little band,
through that trying memorable winter: They were happy as
they never were before. Devotedness knows no fatigue or
privations; and where true love finds labor, even that labor
is loved, said St. Augustine fifteen hundred years ago.

At times, they were indeed richly repaid, as the following little anecdote or real fact will prove.

In his frequent visits to his beloved Indians at Pokagon,
Michigan, Father Sorin one day heard of another settlement of Potawatomi, ninety miles east, in Indiana, who
(sic) had never been visited by any Missionary, and who
had expressed a certain desire to become Christians. Immediately two of the Pottawatomies' best men were dispatched
to the new village, and in three weeks they reported their
new catechumens well instructed, ready for baptism, and
very anxious to see the Missionary. They could not wait;
they were impatient, for fear, they said, to die before becoming the happy children of God.

Very early next morning, the Missionary was journey-
ing in a sleigh, with an interpreter and a driver, towards
Nantawassippi[3] fifty-five miles east of South Bend, to the
residence of an excellent Canadian friend, Mr. Marentet,
at whose house our neophytes were to meet him to receive
Holy Baptism.

It was five P.M. when Father Sorin reached the spot,
and found himself surrounded, before he could get out of
his cutter, nearly half frozen, by nineteen Indians, every
one the very picture of joy and happiness. After supper, an
examination of the little Band was commenced in serious

3. The place was Nottawasippi or Nattawaseppee, now Men-
don, Michigan. See " Missions Attended from Notre Dame, 1842–
1854," 8, Sacred Heart Parish Collection, IPA.

earnestness. Father Sorin was surprised at the thorough knowledge they possessed of the elements of the Christian Doctrine. Then came confession, then Baptism!! . . . finally night prayer, closed by singing in their Indian language. It was nearly twelve, when all on their knees, humbly begged the Missionary's blessing.

Before separating, the hour for Holy Mass was fixed at seven. But they would intreat (sic) the Missionary not to awake, until they sang from below the morning canticle; it was agreed and punctually carried out. Never perhaps had they all slept more sweetly.

At seven an instruction on Holy Communion occupied an hour: then Mass was commenced. Oh! it was a sight, not to be easily forgotten. Commencing by the Instructors, the chief and his wife, the queen as she was called, came slowly and reverentially to receive the Bread of angels; then an aged squaw, over eighty years, and then all, except a little boy, only three years old, the grandson of the old woman who had carried him on her back twelve miles, that he too, might be regenerated in the water of Baptism. Another instruction followed. Who could describe the attention with which it was received?

At eleven the breakfast was served: but not one of the new Christians would do anything else but look at the Missionary, until he had finished his meal. As soon as he rose from the table, the queen stepped towards him, with her husband. "Father," said she, "we have neither gold nor silver to offer you. But pray, do me the favor to accept these vain things, which I prided in too much until this happy morning;" and while uttering these words, she was actually pulling out (sic) from her fingers seven copper rings, which she placed forcibly in Father Sorin's right hand. He thanked her with a trembling voice and with tears in his eyes. Well may it be questioned if he had ever received in Paris or the Belle France, any gift that moved his heart as this spontaneous and sudden Indian generous act[4] did.

4. Here above the line, appears a cross. On the facing page (blank back of p. 372) is a similar cross followed by the words,

Father Sorin would have been delighted to spend the remainder of the day with his new and beloved spiritual children; but he was due at home that evening. By one o'clock he started back with his interpreter and driver. At eleven, he reached his quarters, where he found a good Brother looking for him, in his room, and taking care of a log seven feet long, which he had been pushing into the chimney as it burned away. The journey had been long and cold; but the heart had enjoyed it beyond expression. Such days lengthen a man's life!

At twelve, he was fast asleep in the same bed, on which Father Badin the protopriest, his successor, the saintly Deseille, and the famous Benjamin Petit who died a martyr of his charity for the Indians, had successively rested from their much longer and severer fatigues.

Next morning, he could thank heaven for the blessings and the joys of the previous eventful day, at the very altar, where Father Deseille, an hour before his admirable death, had, with a trembling hand, open (sic) the tabernacle and communicated himself with the Holy viaticum, as no priest could be procured to attend his last moments. *Haec meminisse juvabit.*

Some day probably not far distant, a religious monument will be erected at Notre Dame, to perpetuate the memory of the above glorious names, to which a fourth one no less but much more illustrious, that of the Rt. Rev. Bp. Bruté, shall be added to the great joy of hundreds and thousand(s) honest souls, who knew them to venerate and love them. Sketches have been written of each of them: they form a conspicuous part of the history of the Church of God in the West of the United States. But an especial tribute of respectful gratitude is due them where they labored so faithfully and so efficiently. The best proof their honest and happy survivors can offer of their real appreciation of their merits and of the services rendered by them to the

---

"When he returned to France, in 1846, Father Sorin distributed the 7 Indian rings among the 7 chapels of the Blessed Virgin he knew best, & where they are preserved as interesting mementoes."

cause of Religion and civilization, should be a substantial one, viz.: a lasting monument, for the consolation of the present generation and the instruction of ages to come. "Let the memory of the wicked perish with a noise." The sooner the better; "but let us praise forever the memory of the just; for by it, the living man honors himself."

It would be a disgrace to Notre Dame and St. Joseph County to leave much longer such names unwritten to public gratefulness. Not another spot, on our vast continent, is under such obligations to the modest and yet heroic four names above mentioned.

1. Father Badin, the protopriest of the United States, is known all over the New World, where he spent himself for more than sixty years; but nowhere in the almost boundless field of his labor did he leave his mark and immortalize himself as he did here. Nowhere did he purchase any ground but here. But, as he himself stated to the writer, one day, after ministering to the wants of his dear Indians, while gazing over the two pretty lakes on the shores of which he stood in admiration, a thought flashed to his mind; that such a beautiful spot should be secured for God. What a delightful place for an orphan asylum and a college! Instantly he resolved to buy it. "How well inspired," said he another day to Fr. Sorin, when he returned to Notre Dame fifteen years later, "how well inspired I was, when I entered these 524 acres"!

Should he live yet, he would say the same and bless God the more. When the present state of Notre Dame is compared to that of the primeval forest, entered from the Government, fifty some years ago, by Father Badin, the inspiration of its acquisition ceases to appear a groundless assertion. That it was a providential design, he himself never doubted it. He rejoiced in it, as he never did in any other undertaking. He looked upon it, not as a proof of his personal foresight or sagacity, but as a superior design of which he had been the simple executing tool. So deeply was he convinced of it, that when he revisited it, he gave it all he possessed, viz: six thousand dollars, on which he received a little annuity until he died in 1853.

Here the mustard seed planted by the Missioner's hand grew and gradually, providentially rather, developed into a tree into the branches of which the birds of the air have come to rest and dwell. This is, indeed, Father Badin's principal mission, where his labors have especially blessed (sic).

2. Rev. Louis Deseille. Next in point of time and importance comes the saintly Mr. Deseille, who fixed here his general quarters, as a resident Missionary of the Indians and white Christians, during the five years he lived in the country, until his death, in the fall of 1837. It was he, properly speaking, who created the Mission, and enriched it, not only by his abundant and continual alms to the poor Indians, in Indiana, Michigan and Illinois, but by his incessant apostolic zeal and most edifying life, and above all, possibly, by his memorable angelic death, which alone would for ever place him amongst the holiest Missioners of the Church, and surround his mortal remains and the blessed spot where they rest, with a halo of Sanctity, which has been considered, since forty- five years, as an undoubted pledge of extraordinary blessings upon the labors of those who would come after him, to continue and develop his great work. Who could remember such a death and not say: "Oh! may my last moments be like his!" The possession of such previous remains is, for Notre Dame, a treasure beyond value.

Three times already, since the first day our Religious of the Holy Cross knelt around those venerated remains, have they been religiously removed, each time to occupy a more honorable place. But the outside monument is yet a desideratum. May God enable us soon to show to all our veneration for the saintly predecessor Himself sent to Notre Dame, to lay the foundation of an edifice which he will continue, we trust, to protect and assist unto perfection. He died here in his little log cabin in 1837, but his memory is yet fresh and popular all around. To let it die out when it is so precious to Religion would be an inexcusable folly.

3. The Rev. Benjamin Petit who comes in third on the list remained here but a very short time, scarcely one year, and yet, he seems to be the best known and to have been the most loved. History furnishes such examples of men so richly endowed, so exceptionally drawing everyone and everything to themselves, that when a noble end is aimed at, real zeal finds in nature a help which nothing almost can resist.

Such was, it appears, even from infancy, the third missionary of this western Indian Mission. Richly endowed by nature as all say and trained up by a Mother, equally remarkable for her superior abilities and her piety, he had made brilliant studies in his native city Rennes, where, as a lawyer, he had already secured a flattering prospect of success, when the saintly Bishop Bruté changed all his aspirations, and won his mind and his loving heart to the poor Missions of Indiana.

Two days after his ordination in Vincennes, he was sent here to replace a Saint, as he was called by all that knew him. He saw with his own eyes how deeply the loss of Father Deseille was felt all around, little dreaming then, that in less than twelve months, his own death would plunge so many broken hearts into even a deeper sorrow and more overwhelming affliction, as he was loved already, after such a brief but wonderful exhibition of virtues, of abilities and sacrifices, as none of his predecessors, good and excellent as they were, had ever been loved and admired.

Half a dozen of his letters to his Bishop, or to his Mother, fully justify the universal regrets caused by his untimely demise, which the saintly Bishop Bruté himself called the death of a martyr of charity, and by which he was personally so much affected, that no other cause could be generally assigned for his own death, shortly after this sad loss, than the desolation it created in his heart.

The beautiful pages of the "Annales" and of the *Ave Maria*[5] on Father Petit's memorable career dispense us from

5. See *Ave Maria*, "Missionaries of Indiana—2nd, Rev. B. M.

any further attempt to repeat here what is already familiar to all. What a loss for the mission he loved so well! So much accomplished in one year! And to die at twenty-seven years of age! So much regretted by all who knew him!

Petit," (Dec. 16, 1865), 484–486; (Dec. 23, 1865), 518–520.

INDEX

319

78n.3; established at Orléans,
France, 105; printing of
books by, 220
Congregation of the Sacred
Hearts of Jesus and Mary
and of Perpetual Adoration,
106n.3
Conscription Act of 1863,
286n.4
Constantine, Michigan, 28
Conversions: of passengers
aboard SS *Iowa*, 8; at
St. Peter's Colony, 20; at
Notre Dame du Lac, 38;
of sick people, 49. *See also*
Baptisms
Cooney, Rev. Peter, 276,
291–92, 304
Coquillard, Alexis, xix, 175–76
Coquillard, Mrs. Alexis, 88, 89
Corby, Rev. William, xxiv,
xxvii, 144, 276, 292
Council of Administration,
Notre Dame du Lac, 195,
285, 287, 288, 290
Crops. *See* Farming
Curley, Rev. John, 129, 209

Daniel, Br. (Patrick William
Kelly), 129
Deaths: among Brothers, 57–58,
62, 110, 117, 127, 128–31,
133–34, 151, 158, 280,
290; among Sisters, 58, 60,
76–77, 117, 126–27, 128,
131, 280, 290; during cholera
epidemic in 1849, 86; during
epidemic of 1854, 126–27,
128–32; among apprentices,
127; among students, 127,
131; of orphans, 158–59;
and conversions, 277, 280,
284–85. *See also* Funerals
Defrees, Sen. John Dougherty,
35
de la Hailandiere, Bp. Celestin:
requests for missionaries
made by, xii, xiii, xiv, 1,

13n.14; vocation of, xii;
appointed as bishop of
Vincennes, xiii; Sorin's
correspondence to, xv; and
arrival of missionaries at
Vincennes, xvi, xviii, 1–2,
10, 13–14, 17–19; granting
of land for Notre Dame du
Lac by, xix, 21, 26, 202, 209;
quarrel with Rev. Chartier,
xx, 21, 22; ordinations by,
12n.11; financial support
for Notre Dame du Lac
from, 29; relics of St. Severa
presented by, 40; and transfer
of Novitiate to Indianapolis,
42, 63–64, 73; and Sisters of
the Holy Cross, 46–47; and
missions entrusted to Sorin,
207, 208; and university
charter, 211
Delaune, Rev. Julian, 14, 18,
29, 57, 67–71, 73n.7
Deseille, Rev. Louis, 27, 34,
180n.1, 207, 314, 316, 317
Desert, Sr. Mary of the
(Angelique Godeaux), 86
Detroit, Michigan, 89, 144
Devlin, Mr. (New York
benefactor), 183, 184
Devos, Louis, 133, 151
Dillon, Rev. James, 245, 276,
282, 284, 292, 302
Dillon, Rev. Patrick, 240
Dominic, Br. (Michael Wolf),
126, 128,163, 215–16
Dominican Fathers, 253
Donnet, Cardinal (of Bordeaux),
193
Dowling, Michael, 91
Drouelle, Rev. Victor, 78–79,
80, 81–82, 105, 116, 153,
298, 299, 301
Dubois, Bp. John, 10, 11n.9,
80n.6, 184n.3
Dubuguay, Mr. (Paris
benefactor), 40
Dufal, Bp. Pierre, xxiii, 300–301